Flag, Nation and Symbolism in Europe and America

Although the symbolic and political importance of flags has often been mentioned by scholars of nationalism, there are few in-depth studies of the significance of flags for national identities. This multi-disciplinary collection offers case studies and comparisons of flag history, uses and controversies.

Thomas Hylland Eriksen and Richard Jenkins have brought together over a dozen scholars, from varying national and disciplinary backgrounds, to offer a cluster of readings of flags in their social contexts, mostly contemporary, but also historical. Case studies from Denmark, England, Northern Ireland, Norway, Sweden and the United States explore ways in which flags are contested, stir up powerful emotions, can be commercialised in some contexts but not in others, serve as quasi-religious symbols, and as physical boundary markers; how the same flag can be solemn and formal in one setting, but stand for domestic bliss and informal cultural intimacy in another.

This book will be an invaluable companion for undergraduate and postgraduate students conducting research in the areas of political and economic anthropology, comparative politics and political sociology.

Thomas Hylland Eriksen is Professor of Social Anthropology at the University of Oslo, Norway.

Richard Jenkins is Professor of Sociology at the University of Sheffield, UK.

Flag, Nation and Symbolism in Europe and America

Edited by Thomas Hylland Eriksen
and Richard Jenkins

Routledge
Taylor & Francis Group

LONDON AND NEW YORK

First published 2007
by Routledge
2 Park Square, Milton Park, Abingdon, Oxon OX14 4RN

Simultaneously published in the USA and Canada
by Routledge
270 Madison Ave, New York, NY 10016

Routledge is an imprint of the Taylor & Francis Group, an informa business

Typeset in Sabon by
Keystroke, 28 High Street, Tettenhall, Wolverhampton
Printed and bound in Great Britain by
MPG Books Ltd, Bodmin

British Library Cataloguing in Publication Data
A catalogue record for this book is available from the British Library

Library of Congress Cataloging in Publication Data
Flag, nation and symbolism in Europe and America / [edited by]
  Thomas Hylland Eriksen and Richard Jenkins.
    p. cm.
  1. Flags—Social aspects—Europe—Case studies.   2. Flags—
  Social aspects—United States—Case studies.   3. Emblems,
  National—Social aspects—Europe—Case studies.   4. Emblems,
  National—Social aspects—United States—Case studies.
  5. Nationalism—Europe—Case studies.   6. Nationalism—United
  States—Case studies.   7. Political culture—Europe—Case studies.
  8. Political culture—United States—Case studies.   I. Eriksen,
  Thomas Hylland.   II. Jenkins, Richard, 1952–
  JC347.E86F53 2007
  929.9'2094–dc22 2007018505

ISBN10: 0–415–44404–7 (hbk)
ISBN10: 0–415–45854–4 (pbk)
ISBN10: 0–203–93496–2 (ebk)

ISBN13: 978–0–415–44404–0 (hbk)
ISBN13: 978–0–415–45854–2 (pbk)
ISBN13: 978–0–203–93496–8 (ebk)

Contents

List of figures   vii
Notes on contributors   ix
Preface   xiii

1 Some questions about flags   1
  THOMAS HYLLAND ERIKSEN

2 The origin of European national flags   14
  GABRIELLA ELGENIUS

3 Rebel with(out) a cause? The contested meanings of the
  Confederate battle flag in the American South   31
  JONATHAN LEIB AND GERALD WEBSTER

4 The Star-Spangled Banner and 'whiteness' in American
  national identity   53
  MANUEL MADRIAGA

5 Union Jacks and Union Jills   68
  NICK GROOM

6 Pride and possession, display and destruction   88
  NEIL JARMAN

7 Between the national and the civic: Flagging peace in,
  or a piece of, Northern Ireland?   102
  DOMINIC BRYAN

8 Inarticulate speech of the heart: Nation, flag and emotion
  in Denmark   115
  RICHARD JENKINS

9 A flag for all occasions? The Swedish experience   136
   ORVAR LÖFGREN

10 Nationalism and Unionism in nineteenth-century
   Norwegian flags   146
   OLE KRISTIAN GRIMNES

11 The domestication of a national symbol: The private
   use of flags in Norway   157
   ANNE ERIKSEN

12 Afterword   171
   IVER B. NEUMANN

   Bibliography   175
   Index   189

Figures

3.1   Four flags of the Confederacy   33
6.1   Loyalists flying the Irish Tricolour   93
6.2   An Ulster flag, a Union Jack and loyalist paramilitary flags   95
8.1   Danish flags descending from Heaven   117
8.2   Dannebrog: from the sacred to the profane   133
10.1 Four Union flags from 1844   150

Notes on contributors

Dominic Bryan is Director of the Institute of Irish Studies at Queens University, Belfast, Northern Ireland. Trained as an anthropologist, his research focuses on political rituals, public space, symbols and identity in Northern Ireland. His book *Orange Parades: The Politics of Ritual Tradition and Control* (Pluto, 2000) used theories of ritual to examine parades organised by the Orange Order in Ireland. In ESRC-funded research he is exploring the use of symbols in Northern Ireland during the peace process. He has also undertaken policy-related work with the Community Relations Council, Human Rights Commission and the Parades Commission in Northern Ireland.

Gabriella Elgenius is a Research Fellow at the Department of Sociology at the University of Oxford, UK. Her Ph.D from the London School of Economics was entitled *Expressions of Nationhood: National Symbols and Ceremonies in Contemporary Europe*. Her publications include: 'The Decline of Traditional Social Identities' (with Heath and Martin) in *British Social Attitudes: The 22nd Report*, (2007), 'National Expressions and Diversity in Europe' (*International Journal for Diversity in Organisations, Communities and Nations*, 2007) and 'The Appeal of Nationhood: Celebrating and Commemorating the Nation' (in Sturm and Young (eds) *Nationalism in a Global Era: The Persistence of Nations*, 2007). She is currently working on an ESRC-funded project, evaluating whether or not traditional identities are in decline.

Anne Eriksen is a folklorist and Professor of Cultural History at the University of Oslo, Norway. Her publications include works on collective memory, tradition and understandings of the past. Among her books are: *Det var noe annet under krigen: 2. verdenskrig i norsk kollektiv-tradisjon* ('Things were different during the war: The Second World War in Norwegian collective tradition', 1995), *Historie, minne og myte* ('History, memory, myth', 1999) and *Topografenes verden: Fornminner og fortidsforståelse* ('The Topographers' World: Antiquities and Understandings of the Past', 2007).

Thomas Hylland Eriksen is Professor of Social Anthropology at the University of Oslo, Norway and Research Director of CULCOM (Cultural Complexity in the New Norway), 2004–2009. He has recently been Special Chair in the Anthropology of Human Security at the Free University of Amsterdam (2004–2006). His publications focus on globalisation, identity politics and political symbolism, and include *Ethnicity and Nationalism: Anthropological Perspectives* (second edition, 2001), *Small Places – Large Issues* (second edition, 2002), *A History of Anthropology* (with F. S. Nielsen, 2001), *Tyranny of the Moment* (2001) and *Globalization: The Key Concepts* (2007).

Ole Kristian Grimnes is Emeritus Professor of Modern History at the University of Oslo, Norway. He is the author of numerous books and articles on Norway and the Second World War, among them *Et flyktningesamfunn vokser fram: Nordmenn i Sverige 1940–45* ('The Growth of a Refugee Society: Norwegians in Sweden 1940–45', 1969), *Hjemmefrontens Ledelse* ('The Home Front's Leadership', 1977), *Overfall* ('Conquest', 1984) and *Veien inn i krigen: Regjeringen Nygaardsvolds krigsvedtak i 1940* ('The Way into War: The Nygaardsvold Government's War Decision in 1940', 1987). He has also written a full-length biography of the Norwegian industrialist Sam Eyde, *Den grenseløse gründer* ('The Boundless Entrepreneur', 2001). He has also published some minor articles on the Swedish-Norwegian union and on flags in the era of the union.

Nick Groom is Professor of English at the University of Exeter, UK (Cornwall Campus) and teaches in both Exeter and Cornwall. He has written widely on literature, music, contemporary art, and cultural history in both the academic and popular press, and among his books are *The Forger's Shadow: How Forgery Changed the Course of Literature* (2002) and *The Union Jack: The Story of the British Flag* (2006). He is currently working on representations of the British environment.

Neil Jarman is the Director of the Institute for Conflict Research, an independent policy research centre based in Belfast, Northern Ireland. He is an anthropologist by training and has carried out research on a wide range of issues associated with the transition from political violence to a more peaceful and democratic society. He has written extensively on the use of cultural artefacts and practices in the process of developing and sustaining collective social identity. His publications include *Material Conflicts* (Berg 1997) and *Displaying Faith* (Institute for Irish Studies 1999).

Richard Jenkins, trained as an anthropologist, is Professor of Sociology at the University of Sheffield, UK. He has done fieldwork in Northern Ireland, England, Wales and Denmark, and his main interests are identity (in many aspects) and the contemporary enchantments of modernity.

Among his publications are *Pierre Bourdieu* (second edition, 2002), *Foundations of Sociology* (2002), *Social Identity* (second edition, 2004), *Rethinking Ethnicity* (second edition, 2007) and *Being Danish: National Identity and Everyday Life in an Uncertain World* (forthcoming, 2007/8).

Jonathan Leib is Associate Professor of Geography at Florida State University, USA. His research fields are political geography, cultural geography, and geographies of 'race' and ethnicity, focusing on electoral systems and political representation, political and cultural change in the American South, and the politics of representation on the American South's landscape with respect to Confederate and Civil Rights iconography. Recent major publications include: 'District Composition and State Legislative Votes on the Confederate Battle Emblem' (with G. R. Webster, *Journal of Race and Policy*, 2006), 'Separate Times, Shared Spaces: Arthur Ashe, Monument Avenue and the Politics of Richmond, Virginia's Symbolic Landscape' (*Cultural Geographies*, 2002) and 'Florida's Residual Votes, Voting Technology, and the 2000 Election' (with J. Dittmer, *Political Geography*, 2002).

Orvar Löfgren is Professor of European Ethnology at the University of Lund, Sweden. He has done research on national identity and trans-national processes. Currrently he is working on a project about 'the cultural production of the inconspicuous': routines, daydreaming, and other mundane activities. Among his recent books are *On Holiday: A History of Vacationing* (1999), an ethnography of university life entitled *Hur blir man klok på universitetet?* ('How Does One Become Wise at University?', with Billy Ehn, 2004), and the volume *Magic, Culture and the New Economy* (edited, with Robert Willim, 2005).

Manuel Madriaga is a Research Fellow at Sheffield Hallam University, conducting fieldwork in the United Kingdom. Prior to this post, he pursued and completed his Ph.D in Sociological Studies at the University of Sheffield. Among his publications are: 'Understanding the Symbolic Idea of the American Dream and its Relationship with the Category of "Whiteness"' (*Sociological Research Online*, 2005) and 'Enduring Disablism: Students with Dyslexia and their Pathways into U.K. Higher Education and Beyond' (*Disability and Society*, 2007).

Iver B. Neumann is Professor of Russian Studies at Oslo University, Norway. He holds a master's degree in Social Anthropology from Oslo University and a doctoral degree in politics from Oxford University, UK. His books include *Uses of the Other: 'The East' in European Identity Formation* (University of Minnesota Press, 1999, Russian edition 2004) and, most recently, *Harry Potter and International Relations* (edited, with Daniel Nexon, Rowman & Littlefield, 2006).

Gerald R. Webster is Professor of Geography at the University of Wyoming, USA where he chairs the Department of Geography. His research interests are largely in political geography, and focus on political redistricting, electoral geography, secessionist groups, political iconography and nationalism. Recent publications include: 'The Confederate Battle Flag and the Neo-Confederate Movement in the South' (with J. I. Leib, in *The Neo-Confederate Movement in the United States*, ed. E. Hague *et al.*, 2007), 'If At First You Don't Secede, Try, Try Again: Secession, Hate, and the League of the South' (in *Spaces of Hate: Geographies of Discrimination and Intolerance in the U.S.A.*, ed. C. Flint, 2004), and 'Political Culture, Religion and the Confederate Battle Flag Debate in Alabama' (with J. I. Leib, *Journal of Cultural Geography*, 2002).

Preface

The idea for this book emerged from a conversation between the editors, following a lecture by Jenkins in which he had described some aspects of Danish flag use. It struck us that there did not seem to be much comparative discussion of flags. In fact, there did not seem to be much research or analytical commentary on flags at all. As a result, we decided to organise a small conference with a view to a subsequent publication. This was held in Oslo in November 2005.

This book contains nearly all the contributions to the conference, plus a chapter that we subsequently commissioned from Gabriella Elgenius, which outlines the history of European flags. Since, as we have already suggested, few in-depth studies exist of the importance of flags for national identification, we hope that this book is in some ways pioneering. At the very least we hope that it will stimulate a new debate in the social sciences about flags, and symbolism more broadly, and national identity.

In some other ways, however, we may be criticised for stating the obvious. Because, actually, it is not as if the political and symbolic importance of flags has been ignored hitherto. Yet, in most cases – with the notable exception of the American flag, which has been extensively studied – flags are only mentioned in passing in most social science studies of nationalism. Moreover, national differences in the meaning, political significance and uses of flags are rarely studied at all.

In bringing together a dozen or so scholars, from varying national and disciplinary backgrounds – anthropology, ethnology, folklore, geography, history, political science and sociology – this collection offers a cluster of close readings of flags in their social contexts, mostly contemporary, but also historical. These studies move beyond the trivial fact that a flag 'is more than a mere piece of cloth' (because so much is obvious). Case studies from Britain, Denmark, Northern Ireland, Norway, Sweden and the United States illustrate the many ways in which flags are contested, stir up powerful emotions, can in some contexts be commercialised (although not in others), serve as quasi-religious symbols, and construct and dramatise physical and ethnic boundaries. The same flag can be solemn and formal in one setting, but stand for domestic bliss and informal cultural intimacy in another.

Telling historical detail indicates something of the many ways in which flags are part of processes of modern nationalism and nation-building, on the one hand, and are implicated in fundamental aspects of human group cohesion, through shared symbolism and identification, on the other.

The limited geographical scope of this collection indicates the need for another book (or maybe two) to take on, for example, Eastern European and post-colonial flags. There is also a need to explore the flags of commercial organisations, for example, or religious flags, and how these flags and their uses articulate with national flags and with each other. Questions can be asked about why there are simply more flags, of all kinds, in some places than in others. We are only too aware that the present collection is but a beginning.

Finally, we are grateful to all the participants in the original meeting in Oslo for their contributions to the discussions there, without which the present collection of papers would have looked rather different. We also acknowledge the support of the Cultural Complexity programme of the University of Oslo for the conference and this subsequent publication.

Thomas Hylland Eriksen
Richard Jenkins
Oslo and Sheffield, March 2007

1 Some questions about flags

Thomas Hylland Eriksen

Samuel Huntington begins his controversial book on 'civilisational clashes' (Huntington 1996) with a reflection about flags and cultural identity, retelling an anecdote about an international scholarly meeting in Moscow in 1992, where the Russian hosts had accidentally hung their national flag upside-down. Signifying uncertainty on the part of the reinvented Russians, who had been Soviets only a couple of years earlier, the event was – in Huntington's view – about a stage of transition. Further down the page, he notes that 'more and more the flags are flying high and true', indicating a return of ethnic nationalism in Eastern Europe after communism (but see Kolstø 2006 for a more complex account).

Huntington goes on to relate a few more anecdotes about flags and their importance as symbols of cultural identity in the modern world. He mentions the inhabitants of Sarajevo who, at the height of the siege of the city in 1994, waved Saudi Arabian and Turkish flags instead of Western ones, and thereby 'identified themselves with their fellow Muslims' (Huntington 2006: 19). However, it could equally well be argued that the demonstration was meant to voice dissatisfaction over Western attempts to stop the war, not a wish to align with Muslim countries. As Sarajevans today are quick to point out, when they were forced into exile during the war, nearly everybody went to Western Europe, not to Libya or Saudi Arabia.

Huntington also mentions a demonstration in Los Angeles where Mexican immigrants waved Mexican flags in a bid to demand equal rights. When it was commented that they should have waved US flags instead, some of them did, a couple of weeks later, but carried them upside down.

The theory of an imminent 'clash of civilisations' has been criticised for its simplistic view of culture and deterministic view of conflict by very many scholars in the field, and there is no need to reiterate the arguments. However, Huntington is right when he points to the importance of community symbols and the continued power of postulated primordial – ethnic, cultural, religious, national or regional – attachments in the contemporary world. It is also a matter of some interest that he chooses to begin his book with a brief rumination on the symbolic importance of the flag.

The flag, for all its rich symbolic and political connotations, its long history harking back to medieval heraldry, its ubiquity and emotional power, has been relatively neglected in research on nationalism.[1] Most theorists of nationalism make passing references to flags as symbols of the nation, but rarely treat the flag systematically (Billig 1995 is an exception here, and it must be added that a substantial literature on the American flag exists). The flag is nonetheless a pillar of nationhood, along with institutions such as the population census (Anderson 1991; Kertzer and Arel 2002), the universal educational system (Gellner 1983; Meyer *et al.* 1992), the shared historical narrative (Hobsbawm 1990; Smith 1991), and so on. Yet flags have been poorly theorised so far, and have scarcely been treated comparatively (although see Elgenius 2005a).

This volume brings together a group of scholars from different academic disciplines – anthropology, folklore studies, geography, history, literature, political science, sociology – who make a collective attempt to give flags their proper place in the theory of nationalism. All the main cases are taken from a cluster of culturally closely related societies; Scandinavia, the UK including Northern Ireland, and the USA. There are, in other words, no studies of flag issues in post-colonial countries or Eastern Europe, to mention two obviously different contexts from the ones we have concentrated on. Certainly, some dimensions would have been added if we had decided to broaden the canvas. Controversies over flags in post-communist societies, which include both new and old states, would have brought conflict of a different kind into the discussion; and third world countries with no pre-colonial flag history illuminate, through the indifference often displayed towards the flag among the citizenry, the gulf between state and society in many new countries.

Our decision to restrict ourselves to discussing flag issues from a group of North Atlantic societies nevertheless has some advantages. It limits the range of substantial issues raised, but may, as a compensation, lead to a focus on the *nature* of the flag, showing what a flag *is*, rather than showing what flags *can be* in a number of sharply contrasting cases. Flags are symbolic containers, but what do they contain?

This much said, it should be added that the variety of perspectives and substantial issues raised in this book is, in our view, perfectly adequate. Who outside the region would have guessed, for example, that flag use and perceptions of the flag differ so enormously between the three Scandinavian countries? The contrast between the ambivalent, often lukewarm attitude to the St George's Cross in England and the huge density and variety of flags among Protestants in Northern Ireland, politically part of the same country, is also thought-provoking. The enthusiasm displayed for the Southern Cross in parts of the United States, furthermore, contrasts sharply with the complex attitudes to the Stars and Stripes, a flag which signifies a different kind of imagined community, prevailing among other Americans. This handful of studies from Northern Europe and the USA brings out enough variety as it is, and hopefully they will inspire scholars working in other parts of the world to undertake similar endeavours.

Flags as condensed symbols

Durkheim and Mauss, in their *Primitive Classification*, first published in 1903 (Durkheim and Mauss 1963/1903), commented on the analogy between primitive totems and flags. A totem is usually an object (more rarely a naturally occurring phenomenon such as lightning) which signifies shared identity, mutual obligations and certain exclusive norms, such as food taboos, among the members of a kin group in many traditional societies in Australia, Africa and the Americas. As Lévi-Strauss (1962) showed in his magisterial treatment of totemism, the plants and animals which become totemic are taken on not because they are economically useful, but because they are 'good to think with' (*bons à penser*). They shape thought about the nature of society, its (presumed) natural divisions and internal relationships, *and* the relationship between society and nature.

Others working in traditional societies have also occasionally pointed out parallels between symbols of cohesion there and in modern nation-states. For example, one of Victor Turner's Ndembu-educated informants told him, in an attempt to explain the central place and multiple meanings of a particular tree species (the 'milk tree') in Ndembu culture, that these trees were like the flags of the white people (Turner 1967).

In the European Middle Ages, flags had an instrumental function, in that they made it possible to distinguish between friends and enemies on the battle ground. However, heraldic flags were also associated with kinship, origins and place. Aristocratic families had their flags, powerful Scottish families had their tartans, and many Europeans belonging to the establishment had their coat of arms.

In the modern era of the nation-state, with which this book is concerned, flags signify, at an abstract large scale, some of the same things that totems and heraldic symbols have done in the past, but – in the case of national flags – they signify the metaphoric kin group of the nation rather than other groups. As all the chapters in this book show, disputes over flag design, which flag to use, and how to use it, reveal conflicts which are ultimately concerned with the nature of 'we-hood'. Flags are, in Turner's terminology, *condensed symbols*, or *key symbols* (Ortner 1973). They compress a broad range of meanings and are rich in aesthetic and emotional connotations. For example, when my son decided to become an Arsenal supporter, at the age of eight, I suspected the underlying reason was that our local Oslo club, FC Lyn, where he is an active player, uses the same red and white colours as Arsenal.

It is impossible to express the condensed meanings expressed through flags because they differ so in their cultural significance and substantial meaning. In many countries, flags have little importance in everyday life, and are associated with the state, not the people. In some societies, such as twentieth-century Sweden, flags were unwaved, to use Billig's (1995) useful term. Overt nationalism was considered vulgar, but at the same time, the patriotism of the Swedes was never in doubt. In neighbouring Norway, flags were everywhere during the same period, leading many Swedes to suspect Norwegians of being victims to childish and ultimately destructive nationalist sentiments. Yet, the very ubiquity of Norwegian flags meant that they were uncontroversial, multivocal and quotidian. When Norwegians see a flag, some think about ice-cream (a rare treat in the 1950s, but abundant on Constitution Day, along with thousands of flags); some associate it with the achievements of the national athletes (usually in winter sports); others, probably many, think about the pure air and open spaces of Norwegian nature; while a few associate it with Christmas, since Norwegian Christmas trees are decorated (albeit not exclusively) with streams of tiny flags.

As a result of the omnipresence of the flag, it was impossible for extreme right-wing groups in Norway to appropriate the flag. In Sweden, where flag use was less everyday, neo-nazis were, especially in the 1980s, prone to use the Swedish flag as a symbol of racism and ethnic nationalism. Discovering that they were about to lose a main symbol of the country, other Swedes re-appropriated the flag, waved or unwaved as the case might be (see Löfgren's chapter in this collection).

In Denmark, by contrast again, the flag is associated with *hygge*, cosiness, and the good life. As Jenkins shows in his chapter in this collection (see also Jenkins 1998), Danish flags appear on tins of ham, on beer bottles, hanging from the ceiling in shopping centres and in a lot of other contexts which encourage consumption. The flag somehow makes you want to enjoy your-self through consuming. In the neighbouring countries, this meaning is not conferred on the flag: in Sweden, the Danish practice is seen as slightly cheesy, in Norway as profaning a sacred symbol.

There is, in other words, no single recipe for creating an efficient unifying symbol in a complex society, where the inhabitants are in most respect quite different from each other. Both the unwaved flags of Sweden, the noisily waved Norwegian ones and the commercialised Danish flags seem to bolster and confirm the sense of identification among most of the inhabitants. To what extent immigrants and other ethnic minorities identify with the flag is a different question. In 2005, there was a stir in the Oslo press when mem-bers of the indigenous Sámi minority wished to use the Sámi flag during the 17th May (Constitution Day) parade. People who argued against the idea were not against including the Sámi in the Norwegian nation; on the contrary, they felt that the Norwegian cross (a tricolour inspired by the Danish and Swedish flags) was wide enough in its symbolic connotations to include every citizen regardless of ethnic identity.

In spite of the many variations, a few common denominators are never-theless minimal requirements for a flag to serve as a basis for identification for a sprawling and diverse citizenship. First, the shared identity must be based on something else in addition to the flag. In itself, a flag does nothing; if it doesn't work emotionally, it is nothing more than a piece of cloth. This can be the case for the majority of the population in many post-colonial African countries, many of them ethnically diverse, where the state has a weak legitimacy, where there may be no shared language and few public arenas for the enactment of abstract solidarity (such as religion or international sport).

Second, the flag must be as empty a vessel as possible; it ought to be possible to fill it with many things. If it is associated with particular regional, political, religious or ethnic interests in a diverse country, it is bound to be divisive. Or, if the country is largely homogeneous, it may still work as a unifying symbol, but at the cost of categorically excluding the minorities. To take a Swedish example again: in the mid-1970s, Sweden had two athletes of global significance. The alpine skier Ingmar Stenmark won everything in his field, and the tennis player Björn Borg won about half of the Grand Slam tournaments for several successive years. Still, Stenmark became a national symbol, while Borg did not. The reason is probably that Stenmark functioned as an empty symbol, a bit like royalty who (ideally, if not in practice) behave modestly, have uncontroversial private lives and stay out of politics. Nobody knew anything about Stenmark, except for his unusual skills in racing fast down a snowclad hill. Borg, representing a more powerful and prestigious sport, ought to have become a national symbol by virtue of his achievements, but did not. The reason is probably that his personality was too distinctive and therefore controversial. At a tender age, Borg became associated with a hedonistic lifestyle; he was a tax refugee living in Monaco much of the time, he drove fast cars and was seen with far too many, far too glamorous women. Sweden was divided over Borg because he offered substance, whereas with Stenmark there was no argument over anything. Now, a flag, in order to unite people who are otherwise very different, must be capable of making them *feel similar before the flag*. It should work like a Rorschach test, or as Neumann says in his chapter in this book, it should ideally 'be all things to all people, anytime, anywhere'. Indeed, when Ortner (1973: 1339–40) usefully distinguished between 'summarising' and 'elaborating' symbols, she invoked the American flag as an exemplar of the former, standing for 'a conglomerate of ideas and feelings'.

Third, ambiguity must vanish at the boundary. Most border crossings in the world are marked with flagpoles on both sides. There should be no doubt as to which side you are on. Some of the flag controversies dealt with in this book – notably the Confederate battle flag in the USA, dealt with by Leib and Webster, and the omnipresence of flags in Belfast discussed by Bryan and Jarman – show either that loyalties are disputed, or that they are absolute but entrenched in a sea of people waving other flags.

The symbolism of boundaries

The multivocality of flags is evident everywhere, but so are their excluding and boundary-marking qualities. Encompassing many cultural meanings, they also signify social boundaries. In Grimnes' discussion of the invention and phenomenological transformation of the Norwegian flag, it becomes clear that not only was the new Norwegian flag an affront to Swedes (who had become accustomed to living in a union with their lesser neighbour), but it also divided the domestic population between Norwegian nationalists and Scandinavian nationalists. When a flag has established itself as authoritative, there is no turning back.

At the same time, different flags may co-exist. In Britain, as noted by Groom, the recent re-emergence of the cross of St George, the English flag, has scarcely made the Union Jack obsolete (see also Groom 2006). Instead, there have been suggestions from ethnic minorities to include some thin black stripes in the latter, to remind the citizens of the living legacy of colonialism. The Union Jack[2] is already an amalgam of three pre-existing flags, the crosses of St George (England), St Andrew (Scotland) and St Patrick (Ireland); the argument is that a fourth 'cross' might be added, for the sake of contemporary relevance.

A more radical case can be witnessed daily in cities like Barcelona, where four flags may often be seen side by side: the city flag of Barcelona (signifying place), the Catalonian flag (signifying ethnicity and language), the Spanish flag (signifying a federal union), and the flag of the European Union (signifying international integration). Depicting the identities of city-dwellers as a series of concentric circles, this multiple flag use suggests that even the multivocality of a single flag cannot do justice to all the moral obligations and levels of belonging experienced by a city-dweller. One might add the flags of Barcelona Football Team and the UN flag, making things even more complex; but one may also note that the significance of each flag varies situationally.

Flags signifying different identities may nevertheless conflict with each other. In countries with strong socialist and trade union movements, the red flags waved on May Day stand in an uneasy relationship with the national flag, which for many signifies vertical solidarity and treason to the class cause.

In any case, the flexibility of a flag allows diverse groups to identify with it, provided there are also other bases of solidarity. A few years ago, a Norwegian of Pakistani origin allowed herself to be photographed naked, but painted with the colours of the Norwegian flag, on the front page of a newspaper's Saturday magazine. By doing this, she said several things at once: people of Pakistani origin can be Norwegian, and it is okay for a girl with a Muslim background to pose in the nude. The Danish pop group Shubi-dua, composed entirely of ethnic Danes, communicated something very different when they used the Danish flag on the cover of one of their albums. As Jenkins points out, the Danish flag 'is in fact many flags'; by posing the way she did, the Pakistani-Norwegian invented a new Norwegian flag which had probably never even been imagined before her stunt. She may have enlarged the compass of Norwegianness, but simultaneously reduced the cohesion of the substantial Pakistani-Norwegian community.

Sometimes, the signification of flags may be extended metaphorically. While Palestinian and Israeli flags have obvious meanings in the Middle East and in areas elsewhere populated by Arabs or Jews, it is less obvious that they should be used in Belfast. Nevertheless, Palestinian flags are occasionally seen, waving in the wind or painted on walls, in Belfast (Bryan 2000; Jarman 1997), since Northern Irish Catholics sometimes interpret the Protestant–Catholic relationship as analogous to the Israeli–Palestinian one. Flags can, in other words, even be transposed to alien contexts, and this may not be as uncommon as it seems at first blush. American flags are sometimes used by non-Americans in places far from the USA, to demarcate a point of view which is not necessarily overtly political, but could be mainly aesthetic or cultural.

Notwithstanding the unifying character of flags, flags also naturally divide, or rather come to signify divisions as well as the unity of a nation. Moreover, interest groups may try to monopolise the use of the flag, to appropriate it for their purposes. In 1994, two important events involving national sentiment took place in Norway: the Winter Olympics in Lillehammer (February), and the referendum over European Union membership (November). Flags were in widespread use on both occasions; at Lillehammer, thousands of spectators even had their faces decorated with the Norwegian cross. Interestingly, the people who used the flags on the two occasions probably overlapped only partly, and the flags was invoked for completely different purposes. At Lillehammer, the driving force was commercial and outward-looking; the motivation was to give Norway its fifteen minutes of fame and to attract foreign tourists. At the referendum, the purpose was inward-looking and political; used almost exclusively by the 'No' side, flags were taken to signify sovereignty and independence from the Union. These brief vignettes indicate both the multivocality of flags and their divisive potential.

Waved and unwaved flags

To what extent active and ostentatious flag use signifies a degree of commitment to a community is debatable, as Löfgren's Swedish material suggests. Billig has argued that symbols may be at their most efficient when they are not noticed: the unwaved, unnoticed flag hanging outside official buildings, taken for granted by passers-by, testifies to a deeper and more confident national identity than fervently waved flags. This view has been challenged by Kolstø (2006), who points out that 'massive' flag-waving takes place in the post-9/11 United States and, it may be added, flag-waving is also occasionally conspicuous in a well-established country like France, where the degree of national identity is, overall, high for the majority.

Billig's description of 'banal' nationalism, the everyday and taken-for-granted – the weather forecast, the playing of the national anthem, the patriotism of sport commentators on television – is original and important. A country which doesn't have to remind itself all the time that it is a country, because it knows that it is one, is usually better integrated, and its state enjoys a higher degree of legitimacy, than one where state propaganda and ostentatious displays of patriotism are the order of the day. In Mauritius, to mention a post-colonial country with which I am familiar, flags are rarely used in private contexts. They appear in government publications, in 'responsible' media, in front of public buildings such as ministries and schools, but no Mauritian in his right mind would – like Scandinavians – own a private flagpole to hoist the Mauritian flag on the President's birthday. In Norway, where the informal nationalism of the *demos* runs deep, and flagpoles are common, naked flagpoles on Constitution Day are always noticed, and unspoken alliances are formed between those who hoist their flags on May Day.

Billig's contrast between the waved and the unwaved is reminiscent of Geertz's (1973) comparison between 'deep' and 'shallow' play. In his celebrated account of the Balinese cockfight, Geertz argues that the participants who actively bet on the roosters, who may own a rooster themselves, and who stand in the front row during a fight, cheering the poor combatants on in loud voices, engage in 'deeper' play than the others and are in a better position to understand the nature of the ritual.

We all understand intuitively what Geertz means; listening to a concert in deep concentration is much more rewarding than chatting with your friends at the bar while the band plays. However, Billig's material, and several of the chapters in this book, make the argument more complicated. In fact, Billig seems to argue that the 'shallow' play of near-indifference before the flag works at a deeper level than ostentatious flag-waving. Kapferer (1984) has criticised Geertz along similar (but not identical) lines when noting, in a discussion of an exorcism in Sri Lanka, that the people who watch from a distance are in the best position to reflect on the ritual, moving between an insider's and an outsider's perspective.

There is no decisive answer to this question, and besides, Geertz was interested not in reflexivity, but in degrees of emotional immersion. In any case, some of the most committed flag-wavers presented in this book (cf. Jarman and Bryan on Northern Ireland, Leib and Webster on Southern Cross enthusiasts) obviously have a reflexive and reasoned (if also deeply emotional) relationship to the flag. At the same time, they are all part of contexts where flag use is contested and controversial, which means that it cannot be taken for granted. In many countries, citizens don't even notice it when they see the national flag, but in Northern Ireland they do.

The situation in Sweden for most of the twentieth century (before recent globalisation, EU membership and substantial immigration) would clearly be that of the unwaved flag. A Mauritian poet, who always used the sea as a metaphor in his poetry, sat with his back to the ocean while being interviewed, and commented that he didn't have to see the ocean as long as he knew that it was there.

A third kind of context, which transcends the shallow–deep and waved–unwaved dichotomies, is that of massive commercialisation of the flag. Groom and Jenkins show, in their chapters, how the Union Jack and *Dannebrog* are used in marketing contexts. The Union Jack was in fact considered sexy for a while, appearing on beer mugs, fashionable t-shirts and knickers in the shops of Carnaby Street. It is still treated in a much more relaxed way than most other national flags, appearing on all kinds of tourist trinkets sold in Britain. Foreigners who see the Union Jack may associate it with the Beatles, with English football, Big Ben or the Buckingham Palace. Neither German nor Dutch nor French flags have quite the same connotations, although the Italian tricolour has a strong association with food.

The presence of a great number of unwaved, barely noticed flags may indicate a strong, confident and therefore implicit national identity, but it may also signify the opposite, not least in those Third World countries where flags are associated with a remote and useless government. Similarly, fervent flag-waving may suggest great national enthusiasm, but it can also bear witness to ruthless exploitation by a tyrannical state forcing citizens to feign loyalty. Omnipresence of flags shows the need, either by the state or by parts of the *demos*, to give material evidence for a postulated imagined community.

State and civil society

It is necessary to distinguish between flag-waving from above and from below (see Eriksen 1993, on formal and informal nationalism). None of the chapters of this book, with the partial exception of Elgenius' overview, discuss state efforts to instil patriotism, in otherwise fragmented populations, through flags. This can be a risky endeavour, as Kolstø points out in a comparative discussion of the new Russian and Bosnian flags (Kolstø 2006), since, in 'new, insecure nations the flags . . . often fail to fulfil their most important function as promoters of national unity. On the contrary, they often bring to the fore strong divisions' (Kolstø 2006: 679). Flag use from above may thus be met with indifference, cynicism or downright hostility. However, divisiveness may equally well come about in societies undergoing change, or where social movements have created tension between established elites and other groups. In France, regional flags may often be seen in rural areas, which can be interpreted as a quiet rebellion against the centralised state. 'New Danes', many of them Muslims who neither drink alcohol nor eat pork, are unlikely to identify strongly with the *Dannebrog*, a symbol used on Faxe beer cans and tins of ham.

The civil society element, involving flag use from below, is strong in all the countries discussed in this book. Flags may be contested (the American Deep South, Northern Ireland), their inclusiveness may be variable (immigrants may not identify with the Norwegian flag, Scots dislike the Union Jack), but their use is largely informal. Flag pins are worn on lapels in the USA on the Fourth of July, Swedes and Norwegians hoist their flags on special occasions (which could be as private as a birthday in the family), supporters of the Confederate flag use it in ways often deemed provocative by others, and during the 'marching season', flags of very many kinds can be seen in the Protestant areas of Belfast, often to the despair of the political authorities. In Great Britain, admittedly, the situation is more complicated. The Cross of St George is becoming increasingly familiar in England itself, the Union Jack being something often treated with humour and irreverence, or downright hostility (as on some classic punk record sleeves).

By contrast, the civil society element, or informal nationalism, is weak in many other countries. In Mauritius, the only occasion where I have seen a large number of small Mauritian flags carried voluntarily by ordinary people has been in connection with major sport events. It is through entering relationships with non-Mauritians that Mauritian identity becomes relevant. And during the break-up of East African collaboration over railways and air traffic in the mid-1970s, for example, which led to a cooling of the relationship between Kenya, Uganda and Tanzania, lots of Kenyans identified *as* Kenyans, something many of them had never done before.

Like all symbols of identity, flags are invested with emotions, but they only work when the entity represented by the flag is legitimate, be it an existing state (e.g. Ireland), a projected state (e.g. Palestine or Khalistan) or a competitor to the state (e.g. Catalonia or the southern states represented through the Southern Cross). In other words, the degree of intensity in flag use varies with the degree to which the identity represented through it is challenged, and with the extent of personal emotional resources invested into it.

Just like the ritual symbols described by Victor Turner (1967), flags representing modern nation-states have an *emotional* and an *instrumental* pole in their range of signification. The emotional pole attaches the individual to an abstract collective entity, a metaphoric kin group. The instrumental pole may be political or commercial, intended to mobilise for conflict or to integrate peacefully. Symbols of unity, flags nevertheless always have divisive potential within the group and outwards, and the less ambivalent and multivocal a flag becomes in political practice, the higher its conflict potential. Ambiguity tends to go away at relational boundary markers.

Flags and conflict

Even if the question 'Who are we?' has a straightforward answer, the related question 'What are we?' may be undecided. Even in Iceland, probably the most ethnically homogeneous country in Europe, there are self-professed pagans who denounce the Christian connotations of the Icelandic cross. No functional flag is left entirely at peace, since all delineations and substantiations of imagined communities are contestable.

The pages of this book are full of conflict. Madriaga describes the ambivalence felt by many 'non-white' Americans towards the Stars and Stripes. Bryan discusses the emotion and hostility associated with both UK and Irish state and popular flags in Northern Ireland (a case of formal nationalisms opposed to informal nationalisms). Jarman talks of Belfast in the marching season as a city in a state of emergency, where home turf is demarcated through flags. Groom speaks of the Union Jack as a symbol surrounded by a mixture of hostility and indifference. Leib and Webster describe the Confederate battle flag as a symbol reminding some of their proud Southern heritage, others of the shameful past and menacing present. The Confederate flag also spurs unending debate about who is entitled to see themselves as Southerners. Anne Eriksen, analysing a singular event taking place in a private context, considers the possible reactions to a woman shooting the top off a Norwegian flag pole, while Grimnes vividly recreates the flag controversies in Norway, and between Sweden and Norway, during Union times. Jenkins shows that the many Danish flags can be at odds with each other, and Löfgren suggests a split between immigrant-friendly and immigrant-hostile Swedes, regarding norms regulating proper flag use.

A problem with flags, as Kolstø (2006: 679) acccurately puts it, is that 'symbols that are rooted in a cultural past will more often than not be more divisive than unifying since different ethnic and political groups often hark back to different pasts.' The hidden meanings of flags, which thus are not, in practice, as empty vessels as they may seem in theory, are both historically rooted and based on contemporary usage or interpretation. There is no historical or intrinsic reason why the Italian tricolour should make me think about Barolo wines and fresh pasta, but it does. There is also nothing intrinsic about the American flag which makes people all over the world react to it with a complex emotion involving both admiration, envy and fear.

As Madriaga argues, the Stars and Stripes has hidden connotations of whiteness. At the same time, flag-burning is associated with that flag and not many others. Even in Sweden, Löfgren remarks, disgruntled, politicised youths are more likely to burn the American flag than the Swedish one. Here the American flag is taken to signify geopolitical conflicts, just as the Palestinian flag (along with the Arafat headdress) is metonymic of the struggle of oppressed people everywhere.

Sometimes, flags and the conflicts they connote are left dormant for most of the year, flaring up seasonally, as in Northern Ireland. As Jarman describes it, the flags are left on their poles, as mnemonic traces of the conflict, outside the marching season, eventually becoming bedraggled displays resembling rags more than flags. They are then replaced with new flags in time for the next marching season. Similarly, Catalonian flags are never as conspiciously displayed in Barcelona as during federal election campaigns or before a football match between Barcelona and Real Madrid.

Flags can be used in peaceful and banal, even childish, displays and yet retain their menacing character for outsiders. Löfgren mentions that in the early twentieth century, German miniature flags were placed on sandcastles in the disputed areas of southern Jutland, frightening adult Danes more than their children.

Another kind of conflict surrounding flag use concerns the choice of flags for new countries. Grimnes' account of the nineteenth-century flag controversies in Norway brings this out. A wrong step, and one is a traitor. Interestingly, during the German occupation of Norway in World War II, the Norwegian flag remained a symbol of the resistance, not of Quisling's puppet government – in spite of the latter's deep nationalist sentiments and ambitions.

Some countries have debates, frequently in the informal, everyday sphere of life, about the true meaning of their flags. Such opinionated gossip brings out not only the multivocality of flags, but also their conflict potential. The Norwegian historian Tor Bomann-Larsen, who specialises in arctic explorers and royalty, claims that the so-called cross in the Norwegian flag is really a depiction of a pair of skis.

On a slightly more serious note, I know several Mauritians who question the official explanation of their flag. The Mauritian flag consists of four horizontal stripes – red, blue, yellow and green. Officially, the red band stands for the country's struggle for independence, the blue symbolises the Indian Ocean, the yellow stands for hope for the future, and the green represents the lush vegetation and agriculture. At least one interpretation exists which departs radically from this official one. The main divisive discourse in Mauritius, and arguably its deepest political conflict, concerns ethnicity. So the red is said to stand for the Hindus, the blue for the Franco-Mauritians (and presumably, their traditional clients, the Afro-Mauritians or Creoles), the yellow for the Chinese, and the green for the Muslims. Far from depicting the flag as a unifying symbol, this interpretation shows the potency of flags as condensed symbols with rich connotations of conflict and divisiveness.

Flags and the sacred

The final major theme dealt with in this book concerns the flag as a sacred symbol. Carolyn Marvin, an American professor and flag scholar, once set fire to an American flag in front of her class, not unsurprisingly inspiring powerful emotional reactions among the students. Distinguishing between vexillodules and vexillophobes – flag-lovers and flag-haters – Marvin (2005) argues that both share a view of the flag as a mystical object invested with magical powers. Vexillophobes confess that 'this flag-waving terrifies me', seeing the flag as a false god with diabolic powers. Vexillodules, on the other hand, will have no improper flag usage and see it as a magical object capable of warding off evil.

In many countries, flag-burning is actually illegal. There are strong norms regulating flag use in a country like Norway, some of them written down in official brochures. A flag should never touch the ground, so when lowering your flag at sundown (another norm – flags should be hoisted at dawn and lowered at dusk; they should never fly in the dark) you need considerable dexterity to prevent pollution. Parents of young children who wave small Norwegian flags in Constitution Day parades never fail to reproach the children, who tend to be tired by mid-morning, for letting their little flags hang down towards the ground.

Usually, the sacred character of the flag is contextual. Presumably, the Union Jacks flying from British naval ships leaving for the Falklands/ Malvinas in 1982 had a sacred character to many British, who need not have problems tolerating beer mugs carrying the same symbol. In general, flags take on a sacred character in sport and military events, as well as in ritual celebrations of nationhood.

Using flags in an emotionally relaxed, even jocular manner, can be uncontroversial – perhaps mostly so in countries with few die-hard vexillo-phobes or vexillodules. In some countries, the flag of the neighbouring country can be purchased in the form of toilet paper; it is unclear whether this is an attempt to divest the neighbour's flag of its magical power, or if it is meant as a general comment on flag fetishism. Be this as it may, disposable flags are culturally problematic in countries where the magical properties of the flag are taken seriously. Before the Olympic Winter Games in Sapporo in 1972, moreover, a Norwegian firm placed advertisements featuring the butt of a used tampon against a white background above a caption wishing the athletes – 'and particularly the Japanese female ones' – good luck. The reference to the Japanese flag was unmistakable, and was noticed by, amongst others, the local Japanese embassy, which promptly filed an official complaint.

Let me end with a recent example illustrating the sacred character of flags. During the famous 'cartoon controversy' in late winter 2006, in which many Muslims felt offended because a Danish newspaper (and later a Norwegian rag) had published caricatures of the Prophet Muhammad, home-made Danish and Norwegian flags were ritually burned in public spaces across the Middle East. However, as the Norwegian newspapers were quick to point out, the flag-burners had got neither the proportions nor the colours right. The navy blue of the Norwegian cross (nowadays identifiable as RGB #002868) was too light, the blue and white stripes were too thick, and the flag-burners had deviated from the strict 22:16 proportions. It transpired from some of the comments passed in Norway at the time that the evil magic conjured by the angry Muslims was bound to fail, since the ritual object they desecrated was not authentic. Had they stolen a real flag from a nearby embassy and proceeded to burn it, reactions might have been different.

Notes

1 For a general introduction to the history and current variety of national flags, see: http://www.allstates-flag.com/fotw/flags/
2 The official name of the Union Jack is the Union flag but this book adopts the commonly accepted usage of Union Jack.

2 The origin of European national flags

Gabriella Elgenius

This chapter commences with an examination of the origin of the modern flag tradition, in order to demonstrate how flags, as markers of identity, have become attached to national communities. By demonstrating that there is a link between pre-modern and national symbolism, we may also explore the process of nation-building by the means of the development of the national flags. The underlying assumption is that national flags have something to tell us about the properties of nation-states,[1] as the flag is the main image by which the nation-state projects itself and constitutes an indicator of political change. Flags represent nations and are powerful symbols to rally around (Billig 1995: 93).

What do we mean by *national* flags?

Before we proceed, we will have to explore the meaning of a *national* symbol, the origin of which depends on how we define the 'nation'. Several aspects can be employed to define this complex concept: a distinctive culture, language, religion, shared history, a political agenda for recognition, economic integration or combinations of these elements. These variables are often the cause of empirical confusion, as they vary from community to community and are also difficult to date. This is why the mass culture and mass participation that emerged in the political system after the French Revolution have become important variables that define modern and inclusive nations of citizens. Thus, if we understand the 'nation' as having developed after 1789 we must conclude that 'national' symbols as such did not exist in earlier times. This does not mean that pre-modern communities had no need to employ symbols in order to represent their societies. On the contrary, symbols that indicate belonging to a community constitute a ubiquitous feature of social life and are not exclusive to nations. However, early symbolic devices were not indicative of nationality in its modern sense, and, even if pre-modern loyalties did exist, it is premature to talk about nations in the Middle Ages. This is a matter neglected by the authors of vexillological literature.[2] Likewise, few scholarly attempts have been made to explore the role of flags from a sociological approach.

For the purpose of this chapter we may say that 'the certain definition of a nation is adherence of its people to common symbols – and first and foremost a national flag' (Smith 1975: 54). This means that although flags adopted prior to 1789 were not 'national' in the modern sense, through their mere existence we may understand the existence of pre-modern loyalties as well as the gradual process of nation formation.[3] Thus the national flag appears as a statement of the 'modern' mass-participant nation of citizens, illustrating people's desire to express a new kind of 'sameness', nationhood and citizenship. More concretely, national flags emerge after having been selected and established by nation-states, nations without states and states without nations. Elites in pursuit of state power play an essential role in this process. However, many flags survived over time and only managed to do so because of their support from and resonance with the people.[4] Whatever variables cause the particular formation of a national community, the national flag reflects the supremacy of the national ideal. It is from this perspective that we approach the subject of this chapter.

The study of vexillology

It is only recently that the history and symbolism of flags, or 'vexillology', has become a separate scientific study.[5] The *vexillum*, a Roman cavalry flag or standard, based on a heraldic shield, was used by a *vexillation* or detachment from the legion. The related term 'vexilloid' refers to other solid objects on poles, examples of which could be feathers, animal figures and signs of the zodiac (*Understanding Global Issues* 1994: 13). These objects were employed as signs of identification for an assembly or a military unit. Early vexilloids were also used in order to identify and mark the presence of a notable person and to communicate the attributes of a person or a god. The first references made in literature about usage of this kind date back to 550 BC in Ancient Egypt, where graphic symbolic representations of the deities were displayed in the form of vexilloids, such as the hawk of Horus or the throne of Isis (Crampton 1992; Smith 1975: Chapter 1). The early vexilloids, in use all over the world, are linked in their function to modern flags as signs of identification, although they represented groups smaller than modern nations.

The following account of the use of flags throughout history is roughly chronologically ordered. That is to say, references will be made to the period before the birth of Christ, to the Christian as well as the non-Christian world before the Crusades (until 1100), to the latter part of the Middle Ages (1100–1500), and to the early modern period (1500–1800). The modern period from 1800 onwards will be dealt with in more detail.

Flag-related symbolism in antiquity

The political, religious and military functions performed by the Roman vexilloids mentioned above are found in many earlier and contemporary civilisations, in Mesopotamia, India, Anatolia, Assyria, Persia and Phoenicia.[6]

In fact, the Phoenicians were the first to put flagstaffs on their ships, flying images of the crescent and disc of the moon goddess Astarte and with decorative streamers. The vexilloids from Persia that date back to 400–300 BC display a totemic animal at the top of the pole, or the kind of cloth flags that had distinctive emblems of eagles, falcons, suns, stars or geometric designs. The totem pole is indeed one of the earliest kinds of emblematic identification, and can be found among the native peoples of America and Australia. As the chief symbol of the clan or family, the totem specified the clan's ancestry in terms of the qualities and traits of a particular animal or plant. The totem was a powerful symbol and the clan believed that its powers were derived directly from it. In this way, vexilloids acquired a 'sacred' meaning early on, although the totemic system varied greatly from one society to another.[7]

The Romans were the first to systematise the use of vexilloids to mark units of an army. However, they were not employed in one exclusive way; several vexilloids were sanctioned at the same time as emblems of identification and as weapons (Smith 1975: 37). The two most famous Roman vexilloids reproduced either the image of the emperor or the eagle. The eagle could appear together with the symbol of Jupiter, the patron of Rome, or with a thunderbolt, symbolism thought to add strength and vision to 'Rome' (Crampton 1992: 111–15; Smith 1975: 34–6). The Romans used different kinds of animals on vexillogical standards until 104 BC, after which the eagle became the sole standard of the Roman legions. Each legion had an eagle, whereas the various detached units also carried a *vexillum* (among the first vexilloids in fabric). The eagle standard would sometimes be thrown into the ranks of the enemy, after which the commander of the legion would order his men to recapture it. The parades of ancient Rome provided the context for the early vexilloids. Lavish parades with standards and soldiers in full battle dress served to compensate for a rather weak distribution of resources, an example followed by other regimes in different places and periods. The eagle standards were honoured as 'sacred' objects, symbolising Rome's divine mission, and flags and regalia captured from vanquished peoples were paraded as proof of Roman conquest. In this process, the vexilloids became associated with notions of honour and divinity, attributes indirectly transferred to the Empire as an extension of Rome (Crampton 1992: 111–15). Another example of the sanctification of the Roman standards was that official recognition had to be given to the vexilloids of foreign troops, serving in the Roman army, within the sanctuary of the Roman Pantheon. 'Sacred' Roman vexilloids were also introduced into the Temple of Jerusalem, by order of Pilate in 26 AD, as a mark of dominance and authority.

The origin of the cloth flag

The Chinese used cloth flags following the development of sericulture around 3000 BC, which made possible the production of light, large, enduring and colourful (painted or dyed) flags for use outdoors. These flags were mainly known for their military use, but also appeared in temples and religious processions. The earliest depiction of a fabric flag is vaguely claimed to date back to 400 BC. It is painted on a wall in a Samnite colony in Paestum in Southern Italy (Crampton 1992: 111ff.; Smith 1975: 34–7). This depiction lacks a distinct design although the shape of the flag itself bears a close resemblance to a modern one. It is not necessary to date the first flag, in this context, but we should note that the modern flag has ancient roots.

The Romans, as far as we know, used two kinds of fabric flags, one with the image of the goddess of victory painted on it, and the other, the *flammula*, consisting of red streamers attached to the spear, marking the presence of a general. Crampton (1992) derives this usage from that of the Greek *phoinikis* (a red cloak), which marked the commander of a ship, a practice later copied by the Romans. Another fabric flag used by the Christian Roman emperors was the *labarum*, a standard employed as early as 400 AD by the Roman Emperor Constantine.[8] The *labarum* was a Christian version of the Roman *vexillum*. It marked an evolution from the latter, as it displayed a portrait of the emperor and his family or other government officials and, atop the staff, the monogram of Christ (the Chi-Rho). The legend about its origin, as told by the fourth-century historian Eusebius in his *Life of Constantine*, has it that the emperor, before the victory over Maxentius in 312, saw a sign of the cross in the sky with the words '*In hoc signo vinces*'.[9]

Although similar in some functions to modern flags, these devices were all portable deities and not flown from flagpoles. In consequence, flags in their modern sense were still to be invented. Nevertheless, flags are related to the units they represent, as signs of identification, whether flown in ancient or modern times.

Flags and banners in the Middle Ages

The Koran's injunction against representational art encouraged the development of flags in the Arab world. These relied heavily on abstract patterns and calligraphic inscriptions – often religious texts – in embroidery, appliqué or painting. Even before the rise of Islam, flags of black and white were used in the early part of the seventh century. From what we know, Mohammed (570–632) used one black and one white flag. The *liwa* (black with a white border) is another flag connected with him. The Arab world developed the tradition of using specific colours and inscriptions for different dynasties and leaders. As dynasties followed one another, contrasting colours were used, in order to differentiate the ruling dynasty from its predecessors.[10] The Arab world contributed significantly to the modern flag tradition by inventing cloth flags with greater adaptability. Their colours (and inscriptions) illustrated an affiliation and affirmation of a 'dominant ethos'.[11] Associating specific colours with dynasties and/or individual leaders reinforced the particular ethos of a political identity and later became the basis for all modern flags. In the case of the early Arab flags, their colours were all chosen to assert legitimacy through association with Mohammed as the Prophet. An interesting difference can be noted with regard to the use of colours by the Chinese and, later, by the Arabs; whereas the Chinese identified every colour with a philosophical or religious concept, the Arabs associated specific colours with dynasties and individual leaders (Smith 1975: 42).

In the West, flags were introduced during the Crusades, inspired by Arab military banners,[12] and derived from the struggles between Christians and Muslims (Smith 1975; *Understanding Global Issues* 1994: 13). In the Christian world the practice of bestowing banners previously blessed by the Pope became a tradition of high significance at this time and followed the ceremonial forms set by pre-Christian Rome. These banners were generally called *pallia* and, like the cloak of Mohammed (see note 10), they were originally garments. It is interesting to note that *pallia* were dedicated to St Augustine (354–430), Charlemagne (742–814), and William the Conqueror (1028–1087). The cloak of St Martin was another garment that was turned into a flag, which later became a cult object of Frankish kings and even influenced the choice of blue as part of the modern French tricolour (Crampton 1992: 112).

Meanwhile the power that finally led to the creation of the Mongol Empire arose in Asia. Many of the Mongol standards displayed a device, a 'flaming trident', reproducing the blades of a trident with flames surrounding them. The flag of the Khan himself consisted of nine yak-tails hanging from a rack of crossbars. After the conquest of China lateral flags were used, still with the horsetail and the flaming trident. The use of flags by the forces of Genghis Khan (ca 1155–1227) was significant for the development of a world-wide flag tradition, in that a special flag, actually called 'banner', came to be connected with each regiment (Crampton 1992: 113).

It is thus evident from the first cloth flags in the Arab, Asian and Christian worlds that the practice of flagging one's beliefs and purposes has been in use for a very long time, regardless of material and form.[13]

Heraldry: seals, livery colours and badges

In the context of the Middle Ages we must also take into consideration that vexillology has been looked upon as a branch of heraldry[14] and that many national flags, their colours and designs, have been influenced by coats of arms which were originally used to identify soldiers on the battlefield (Tenora n.d.). Moreover, from the extension of heraldry to Christianity, in the use of arms on the seals of ecclesiastics, another early collective principle can be deduced. Seals from the twelfth century onward were not necessarily used to identify individuals. Instead, they symbolised the body that the ecclesiastics represented, in similar fashion to modern expressions of nations, cities or educational establishments. Similarities are also to be found in the ceremonial forms of the ritualistic tournaments in the Middle Ages – where coats of arms, livery colours and badges[15] were displayed in a context of strength and distinction – and the competitive arenas of international sporting events.

The first badge used during the Crusades was the cross, which could be worn as a garment on the chest or back of the warrior. The imperial war flag of the Holy Roman Empire (from 800 onwards) displayed a white cross on red, symbolising the holy cause in which the battle was fought (FOTW 1995, 2004). Different colours were in use for crusaders from different regions as early as 1188, a distinction suggesting that differentiation based on pre-modern loyalties emerged very early. It was also decided, in 1188, that King Philip Augustus of France was to have his own colours displayed on his cross flag (red cross on white), as were King Henry II of England (white cross on red) and Count Philip of Flanders (green cross on white). These colours were later reversed and, while the reason for this remains unclear, England embarked on a continuous tradition of a red cross on white from 1277, whereas France displayed a white cross, first on a red, then on a blue flag (Crampton 1992: 111–15; Notholt 1996; Smith 1975: 130–9, 180–9). From this practice and time emerged the famous and significant cross flags, such as St George's cross (red cross on white), the cross of St Denis (a white cross on red), and the cross flag of the Teutonic Knights (black cross on white). The Crusader flag, displaying a white cross on red, was originally used by Christians against European 'pagans' and was later employed by the Holy Roman Empire in battle.

The influence of heraldry on modern flags has been substantial, and the effectiveness of the symbolism owes something to the simplicity, distinctiveness and originality of heraldic colours and designs. The first cross flags indicated primarily that the military operations of the crusaders were sanctioned by the Pope. However, it is clear that these flags acquired territorial associations as time went by.

Early modern flags

Many present national flags are derived from the 'arms of dominion' (arms of the realm used by the rulers of empires, kingdoms, principalities and states), either in terms of being armorial flags[16] or displaying the livery colours of these arms, for example the flags of Austria, Spain, Poland, Sweden, Hungary, Malta, Belgium and Luxembourg. The heraldic tradition tied the ruling elites to a specific territory via the arms of dominion, and town flags were associated with 'local rights'. Thus, the hereditary principle of the heraldic coat of arms has, to some extent, been transferred to national 'inheritance', via monarchical rights. For example, there is a legend of the creation of the Austrian flag (a tricolour with horizontal stripes of red, white and red) that found its present form with the dissolution of the Austro-Hungarian Empire in 1918. The legend has it that the red-white-red stripes have their origin in the Third Crusade of 1189–92, when Duke Leopold V of Austria fought in the bloody Battle of Acre (Ptolemais) of 1191. The white stripe in the middle symbolises the only part of his costume that remained white after his belt had been removed. Alternatively, the red and white colours came originally from the arms of Duke Frederick II of Austria in 1230, which depict the spread black eagle of the Holy Roman Empire with the shield of Austria's national colours (red and white) at its centre.

The several kinds of alternating symbolism indicate that various forms of loyalty existed before standardised measures were taken towards a more uniform mode of representation. For example, the use of the arms of dominion of England (the three lions) gradually became restricted so that it could be flown only by the monarchs or their appointed agents. This process started after the Crusades, when the nobility recognised that it would never enjoy the same 'divine sanction' as the clergy, and insisted on maintaining their coats of arms and transforming them into a formal system restricting their usage. The systematisation of heraldic coats of arms became a matter for professional heralds, whose task it was to establish the hereditary and personal nature of the arms. As the system was elaborated, it continued with specifications such as relating the size of flags to rank (Smith 1975: 44–6). With heraldry's loss of practical relevance on the battlefield, and with the growth of new social classes, novel means of representation were needed to fill the void. The cross of St George, originally seen as a less important flag, became, as a result, the flag to symbolise England, and the English trading companies started to use St George as a basis for their own flags and in order to identify themselves at sea.

Sharp ideological divisions (religious, dynastic and pre-national), and the military encounters based on these during the fifteenth and sixteenth centuries, were reflected in the flags and banners carried by the troops. As a result, these new groupings came to be identified with certain colours, which provided the foundation for the elaboration of what were to become the 'new' tri- and bicolour flags, adopted by the revolutions preceding modern nation-states a few centuries later. In times of constant warfare these colours, emerging from the crusader flags or the livery colours of individual monarchs and noblemen, gained more symbolic value and their attributed associations slowly became more national in character, in terms of their associations with groups of 'people'.[17] The banners and standards of the time, however, were not comparable to the flags of modern times in their usage, size or design, and did not represent a citizenry or a mass-participant body of 'equals'. Notwithstanding this, the early designs were clearly predecessors to modern flags, symbolising pre-modern loyalties to specific rulers. The 'people' were still part of smaller communities or corporations and were, consequently, represented through church banners and guild flags. In general, we may conclude that symbolic representation during the Middle Ages and the early modern period was still exclusive. Likewise, it operated on two different levels of society, which illustrates the lack of communication between the elite – the nobility and the sovereigns – and the people. These two levels were to be integrated, at least officially, in the final version of the modern national flag.

As a general rule, a contrast can be found between the two kinds of flags that emerged after the sixteenth century: on the one hand, the elaborate and complex designs of flags connected to armorial bearings, and, on the other, simpler flag designs. The latter inspired the new and popular system of elementary flag designs which served as the bases for modern ones. The complex honorific flags preserved for the magnates and the more simple flags figured side by side on land as two different and distinctive symbols of identification. A crucial reason for the standardisation of flag designs, corresponding to the need for a signal system at sea, was the growth of standing armies and the need for 'ordering infantry by company and battalion' (Hulme 1915: 127–40). Subsequently the cross of St Denis started to figure on France's infantry colours, whereas the English made use of the red cross of St George, which provided an indication of growing notions of differentiation between peoples.

Although the mobilisation of the masses into politics was a precondition for people to be represented by national flags, pre-modern loyalties in one form or another existed long before 1789. Some flags appeared early on the political scene and several flags managed to survive from the Middle Ages into modern times. These pre-modern flags point to the establishment of the symbolic system that was to be introduced for all national communities in modern times: (the perception of) one nation, one flag. In this way the pre-modern nations were pioneers of flag usage and created a symbolic pattern that other nations were to follow. Within this symbolism notions of 'success' and 'honour' were transferred to the flag, much as in Roman times. The modern flags that have survived from the latter part of the Middle Ages and the early modern period are those of Denmark, Switzerland, Sweden, England, Scotland and The Netherlands.

Religious and monarchical representation: cross flags

The English cross of St George and the Danish *Dannebrog* are the only flags that as national flags can claim a direct link to the Crusader cross. Thus, the first known cloth flags (the cross flags) in the Christian tradition constitute an important link between, on the one hand, the earlier representation of religiously sanctioned communities, and, on the other, the national communities of our times. This original form of representation developed from religious (together with, or via, monarchical) representation to national symbolism.

The cross flag constitutes the 'archetypical European' flag. The Danish flag, from which all the other Scandinavian cross flags have originated, is attested to in the arms of King Valdemar IV Atterdag (reigning 1340–75), and a legend of 'chosenness' endorses its origin. According to legend, King Valdemar II (1170–1241) had a vision of a white crucifix in the darkening sky on the eve of the Battle of Lyndanisse on 15 June 1219, a vision taken as a sign of Christ's protection during the battle against the pagan Estonians. In a similar fashion, the flag is also said to have fallen from heaven, thereby accounting for the turning of defeat into victory (Crampton 1992; Devereux 1992). The Danish legend bears a striking resemblance to the legend, referred to earlier, of the cross and the monogram of Christ that appeared in the sky before the Emperor Constantine's victory over Maxentius in 312. In the Danish case ancient symbolic representation may have acted as inspiration. The design of the Danish cross flag is likely to have been derived from the war ensign used by the Holy Roman Empire and its provinces, a white cross on a red background (Notholt 1995).

The cross of St George has already been accounted for, but we may add that its origin has been traced back to 1348, when Edward III made St George the patron saint of the Order of the Garter. It was not until the Battle of Agincourt in 1415 that Henry V ordered all the soldiers siding with the English to wear a band with the colours of St George.[18]

Another 'archetypical European' flag that was in use in medieval Europe is the Swiss cross (a white couped cross on a red background, square in shape). A version of the present flag, a red flag with a narrow white cross in its canton (Smith 2004), was used in early medieval Europe by Schwyz, one of the three cantons forming the original league of 1291, but not adopted until the first Confederation of Schwyz, Lucerne, Nidwalden and Uri, in 1480. The use of this flag was restricted prior to 1848, when the modern version was adopted (Crampton 1989), although it had been used in the struggle against the Holy Roman Empire at the Battle of Laupen. It is thus interesting to note that the flags used in the wars between the Confederation and the Empire were both red flags with a white cross, the design of the cross being the only differentiating element, as if to say that we are the *same* (equal) but *different*.

Moving on to the other cross flags, adopted somewhat later, the design of the Swedish flag, a yellow cross on blue, was inspired by its Danish predecessor, whereas its colours were derived from the Swedish coat of arms (Bergsten 1997; Engene 1996; Nevéus 1992, 1993; Swedish Institute 1997). Again, the exact age of the Swedish cross is not known, but the oldest depiction is traced to the sixteenth century. The cross flag is thought to date from the accession of King Gustav Vasa (1496–1560) in 1523, but it may well have been adopted three years earlier in 1520, when Sweden fought against its arch-enemy, Denmark. A royal warrant decreed in 1569 that all Swedish battle standards and banners must bear the yellow cross.

A break with tradition: tricolours, revolutions and republics

The Dutch example is interesting as it signifies a first step towards a new era in which a new type of community was encouraged by means of flags (FOTW 2003; Smith 1975: 156–63, Netherlands Ministry of Foreign Affairs

1999). The Dutch *Princevlag* emerged as a flag of resistance and as a symbol of liberty, and appeared during the struggle for independence from Spain (1568–1648), the 80 years of warfare that led to the formation of the United Provinces of the Netherlands. The first Dutch tricolour displayed the colours orange, white and blue, originated from the livery colours of the House of Orange, and was adopted by supporters of William of Orange (who reigned from 1572–84). From 1597 onwards it was used as the sole Dutch flag, although in the first decades of the Republic (created in 1581 and recognised as independent in 1648), 'red' replaced 'orange' (1630–60) as a sign of political change and growing dissociation from the House of Orange. The red, white and blue tricolour was abolished when the Netherlands was annexed by France in 1810, but was reintroduced in 1815, after the over-throw of Napoleon. Ironically, it was the Dutch tricolour that had originally inspired the French flag, and provided Peter the Great of Russia with a model for the Russian design in the order of white, blue and red (Devereux 1992), and the French and Russian tricolours were to influence many other Euro-pean nations in their choice of flags. The early tricolours came to symbolise the struggle against oppression and the colours (red, white and blue) become known as the three 'colours of liberty'.

Modern national flags

The end of the eighteenth century marks the official appearance of 'national' flags. The establishment of these was in some cases a gradual process, and official recognition would only come after designs and colours had gained some sort of symbolic value for elites and/or people (Smith 1975: 53). As we have seen, many countries had more than one flag denoting 'belonging' before modern times. Varieties of flags referred to vague notions of 'national-ity' and were, in their various designs, used at sea by warships, unarmed vessels and privately owned craft, and on land by state buildings, private businesses and individuals. The first attempts to renegotiate their symbolic representation were made by governing elites, or at times because of popular demand.

The impact of the American (1775–83) and the French (1789) Revolutions needs to be recognised as one context in which flags emerged as political symbols in modern times. Talocci (1995) emphasises that the concept of the 'national flag' is the direct consequence of political developments after the American and the French Revolutions, when the idea of the flag representing the country and its people emerged. Since Europe is the main focus of this chapter, the origin of the American flag will only briefly be mentioned. The American flag was adopted to represent a multi-ethnic people and symbol-ised, first and foremost, the attempt to break free from colonial domination. At the same time the 'Stars and Stripes' flag made a significant contribution to the modern flag tradition, in the idea of a flag representing a 'whole popu-lation' as well as its government, and it also reflected the more egalitarian ideas of the time. The 'Stars and Stripes' was created on 14 July 1777 – by whom and where remains unclear – and it was used in different forms during the remainder of the War of Independence.[19] It is worth noting that America did not have a flag representing it (or the colonies) prior to the conflicts with England.

Developments in France demonstrated a clear break with the *ancien régime* and popular demand for participation in the political process. Prior to the outbreak of the Revolution, the flags of the Bourbon dynasty had been mainly white, as in the case of the two important flags, the Naval Ensign and the Royal Standard, the latter also displaying the golden fleur-de-lis and the royal arms. Besides, individual flags of red, white and blue had been in use long before the Revolution, and combinations of these three colours also had a past as royal livery colours.

The process of renegotiating the official representation of France began with the introduction of cockades.[20] From 1789 onwards, the troops of the Paris Militia – later the National Guard – were required to wear the livery colours of Paris: blue and red (white was added shortly afterwards); and an official naval flag of red, white and blue was adopted in October 1790.[21] The final form of the tricolour design during the first Revolutionary period dates from 1794, when the modern *Tricolore* was substituted for the two previous flags, the Jack and the Ensign, flown at sea and exhibiting vertical stripes of blue, white and red, which were meant to symbolise the new notion of nationhood (Girardet 1998; Smith 1975: 130–9, 2004a).

The many uprisings in nineteenth-century Europe were inspired by the French Revolution and had important effects on the development of national symbolism. The tricolour appeared, for example, in Germany (black, red and gold) as early as the War of Liberation (1813–14), fought against France, when it became a mark of resistance against French administration and domination. The hundreds of German-speaking states belonging to the Holy Roman Empire, until it ceased to exist in 1806, fought for unification under the tricolour as a symbol of liberty during the Napoleonic Wars. The German colours originated primarily from the uniforms of the Lützowian Free Corps (black with gold and red details), who started the resistance, and their influence was later reinforced when they were displayed in the patriotic rallies at Warburg Castle (1817) and Hambach (1832). The German tricolour was adopted by the new German parliament in 1848; in 1867 Bismarck's tricolour of black, white and red superseded it, but the original tricolour was restored with the Weimar Republic in 1919–33 (Hattenauer 1990; Smith 1975: 114–23, 2004b).

The revolutions of 1848–9 followed, in many ways, the French pattern of public revolt since 1789, and the same symbolism was adopted. The tricolour flag became the mark of revolution, and several new tricolour flags appeared in 1848, combining the 'winning' formula of 1789 with national colours and traditions. Thus, tricolours were adopted in Romania, Hungary and Schleswig-Holstein in 1848. The tricolour flag also appeared the same year in Slovakia, imitating the Russian colours, and in Ireland, where the choice of colours was made with unification in mind: 'white' to express peace and unity between the traditional 'green' of Ireland and the 'orange' of the supporters of the late King William of Orange (Hayes-McCoy 1979; Morely 1998; Smith 1975: 156–63). The tricolour appeared in Italy and produced symbolic changes in Parma, Venice and Naples. Savoy-Sardinia established the tricolour as early as March 1848 (adding the shield of Savoy with a blue border), and it was hoisted again in 1859 with the movement to free 'Italy' from Austrian oppression. With some modifications, the tricolour flag was adopted by the unified Kingdom of Italy in 1861. Several of the tricolours flown during the revolutionary year 1848 were lowered in 1849, but some of them have since been restored (Crampton 1992: 127–8).

For many European nations, gaining independence was a long process and the adoption of national flags became the symbol of this struggle. An illustrative example is Norway, which tried to achieve independence from Denmark in 1814, under a red flag with a white cross (like that of the Danes) bearing the Norwegian arms (a golden crowned lion holding an axe). As Norway entered the union with Sweden (1814) the country was reduced to using the Swedish flag with a specific 'union symbol'. The present Norwegian flag dates from 1821, when the white Danish cross on red was overlaid by a blue cross – colours inspired by the French *Tricolore* (Engene 1997a, 1997b; Grimnes, this volume; Smith 2004c).

The disintegration of the Soviet Union saw a resurgence of nationalism in Eastern Europe, spanning a continuum from genocide and ethnic conflict to a struggle for democracy and self-determination. In the midst of all this it may seem a somewhat odd development that national aspirations would also concentrate on symbolic manifestations. Many countries in Central and Eastern Europe redefined themselves, their past and their present, through a process of selecting new national symbols (flags, anthems and national days) from 1989 onwards.

Illuminating examples include the flags of the Baltic states that were restored in 1989 (their national flags of 1918), the adoption of the horizontal Croatian tricolour (red, white and blue) with the chequered shield (Ignatieff 1993: 18), and the flag in Bosnia-Herzegovina in 1998.[22] Looking back, it seems appropriate that the symbol of the 1989 revolution in the GDR, which led to the fall of the Berlin Wall on 9 November, was the flag with the communist emblem cut out of it. The same kind of symbolism was also used in Romania and Bulgaria. Ignatieff, however, writes, 'A state that has a flag with a hole in it is a state that no longer knows what it is' (*ibid.*: 45). Perhaps the interpretation ought to be that a state with a hole in its flag is changing the course of its future and redefining itself via its main national symbol. As Firth argues:

A new national flag is a potent symbol, a highly condensed focus of sentiment which emphasizes the independence of the newly created unit

... it is significant that the entry of the many new states to the United
Nations has always been accompanied by ... the display of their new
flags.

(Firth 1973: 347)

The changes we witnessed in Central and Eastern Europe, where national
borders during the many conflicts of independence had been challenged and
defended, brought about a new symbolic regime of flags which display, *inter
alia*, the pan-Slavic colours of the Russian tricolour. These cases stand in
contrast to examples such as Britain, France, Sweden and Denmark, where
national symbolism has been retained irrespective of border adjustments,
and whose national symbols are taken for granted, because they are no
longer, to the same extent, associated with political controversy.

The national flag refers, through its mere existence, to claims of historical
continuity and established rights to a designated territory, passed from one
generation to another. In other words, claims of a national past and heritage
attached to a historic ancestral territory cannot be dismissed in the modern
world. The conflicts in the Balkans that resulted from such claims during
the 1990s were in part expressed through newly established national flags,
and, more recently, in the renegotiation of nationhood as expressed via the
flag in Ukraine in 2005, during what has become known as the 'Orange
Revolution'.

Concluding remarks: continuity and narrative

Symbolic devices such as flags have long been employed to communicate
meaning and to identify groups and territories. At the same time, they have
also been used to differentiate communities from each other and to visualise
the relationship between 'us' and 'others'. Society depends on a shared
medium of discourse and the use of medieval cross flags by states such as
England, Denmark, Savoy, Spain, Milan, Padua, Genoa and Russia was to
symbolise the holy mission of Christianity, against non-Christians. Some of
these cross flags survived into modern times when they came to represent the
national communities of, for example, England, Denmark and Switzerland.

The national flags of Europe are intimately linked to the formation of
nations and states. Flags are used to legitimise sovereignty and to illustrate
distinctiveness. The novelty of the modern 'national' flag, compared to earlier
practices of identification, reflected the egalitarian ideas of the modern nation,
in contrast to the symbols of earlier societies. By definition, the national flag
was to be available to all citizens and not exclusively to a small privileged
group, or on special occasions. Subsequently, the flag became a subject of
modification, as national goals or the means of achieving these altered.
Moreover, the national flag became an instrument of political action and a
symbol of 'independence', 'liberation' and 'freedom'. Various private notions

of the nation could also be expressed through the flag, which allowed the object to kindle devotion.

In conclusion, a few significant aspects of the European flags will be highlighted in terms of their prototypes, origins, transformations, flag families and symbolic narratives. Firstly, the main European national flag prototypes are the Danish/English cross flags and the Dutch tricolour. The Danish and the Dutch flags survived into modern times and came to represent the modern nations and also influenced many other flags. St George's Cross of England is also influential, but it did not remain the sole national flag after the formation of the United Kingdom. All the Scandinavian cross flags were inspired by the Danish flag. Modelled on the Dutch tricolour, the French and the Russian tricolours subsequently inspired the tricolours that became established in the nineteenth and twentieth centuries. The colours of the French tricolour, symbolising the ideals of the Revolution, have been extraordinarily influential, inspiring many other tricolours, but also the colours of cross flags, such as the Norwegian and Icelandic flags. The colours red, white and blue became recognised as the pan-Slavic colours, and were later associated with the nineteenth-century movement recognising a common ethnic background for the eastern, western and southern Slavs, a movement rejected by the competing national identities which emerged in the twentieth century.

Secondly, European flags may be categorised in accordance with their immediate origins, as symbols of warfare, revolution, independence, or state-reconstitution. The earliest flags are symbols of *warfare* (of which some appeared as cross flags or as naval flags), as in the cases of Denmark, Sweden, England, Switzerland, The Netherlands and Russia. The flags of *revolution* (and political upheaval) are those of France, Italy, Germany, Portugal, Spain and the former communist countries (variations on the Red Flag for the latter). The flags of *independence* include those of The Netherlands, Belgium, Greece, Hungary, Finland, Bulgaria, Norway, Ireland, Poland, Lithuania, Estonia, Latvia, Iceland, Croatia and Slovenia.[23] Many flags also appear as flags of *state-reconstitution* during the formation of unions and the dissolution of the empires, as with the United Kingdom (the Union Jack), Romania, Finland, Austria, the Federal Republic of Yugoslavia, Czechoslovakia, Germany, Russia, the Czech Republic and Slovakia.

Thirdly, national flags continue to reflect the political realities of nations and are introduced and promulgated during, or after, significant national events. As a general rule, the history of the flag provides an understanding of the (subjective) history of the nation. Generally speaking, the major changes in the development and symbolism of European flags are connected to revolution, occupation, independence and union; transformations from monarchies to republics (Netherlands, France, Italy, Russia) and *vice versa* (France 1814, Italy 1861); communist domination (the Baltic States, Central and Eastern Europe) and anti-communist transformations (the removal of communist emblems); and fascism (Italy and Germany and their satellite states during World War II) and anti-fascist transformations (with national flags readopted). Changes in national symbolism take place when the associations attaching to nation and nationhood are renegotiated.

Finally, national flags constitute 'national narratives' and can be classified in accordance with different symbolic groups or flag-families. A detailed account of this analysis is beyond the scope of this chapter (see Elgenius 2005a, 2007). The main flag types can be identified as *cross flags*, *tricolours* and *heraldic flags*; these have originated in different periods of times and are linked by common traditions. The third group, which I call heraldic flags, mainly includes *younger* national flags displaying heraldic colours or devices that are claimed to have originated in the Middle Ages.[24] Clearly, some cross flags and tricolours have been influenced by coats of arms and livery colours, but these flags were primarily adopted with religious or revolutionary aims in mind, following specific thematic patterns and designs.

Notes

1   For a typology of national flags in Europe, and details about their origins, development and usage, see Elgenius 2005a. For a discussion of the complex process of nation-building and the establishment of the national flags and holidays in France, Britain, Norway and Germany, see Elgenius 2005b.

2   See: Crampton 1989 and 1992; Hulme 1915; Preble 1980; Smith 1975 and 1969. Available sources on flags are of different age and quality. W. Smith's study of 1969 and his opus of 1975 are, so far, the most comprehensive study of flags. With regard to recent developments and flag-related matters, the website 'Flags of the World', a member of the Fédération Internationale des Associations Vexillologiques (FIAV), supplies a bank of articles: http://www.crwflags.com/fotw/flags

3   It is not the aim of this chapter to define the nation, other than as a 'working definition' only. The 'nation' refers here to a social group and its sense of shared cultural and/or political experiences, but also to its overall adherence to a complex of symbols that constitutes the boundaries between 'us' and 'them' (Elgenius 2005a).

4   For a detailed survey of European flags, see Elgenius 2005a: 73–9.

5   The term 'vexillology' was coined by W. Smith and has been a separate study since the 1960s.

6   As regards the earlier civilisations, astral symbols with religious significance appeared in Indian and Mesopotamian cultures around 2000 BC. Two emblems that have continued to be reproduced throughout time, the Babylonian stele of Ur Nammu and a representation of the crescent moon and the rayed star of Shamash (the sun god) have been dated to this time, 2100 BC. The standards of the Anatolian civilisation (2000–1000 BC) were linked to stags, whereas the Assyrians until 640 BC used standards with bulls and the emblem of Assur, the divine archer of the Sun (a winged disc). Later, the Persians in 500–400 BC used the winged disc in a more elaborate form. A sun and moon standard is recorded (how remains unknown) in Phoenicia from 500 BC onwards, an era during which a signal flag marked the ship of an admiral or communicated a command to attack (Crampton 1992: 111–16; Smith 1975: 38ff.).

7   The totemic system varied as much as the theories trying to explain it (e.g. Durkheim 1976; Evans-Pritchard 1965: 48–77).

8 The *labarum* itself is described as a jewelled square purple cloth, hanging from the crossbar of a long gilded pike, with a golden wreath with the cross monogram displayed on the top of the spear. The *labarum* has been dated thanks to the documentation of coins issued at Constantinople after Constantine's victory over Licinus in 324 (Hulme 1915: 2–3, 51).

9 'In this sign thou shalt conquer' (Crampton 1992: 111ff.).

10 'Red' was associated with the two caliphs (Arabic: *chalifa*, 'successors'), Abu Bakr, who initiated the caliphate, and Umar. White flags were used by the Ummayads, in commemoration of Mohammed. The Abbassids, who transferred the capital from Damascus to Baghdad, chose the contrasting colour of black, with the justification that this was after all the true colour of Mohammed's flag. Subsequently the Fatimids selected green (the flag is called *borda*), by tradition the colour of the cloak used by Mohammed. The so-called 'Secessionists' – the Kharijites – were represented by red, used earlier, and later also used by the Ottomans (Smith 1975).

11 One example is the banner attributed to the Moorish State of Granada in the eighth century, which displayed the inscription 'There is no conqueror but God' on a red background.

12 A banner refers to a cloth stretched between two anchor points bearing a slogan, or a flag with heraldic arms, or a flag carried by a military unit ('Glossary of Flag Terms': http://fotw.digibel.be/flags/flagglos.html).

13 It is impossible to provide a precise date for the first cloth flags, since fabric flags have not been preserved from the Middle Ages (Smith 1975: 37–8ff.).

14 Woodcock and Robinson define heraldry as the 'systematic hereditary use of an arrangement of charges and devices on a shield' (1990: 1). Heraldic devices and colours emerged in the mid-twelfth century, over a wide area of Europe.

15 Livery colours are the main colours of the field (background) and on the principal charge (motive) of a coat of arms. A 'badge' is a distinctive emblem added to a flag or used on its own (Crampton 1989: 133; Smith 1975: 13).

16 An 'armorial flag' corresponds exactly to the shield of the coat of arms.

17 Smith illustrates how the Crusader cross (red couped cross on white), originally adopted as a Christian symbol, influenced the development of three main streams of cross flags, some of which were used in the Middle Ages, others not until the modern period. In the first version we find a coloured cross on white, as in the cross flags adopted by England, Genoa, Milan, Padua, Sardinia (red cross on white), by Finland (blue cross on white) or by Nantes (black cross on white). The second version of the Crusader cross is a white cross on a coloured background, such as a white cross on red displayed in the flags of Denmark, Savoy, Malta and Vienna, and the white cross on blue used in the flags of France and Greece, and the yellow cross on blue adopted by Sweden. Thirdly, the original Saltire cross (red diagonal cross on white) was used by Ireland (St Patrick's cross) and by Spain, and served as the inspiration for the white diagonal cross on blue used by Scotland (St Andrew's cross), or the blue diagonal cross on white adopted by Russia, also known as St Andrew's cross (Smith 1975: 46–52).

18 St George's cross is the founding component of the Union Jack, reflecting the reality of the political union of 1801, after the formation of the United Kingdom in 1800. A union flag was initiated as early as 1606, following the personal union of the crowns of Scotland and England, although the independent national cross flags of England and Scotland were still in use on land and were legally formalised in 1707 (Notholt 1996; Smith 1975: 180–9).

19 A special jack had been selected for the colonial governments in 1701, but whether it was in fact used is not clear. It is likely that the colonial civil ships and merchant vessels had their own jack and ensign before 1707, displaying the

Union Jack in the canton of the ensigns. It is noteworthy that one of the first manifestations of American 'resistance' was a Red Ensign with the motto 'Liberty and Union', which was hoisted a year before the Revolution in Taunton, Massachusetts. Even earlier, in 1769, Boston had flown a flag of red and white stripes. The use of the Red Ensign with the motto in the fly constituted together with the Boston striped flag a main starting point for the colonial flags evolution during 1775. In 1776 the flag hoisted in Massachusetts was described as 'English Colours but more Striped', i.e. a British Red Ensign but with white stripes across the field. The number of stars on the American flag has changed with time from 13 to 50 in order to correspond with the increasing number of states. This process commenced after the Declaration of Independence in 1776 (Crampton 1992: 120–9; Marvin and Ingle 1999; Smith 1975: 190–9).

20 A 'cockade' was a rosette (a badge) in livery or national colours and was an important political symbol.

21 Three-quarters of this new war ensign were still white, but its canton (the upper hoist quarter of the flag) repeated the national colours twice: vertical stripes of red, white and blue, thus the reverse of the modern order, were bordered by the same colours. The design of this canton also served separately as a French jack (flown at the bow of a ship).

22 *Flagmaster* 1998; *The Law on the Flag of Bosnia and Herzegovina*, adopted by the Office of the High Representatives, Sarajevo: http://fotw. digibel.be/flags/ ba-law.html

23 The flags of Ukraine and Belarus are also flags of independence.

24 The central elements of heraldic flags are the emblems or colours displayed and these are of a more recent origin compared to cross and tricolour flags. With many of the new heraldic flags we find that the past is used to justify the nation in the present and a more recent date of national independence. Heraldic colours and emblems are used to symbolise a distinct national heritage and, at times, a golden age of sovereignty. When Poland, finally independent in 1918, adopted a new flag, it was based on the old coat of arms dating from the Polish–Lithuanian union (fourteenth century). When independence was declared in 1918, Lithuania, too, originally revived a heraldic banner claimed to date from this period. Myths of heroism are connected to a number of flags using the backing of an ancient past by means of particular colours and old heraldic designs, such as in the case of the Austria flag mentioned earlier.

3 Rebel with(out) a cause?

The contested meanings of the Confederate battle flag in the American South

Jonathan Leib and Gerald Webster

As noted in the introductory chapter of this volume, flags are 'symbolic containers', with most country flags today symbolizing membership in a national citizenry. National flags therefore 'condense' a range of meanings and emotions pertaining to a group's perceived common historical experience, real or imagined cultural homogeneity, and efforts to define a similarity of outlook for the future. Frequently a central purpose for such flags is to highlight centripetal forces of cohesion, to overcome all existing centrifugal forces of disunion. This function is clearly critical in the multi-national states that dominate the roll of existing countries in the world today. As such, flags are a central element of the 'glue' that states develop as part of their sets of national iconography, which may also include myths, heroes, monuments, religious perspectives, language and even sports (Webster 2006). However, the symbolism of a flag does not always disappear when the formal state ceases to exist. Rather, elements of a failed state's iconography such as its flag may persist and develop additional symbolism through time. Such is the case for the flags associated with the short-lived Confederate States of America (1861–5).

The meanings and emotions that are condensed within flags are constructed, enforced and contested over time. Given the power that such symbols can hold over a society, the politics to control and impose the meaning condensed within flags can be intensive. When two or more groups disagree over the meaning of a flag, the group that ultimately controls the 'power of definition', to borrow John Western's phrase (1997: 8), can control an important element in the battle over social relations within its territory. Because its present meaning(s) and symbolism contrast sharply, depending on the demographic group surveyed, the Confederate battle flag provides an excellent example of the vitriolic character of the process of contestation.

Racial divisions have long been the central fault line on the political landscape of the American South. No issue confirms this reality more clearly than the region's controversies over the meanings of the flags of the Confederate States of America (CSA). The most passionate of these debates have centred upon the public display of the Confederate 'battle flag'. Many Southern whites interpret the battle flag as representative of the honourable struggle of their ancestors in the American Civil War, and they view the flag as emblematic of their proud heritage. Other Southern whites interpret the battle flag as representative of their culture generally, and thus as a symbolic container which condenses all that it means to be a (white) Southerner. Oftentimes this interpretation does not directly include reference to the Civil War itself, but principally to the values viewed by many white Southerners as central to the region's Antebellum culture. Others, including both Southern and non-Southern whites, interpret the flag as a generic symbol of rebellion or defiance. On the other hand, a majority of the region's African American citizens view the battle flag as emblematic of the South's efforts to preserve slavery in the Civil War and the region's more recent efforts to deny members of minority groups their rights of citizenship during the Civil Rights Movement. As a result, a substantial majority of African American Southerners view the battle flag as a symbol of racial discrimination, intolerance and hatred.

The history of the Confederate battle flag

The Confederate battle flag is one of the four flags most directly associated with the Confederate States of America (1861–5). It is also known as the 'Rebel Flag', the 'Starry Cross', and the 'Southern Cross' (see Figure 3.1 for this and the other Confederate flags). Though it is the best-known symbol of the short-lived CSA, the Confederate battle flag never served as the official flag of the Confederacy.

The first national flag of the Confederate States of America, also known as the 'Stars and Bars', was flown from 1861 until 1863. The Stars and Bars was designed purposely to be a modification of the United States flag, due to Southern respect for the U.S. national flag. But the resulting similarity soon caused confusion in battle during the early stages of the Civil War, and as the war progressed there was increasing animosity against Northern forces carrying the U.S. national flag. Battlefield confusion eventually led to the adoption of the Rebel Flag as the CSA's battle flag. In 1863, the Stars and Bars was replaced as the Confederacy's national flag as well. The second national flag, also known as the 'Stainless Banner', contained the battle emblem in the upper left corner, with the remainder of the flag being white. While some have suggested that the white field represented the purity of the Confederate cause from a religious perspective, others have contended that the flag's white field was emblematic of the white racist foundations of the CSA. Arguably, the commonplace conflation of racism and religion in the nineteenth-century South suggests that both interpretations are correct (Bonner 2002; Sebasta 2004; Sebasta and Hague 2002; Webster 1997; Webster and Leib 2007). Problems with the Stainless Banner rapidly emerged because it can be confused with a flag of surrender on a windless day. This problem led it to be replaced by the Confederate Congress with the third national flag of the Confederacy, shortly before the end of the war. This

Figure 3.1 Four flags of the Confederacy.

Upper Left: Confederate battle flag ('Rebel flag')

Upper Right: First national flag of the Confederacy, 1861–1863 ('Stars and Bars')

Lower Left: Second national flag of the Confederacy, 1863–1865 ('Stainless Banner')

Lower Right: Third national flag of the Confederacy, 1865

third national flag added a vertical red stripe to the right edge of the white field of the second national flag (Bonner 2002; Cannon 1988; Coski 2005).

While we do not have the space in this chapter for a full discussion, for a variety of reasons after the Civil War the battle emblem became the most recognized symbol of the Confederacy, with the three national flags fading into comparative obscurity (see Webster and Leib 2007; Webster and Webster 1994). First, given the rapid changes to the national flags of the CSA, Southern troops became far more familiar with the battle flag during the Civil War than with the three national flags. Second, the battle flag was commonly used in post-Civil War soldiers' reunions and other festive occasions, adding to its stature and familiarity to the public at large. Third, the battle flag was frequently flown by U.S. military personnel hailing from the South during the Second World War fully 75 years after the end of the Civil War, increasing its familiarity and acceptability to many. Fourth, the battle flag became widely used by white racists during the 'Massive Resistance' to efforts to end racial segregation in the region during the 1950s and 1960s. Fifth, more recently the flag has been widely used by white Southern nationalist and heritage groups. Some of these groups, such as the Council of Conservative Citizens and League of the South, are classified as 'hate groups' by the Southern Poverty Law Center, the leading tracker of hate groups in the U.S. (Hague *et al.* 2007; Webster 2004; Webster and Leib 2007).

Scale and the Confederate battle flag debate

At the core of many contemporary controversies over the Confederate battle flag is the regional identity of the South. Who among the region's population may claim appropriate lineage as a 'Southerner'? Does the term apply to all of those who are from the region, or only to a subset of the region's population, namely, whites? It is critical to point out that these debates over the flag and regional identity are being waged at a number of different geographic scales above and below that of the region of the South. For example, along with the regional scale, recent battle flag controversies have become politicized and publicized at the individual, local, state and even national geographic scales. As a result, regional identity is not solely defined at that geographic scale.

State level

The most widely publicized and strongly contested disputes over the Confederate battle flag have occurred in the states of the American South (Leib *et al.* 2000; Leib and Webster 2002). The most vitriolic controversies have been waged at the state level in the 'Deep South' states of South Carolina (Hill 2002; Prince 2004; Webster and Leib 2001), Alabama (Webster and Leib 2002), Mississippi (Leib and Webster 2003), and Georgia (Leib 1995;

Leib and Webster 2004b). In both Alabama and South Carolina the battle flag flew over the state capitol domes, while in Georgia and Mississippi the battle emblem was incorporated into the state flag. In these controversies, battle flag proponents and opponents have clashed in their attempts to define the values that each state government is sanctioning by allowing the flying of the battle emblem in public spaces.

The battle flag was placed atop the dome of the South Carolina state capitol building in Columbia in 1962. Supporters of the battle flag argue that it was placed on the capitol dome to celebrate the Civil War Centennial. In opposition, others contended that the flag's placement was to underscore the resolve of the state's then exclusively white political leadership to forestall, if not prevent, racial integration (Hill 2002; Prince 2004; Webster and Leib 2001). Black political leaders began demanding that the flag be removed from the dome in the early 1990s, with the debate becoming progressively more heated as the decade progressed. A boycott by the National Association for the Advancement of Colored People (NAACP), and large-scale protests against the flag, finally led to a compromise, which moved the flag off the state house dome to a nearby Confederate soldier's memorial. This outcome was not fully embraced by either pro-flag or anti-flag forces.

The battle flag was placed on top of the Alabama state capitol building in Montgomery in 1963, by then-Governor and fiery segregationist George Wallace. Wallace raised the flag over the state capitol dome immediately prior to a visit by U.S. Attorney General Robert F. Kennedy to discuss efforts to desegregate the University of Alabama in Tuscaloosa. To many, Wallace's act was clearly to signal his intention to defy federal authority over Alabama's segregationist state laws and traditions. The battle flag remained above the state capitol until 1987, when it was temporarily removed, along with the state and federal flags, to make extensive renovations to the building. Prior to the completion of the renovations, African American state legislators successfully filed a lawsuit that prevented the battle flag from being returned to the top of the dome. Instead, the flag currently flies at a Confederate soldier's memorial next to the capitol building on the capitol grounds. In addition, the battle flag flew inside the chambers of the lower House of the Alabama state legislature. In 1999 a black lawmaker successfully negotiated replacing the battle flag within the chambers with the Stars and Bars, the first national flag of the Confederacy. Repeated attempts by pro-flag legislators to return the battle flag to the top of the state capitol dome and to the House's chambers have been unsuccessful (Webster and Leib 2002).

In Georgia, the battle emblem was incorporated into the state flag in 1956, two years after the U.S. Supreme Court's ruling in *Brown v. Board of Education* declared segregated public schools unconstitutional. The evidence suggests that the emblem, dominating the right two-thirds of the flag, was added as an act of defiance against the desegregation efforts of the federal government (Davis 1998; Leib 1995). In 1993, Georgia Governor Zell

Miller unsuccessfully led an effort to remove the battle emblem from the state flag. In 2001, Governor Roy Barnes, backed by black state legislators and Georgia's business community, successfully passed a bill through the legislature creating a new flag, which minimized the size of the battle emblem and placed it in a historical context with other flags that have flown over Georgia during its history. In 2002, Barnes lost re-election, thanks in part to increased turnout among rural whites from southern Georgia, who were angry about his efforts to change the state flag. In 2003, the state's legislative session was dominated by attempts to restore the battle emblem to the state's flag. Opponents of the battle emblem flag were ultimately successful in the floor debate and instead agreed to adopt a new flag resembling the Stars and Bars, along with a state-wide referendum that allowed voters to ratify the choice of this new flag, without presenting voters with the battle emblem state flag as a viable alternative. While still resembling *a* Confederate flag, battle emblem opponents saw this new Stars and Bars flag as less objectionable than the one dominated by the battle emblem. In 2004 this new flag was approved overwhelmingly in the public referendum, with support from both white and black Georgia voters (Leib 1995; Leib and Webster 2004b, 2006).

The battle emblem was added to the Mississippi state flag in 1894. In 2000, the Mississippi State Supreme Court issued a ruling emanating from a lawsuit, first filed in 1994, which sought the elimination of the battle emblem from the state flag. Rather than ruling directly on the legality of the battle emblem, the Court found instead that the state did not have an official state flag, because the flag as adopted by the state legislature in 1894 was not included in a 1906 revision of the state's constitution (*Mississippi Division of the United Sons of Confederate Veterans v. Mississippi State Conference of NAACP Branches* 2000). In reaction to this finding, the Mississippi state legislature provided for a public referendum in 2001 that asked the state's voters to choose between the 1894 battle-emblem state flag or a newly designed flag. With the international and national media closely following the campaign, the Mississippi electorate voted to retain the battle emblem flag by a two-to-one margin, with race being the dominant fault line in the vote (Leib and Webster 2002, 2003).

Individual

Controversy over the battle flag's symbolism has occurred at other geographical scales, including at the scale of the individual in a variety of contexts. For example, in recent years a number of school districts throughout the region have banned clothing featuring the battle emblem, in order to reduce racial tensions between students (Beirich and Moser 2003; Ford 2003). Some of these bans have been challenged in the court system (Henry 2004). Private businesses have also been affected, not least among these being manufacturers that produce clothing with Confederate symbols including the battle flag (Leib and Dittmer 2006).

One of the most widely publicized cases involving a private company pertained to South Carolina's Maurice Bessinger, owner of the state's largest barbecue restaurant chain and a noted battle flag defender, who in the 1960s was one of the state's most ardent segregationists (Bessinger 2001). In 2000, following the removal of the Confederate battle flag from the top of the South Carolina state house, Bessinger removed the U.S. flags flying outside his restaurants and replaced them with the battle flag and the South Carolina state flag. In spite of growing controversy and negative effects upon his business, Bessinger refused requests to remove the battle flag from outside his restaurants. His refusal, combined with the discovery that he was distributing racist literature at his restaurants, led to what is now a six-year boycott of his barbecue chain and products (Webster and Leib 2007).

Local

Various localities have also been sites in the battle over the flag. For example, protests took place in 2001 in Lake City, Florida, because its municipal seal incorporates the battle flag (Andio 2001), while debate over the flag emerged in 2005 in Maryville, Tennessee, after that city's Board of Education banned the flying of the battle flag by fans at local high school football games (Barker *et al.* 2005). Similarly a long-standing fight along the Mississippi Gulf Coast was settled in 2002, when the electorate of Harrison County voted to keep the battle flag flying as one of an eight-flag display on the beach along the Biloxi/Gulfport Mississippi border (the battle flag representing one of the eight flags that have flown over Mississippi during its history).[1]

The flag has also been used as a symbol protest on the Southern landscape against the commemoration of the Civil Rights Era. For example, in 1997, a monument to Viola Liuzzo, located at the site where she was slain by members of the Ku Klux Klan during the 1965 Voting Rights March from Selma to Montgomery, Alabama, was vandalized, when a battle flag was spray painted over it (Stanton 1998). In 1995, white protesters carried battle flags at the Richmond, Virginia, groundbreaking ceremony for a statue to Arthur Ashe on the city's grandest Confederate memorial site, Monument Avenue (Leib 2002). Four years later, protesters unfurled a giant battle flag at the grand opening ceremony of Richmond's Canal Walk redevelopment project, after a large portrait of Confederate General Robert E. Lee was removed from a series of murals depicting the city's history as one part of the project. The portrait was removed after a complaint from an African American city councilman (Leib 2004).

Regional

At the regional level of the South, a variety of groups have been actively involved in the flag debate. Most prominent have been 'Neo-Confederate' groups, who view the region as the exclusive domain of native Southern white Christians (African Americans are largely if not entirely excluded from their definition of the region), and who seek secession, if necessary, to create their vision of a white Christian South (Hague *et al.* 2005; Webster and Leib 2007). Including the League of the South, the Council of Conservative Citizens and, more recently, the Sons of Confederate Veterans, these groups have actively defended and flown the Confederate battle flag over the past two decades (Potok 2000; Sebasta and Hague 2002; Webster 2004; Webster and Leib 2007). They have also been prominent in local and state-wide controversies about the flag, have worked to defeat legislators they view as anti-battle flag, have lobbied heavily for legislation promoting, protecting and defining the flag's meaning (for example, the SCV has filed lawsuits against state motor vehicle agencies to force them to issue specialty car license plates that feature the battle emblem), and have sponsored projects to place Confederate flags in home-owners' yards and high above interstate highways (Webster and Leib 2001, 2007).

National

While the debate over the Confederate flag is normally seen as a regional issue, it has taken on national importance as well. In 2000 and 2004, the flag became an issue in the U.S. presidential elections, especially in the 2000 Republican primaries and the 2004 Democratic primaries. The U.S. Senate was brought into the debate over Confederate flags in 1993, when the then-only African American member of that body, Senator Carol Moseley-Braun of Illinois, led the fight to stop the chamber from renewing the patent for the insignia of the United Daughters of the Confederacy, which features the first national flag of the Confederacy (Webster and Webster 1994). The passionate debate over the issue foreshadowed more recent controversies about the flag in the region over the past decade.

The meanings of the flag: the power of definition

These various debates and political and legal battles over the right to display Confederate flags might be considered trivial if they did not shed light on the long and tumultuous history of race relations and racial divides in the American South. The region's debates over the flags of the Confederacy indicate a substantial societal cleavage largely defined by race. As we have argued elsewhere, in the region's social relations:

> ... whites constitute the core societal cleavage due to their numeric advantage as well as their historic control over the region's political and economic systems. In contrast, Southern African-Americans constitute the societal periphery, at least from the vantage point of many Southern whites.
>
> (Leib and Webster 2002: 224)

While the salience of this division has lessened in the past couple decades, its long historical social significance has not been eradicated and it clearly continues to affect the Deep South's socio-political structures. This cleavage is particularly striking in public opinion polls, as well as in legislative and popular votes on the Confederate flag issue. For example, public opinion polls in the region find a dramatic racial divide, with many Southern whites wishing to enshrine the flag in public places while most African American Southerners view the battle flag as a racist symbol that should never receive government sanction for display in the region's public places (Leib 1998; Leib and Webster 2002). In earlier work analysing state legislative votes about the public display of the flag in South Carolina, Alabama and Georgia, we found that race was by far the most salient influence on these votes (Leib and Webster 2004b, 2006; Webster and Leib 2001, 2002).

Champions of Southern heritage commonly argue that the Confederate battle flag is an honourable symbol in which all Southerners can take pride. For example, in a recent opinion column in the *Birmingham News* (Alabama), a member of the Sons of Confederate Veterans argued that the battle flag 'ought to be the honored heritage of every Southerner and every American'. He also contended that the flag was an 'acknowledgement of God', represented a 'government of law' and Southern opposition to 'unjust taxation' (Scruggs 2006). The column prompted a series of letters to the editor, with many arguing that the flag had racist overtones due to its use as the battle emblem of Confederate troops in the American Civil War. As one letter writer argued:

> The Confederate flag represents people who wanted to keep my ancestors enslaved because they thought we were no better than a horse or a mule ... Celebrate your ancestors by saying a prayer for them instead of waving that flag around.
>
> (Jeter 2006)

How can these diametrically opposed positions by different Southerners be explained? To aid our understanding the political dynamics of these debates over the Confederate battle flag, the concepts of *iconography* and *public memory* are useful. The concept of iconography was first introduced to geography by the French scholar Jean Gottmann (1952). Gottmann focused on the societal forces that might aid in the reconstruction of states devastated during the Second World War. In his work, iconography referred to a common set of symbols, used to bind a group of people together within a territory. While these icons generally act as centripetal forces, to unify a country's population by providing a common set of national values embraced by the citizens of a state, icons such as the battle flag can also clearly serve as centrifugal forces, dividing a state's population along major cultural and racial cleavages.

Icons and their meanings are socially constructed, and these meanings can be deconstructed 'within a larger complex of cultural, social and political values' (Boime 1998: 2). The contrasts between the competing meanings of icons are rarely, if ever, completely resolved; rather, they are subject to continuous redefinition and debate. Through the use of the concept of public memory, John Bodnar (1992, 1994) has suggested that how the past and its symbols are interpreted, commemorated and represented is as much about shaping how society understands its *present* and *future*, as it is about the past. Bodnar also argues that this process is heavily political, always changing and commonly contested (see also, Johnson 2004). Brooks Simpson, a Civil War historian, has argued that the Neo-Confederate movement, in its strident and very public defence of the Confederacy, its cause and its symbols, is attempting to develop a revisionist history of the Civil War, in a project to redefine the South's public memory (see Levine 2006). As Simpson suggests:

> This is an active attempt to reshape historical memory, an effort by white Southerners to find historical justification for present-day actions. The neo-Confederate movement's ideologues have grasped that if they control how people remember the past, they'll control how people approach the present and the future.
>
> (quoted in Potok 2000: 36)

Thus, rather than simply a fight over the contested meaning of a piece of cloth, the contest to define the meaning of the battle flag is part of a broader war to exert control over societal relations.

The debates over the Confederacy, its foundations and its symbols in the American South represent one part of a series of so-called 'culture wars' that have been waged over the past several decades in the United States, largely over controversial social issues. As Don Mitchell (2000: 5) argues, these culture 'wars are about defining what is legitimate in a society, who is an "insider" and who is an '"outsider". They are about determining the social boundaries that govern our lives.' Andrew Manis notes:

> For contemporary Southerners, perhaps the most hotly contested battleground of the culture wars remains how to deal with the region's Confederate past . . . [and] . . . no segment of this larger concern is more controversial than debates about the Confederate flag.
>
> (2005: 179)

Thus, the fights over who has the power to define the meaning of the flag are about what (and who) is legitimate in society, and most particularly, who is a 'true' Southerner.

The various and contradictory meanings ascribed to the Confederate battle flag in the American South provide the foundation for the region's ongoing controversies over its past, and thus future (Leib 1995, 1998; Leib and Webster 2002, 2004a, 2006; Leib *et al.* 2000; Webster and Leib 2001, 2002, 2007; Webster and Webster 1994). Next, we discuss the flag's contested meanings: as heritage, hell-raising and regional pride, on the one hand, and hatred and racism, on the other.

Heritage, hell-raising and regional pride

As pointed out earlier, many traditional white Southerners view the Confederate battle flag as a symbol of their ancestors' efforts to defend themselves against the invasion of federal military forces during the Civil War. They argue the flag has no racist symbolism, nor is it symbolic of the region's historical oppression of African Americans. Rather, to these flag defenders the battle emblem represents the Confederacy's heroic efforts to defend its homes and way of life against the onslaught of the Union's numerically superior forces. As such, the flag is deemed a symbol of a noble heritage, a viewpoint regularly reiterated on a popular automobile bumper sticker in the region, which declares the flag is a symbol of 'heritage not hate'.

In addition to bumper stickers, the South has a long history of attempting to define and document the flag's meaning. As noted earlier, the battle emblem was incorporated into the Georgia state flag in the late 1950s, as the 100-year anniversary of the Civil War approached. A state brochure prepared to explain the change stated that it was:

> to create a living memorial to the Confederacy ... Embracing the beloved Battle Flag of the Confederacy within our own State emblem portrays in part the unbounded love, admiration, and respect that we of today have for them of yesterday.
>
> (Fortson 1957: 12)

In the 1990s, Georgia battle flag supporters also argued that the 1950s modifications to the state flag were simply to honour the bravery of their ancestors, in recognition of the upcoming centennial celebrations, and not to underscore white defiance against the rapidly emerging Civil Rights Movement. South Carolina political leaders also argued the flag was raised over their state capitol in 1962 solely to celebrate the Civil War centennial. In 1997 a proposed legislative compromise which would have removed the battle flag from the South Carolina capitol dome included language that legally codified the official state's interpretation of the flag's meaning by declaring it 'a nonpolitical symbol of heritage' (quoted in Webster and Leib 2001).

Similarly, after the battle flag was removed from the chamber of the Alabama House of Representatives in 1999 and replaced with the first national flag of the Confederacy, a resolution was introduced by a strong legislative battle flag defender. His resolution proclaimed that the battle flag was the 'only Confederate flag recognized by the state of Alabama' (this in spite of the fact that the first national flag of the Confederacy had flown over Montgomery while the city briefly served as the first capital of the Confederacy, in 1861). His resolution went on to state that 'the Confederate Battle Flag is an important symbol of the Heritage of the South and of the State of Alabama, no less a source of great pride in our American Heritage than the United States Flag' (quoted in Webster and Leib 2002: 9). That there were blatant racial overtones when Governor George Wallace placed the battle flag on the state capitol dome in 1963 is a historical reality seemingly lost on the white legislator.

Today, a variety of Neo-Confederate groups, such as the Sons of Confederate Veterans and the League of the South, passionately uphold the flag as a proud symbol of their white Southern Christian heritage (Webster and Leib 2007). These organizations have received varying degrees of publicity and support in the region and have been able to reach a worldwide audience through their use of the internet (Warf and Grimes 1997; Webster 2004).

A second meaning ascribed to the flag is as 'an all-purpose symbol of revolt, defiance, militancy and even general hell-raising' (Wellikoff 1994: 24). The flag received renewed visibility after the success of the 1939 movie about the Civil War, *Gone With the Wind* (Hale 1998). Shortly thereafter it was used by American military troops from the South during the Second World War, as a rallying symbol against the Axis powers (McElroy 1995). This growing use and subsequent recognition of the battle flag led it to become a popular culture icon by the late 1940s and 1950s. Today the flag is not only flown in the American South, but also elsewhere in the United States as well as abroad. In many cases the flag is intended to symbolize defiance and rebelliousness against the established order or authority generally. Leib suggests that this 'reading of the flag is interesting because it detaches racial issues and racism from the flag, despite that these notions of defiance ascribed to the flag are based on Southern secession in the 1860s' (1998: 233). Or, as one commentator has noted, the flag has become 'the symbolic middle finger' (quoted in Wetzel 2006).

The use of the flag as a symbol of defiance is also tied to the flag's meaning as a symbol of (white) Southern regional pride. For much of the twentieth century, the American South was seen by the rest of the country as America's 'other', a 'backwards', inferior region, especially in the Northern states (Jansson 2003). Flying the battle flag as a proud symbol of the South is an effort by some (white) Southerners to flip this reading of regional relations on its head, by proclaiming the superiority of the South, and displaying 'the symbolic middle finger' to the North. Parallel to this interpretation of the battle flag is its use to celebrate white Southern culture, sometimes with overtones of a 'redneck' version of that culture. The flag has been interpreted this way primarily through its use in mid- to late-twentieth-century popular culture, for example its display on the roof of the car (the 'General Lee') in the popular 1970s television show 'The Dukes of Hazzard' and the 2005 movie by the same name. In this view, the flag is interpreted as a celebration of white Southern culture devoid of any overt racist context. This perspective was advanced in an August 2000 statement by Georgia State Senate Minority Party Leader, Republican Eric Johnson, who defended the battle emblem's inclusion in the Georgia state flag by arguing that 'nobody looks at it as a symbol of hate'. Rather, he argued, to the 'vast majority of Georgians', the flag stands for 'pickup trucks, deer hunting, barefoot girls and boiled peanuts' (quoted in McMurray 2000). In spite of the Senator's claims to the contrary, there is a racial dimension to this rural and masculinist conception of 'southernness', because the accompanying imagery almost universally includes white drivers of pickup trucks, white deer hunters and white barefoot girls, as opposed to images of African Americans in the same circumstances.

Hatred and racism

If some Southerners define the Confederate battle flag as a symbol of heritage and regional pride, others within the region are working to rewrite this definition. The battle flag is viewed by many, including an overwhelming majority of African Americans, as a symbol of racial intolerance and hatred, which was used by Confederate forces during the Civil War as they defended the Southern 'way of life' and slavery. In the 1950s and 1960s, the battle flag was used by those opposing the Civil Rights Movement's demands that the basic rights of U.S. citizenship be extended to the South's African American population. The use of the flag for these purposes increased dramatically after the U.S. Supreme Court's 1954 decision in *Brown v. Board of Education*, which declared segregated public schools unconstitutional. In Alabama in 1956, for example, the flag was a rallying symbol for those whites at the University of Alabama protesting about the first attempt to enrol a black student (Clark 1993). Seven years later Alabama Governor George Wallace raised it over the state capitol to protest the federal government's efforts that eventually desegregated the University. The flag was also used by Governor-elect Wallace during his 1963 inauguration, during which he made his now infamous declaration of 'Segregation now . . . segregation tomorrow . . . segregation forever' (Carter 1995). Writing in 1965 about white Mississippians' use of the flag in their struggle to stop the civil rights advances sought by the state's African American citizens, famed Southern writer Walker Percy noted that 'the Confederate flag, once the battle emblem of brave men . . . has come to stand for raw racism and hoodlum defiance of the law' (1997: 214; see also Cohodas 1997; Eubanks 2003; Walton 1996). Flag opponents also interpret the addition of the battle emblem to the Georgia state flag and the flying of the battle flag over the South Carolina state capitol as indications of each state's white power structure's defiance of the federal government's efforts to secure the full rights of citizenship for the region's African American population.

Due to its use as a symbol of support for slavery in the 1860s and of segregation in the 1960s, the battle flag is viewed as blatantly racist by most Southern blacks. As a result, even when the battle flag is raised by supporters solely in honour of the memory of those soldiers killed in the Civil War, opponents argue that no public sanction for its display should be provided. As signs carried by African American marchers in a January 2000 anti-Confederate battle flag rally at the State House in Columbia, South Carolina read, 'Your heritage is my slavery' (quoted in Leib and Webster 2002: 229).

The unbridled passion that both supporters and opponents feel about the battle emblem is underscored by public statements of Southern politicians. For example, Glenn McConnell, a white leader in the South Carolina State Senate and one of the state's most powerful politicians, argued in 1996 that to remove the flag from the top of the state's capitol dome would be an act of 'cultural genocide' against Southern whites. McConnell, an owner of a Civil War memorabilia store, went so far as to argue that such an act would be analogous to Neville Chamberlain's appeasement of Adolf Hitler in the 1930s. Flag opponents have also employed Nazi imagery in their arguments, equating the flag with a Nazi swastika. As Georgia State Senator Billy McKinney put it in a 1997 flap between New York and Georgia over flying each other's state flags, 'if you really want to get some dander up, put the Nazi flag up. They both [the Nazi flag and Georgia state flag] stand for the same thing' (as quoted in Leib 1998: 234–5).

While some white Southerners may view the flag as a symbol of regional pride, thereby challenging the North's 'othering' of the South as inferior, African American opponents of the flag are challenging the region's history of white dominance. By challenging the long-constructed dominant meaning of the flag in the region, black Southerners are seeking to overcome white Southerners' 'cultural imperialism':

> To experience cultural imperialism means to experience how the dominant meanings of a society render the particular perspective of one's own group invisible at the same time as they stereotype one's group and mark it out as the Other. Cultural imperialism involves the universalization of a dominant group's experience and culture, and its establishment as the norm.
>
> (Young 1990: 58–9)

The insights emerging from critical race theory and whiteness studies during the past decade aid in understanding why some white Southerners cannot comprehend the basis for the region's recent conflict over the battle flag (Leib and Webster 2002; Webster and Leib 2001).[2] From the perspective of many traditional whites in the region, white Southern culture is the norm, and they are charged with the maintenance of its purity. African American Southerners are viewed as the 'other', and thus as inferior, though their regional roots may be longer and deeper. As a result, African American

Southerners are viewed by traditional white Southerners as outsiders, who cannot comprehend the importance of tradition and 'Southern' heritage.

Many pro-flag white Southerners assume that white Southern culture is the 'regional culture', and cannot comprehend (and do not attempt to try to comprehend) why black Southerners do not feel the same emotional attachment to 'Southern' symbols as they do (Leib 2002; Leib and Webster 2002; Webster and Leib 2001). In keeping with whiteness theory, many Southern whites see the battle flag as an inclusive Southern symbol rather than an exclusive symbol of white 'southernness'. Edward Ayers argues that the

> Confederate flag is a topic of such debate and divisiveness in the South today because it denies all that black and white Southerners share, because it reduces the South to a one-time and one-sided political identity.
>
> (1996: 79)

While we might identify qualities that collectively define both black and white Southerners, the Confederate battle flag defines 'southernness' exclusively as 'white Confederate southernness'. By challenging the reading of the flag as a symbol of heritage and pride, flag opponents have highlighted the whiteness of the battle flag and have, by extension, challenged the region's existing white-dominated social relations.

Most prominently, flag opponents challenged the meaning of the flag in those states in which the state government flew the battle emblem, arguing that by doing so these governments were sanctioning a symbol of hatred and racism. In Georgia and Mississippi, opponents tried to remove the battle emblem from the flags of both states, ultimately being successful in Georgia, but unsuccessful in Mississippi. Flag opponents also sought to remove the battle flags flying atop the state capitol buildings in South Carolina and Alabama, arguing that these states were sanctioning hatred and racism by flying the flags above their state capitol domes.

The Alabama and South Carolina controversies also underscore the power of cultural landscapes. Along with studying the meaning of iconographic symbols, the landscapes in which these symbols are situated are themselves embedded with meaning. Thus, we can learn about society not only through the study of symbols themselves such as flags, but also by examining when, where, how and by whom such symbols are placed on the landscape (Johnson 2004; Leib 2002; Mitchell 2000; Schein 2006; Till 2003). As the cases in Alabama and South Carolina demonstrate, the meanings assigned to the flag can change not only with *who* is defining them but also depending on *where* upon the region's landscape the flag is situated (Leib and Webster 2004a). In the South Carolina and Alabama cases, flag opponents sought to remove the flag from atop the state capitol dome, with flag opponents resisting the change. The South Carolina debate during the 1990s was intense and vitriolic, with battle emblem opponents arguing the flag should be taken off the capitol dome and placed at ground level, at a Confederate soldier's monument in front of the state capitol building. They argued that this location would place the flag in an appropriate historical context without providing overt government sanction for the flag's negative meanings. Flag proponents strenuously objected to the change, in spite of the fact that at ground level the flag would be easier for visitors to see than it was flying high over the capitol building (Leib and Webster 2004a).[3] Hence, the meanings assigned to the flag by supporters and opponents alike differed, depending upon where on the state capitol grounds it was placed.

Why has the flag's meaning only become a prominent issue in Southern politics during the past two decades? While African Americans have long questioned the meaning of the flag, vigorous enforcement of the federal Voting Rights Act (1965) in the 1990s dramatically increased the number of African Americans elected to state and local legislative bodies. This increase created a critical mass of flag opponents to challenge government-approved displays of the battle flag in the region's public spaces (Leib and Webster 2006). Secondly, in the 1990s several Southern states and localities increased their efforts to attract foreign investment in the form of industrial branch plants of foreign corporations. High-profile competition among states in the South occurred especially for German, Japanese and Korean automakers seeking to locate plants in the United States. State economic development officials and some political leaders in the South believed that foreign companies would interpret the meaning of the flag as a symbol of hatred and racism, thereby equating the prevalence of the flag with poor race relations and a poor business climate, and therefore withhold their investments in states where the flag was prevalent. Such arguments first arose in 1993 when it was alleged that one reason for Mercedes-Benz's selection of Alabama over South Carolina for the site of its first North American automobile plant was that the latter continued to fly the battle flag from the top of its state capitol dome (Webster and Leib 2001). Similar concerns that flying the battle flag could be detrimental to outside investment and economic development were also raised in the battle flag debates in Alabama, Georgia and Mississippi (Leib and Webster 2002). As the head of Mississippi's Chamber of Commerce argued in 2001, during the effort to remove the battle emblem from that state's flag, the 'issue isn't about black or white . . . It's about green [the colour of U.S. paper currency], about bringing jobs to Mississippi' (quoted in Blackmon 2001).

Defining the meaning of the flag in popular culture

Parallel to the efforts to define the meaning of the battle flag in the politics of the South are efforts to control its meaning in popular culture, most notably in the region's sports and music. For example, the flag has long been associated with country music, a genre historically dominated by white Southerners. The flag has been a prominent symbol for a variety of country artists, including Hank Williams, Jr. and the band Alabama, as well as Southern rock groups such as Lynyrd Skynyrd. Many of these groups see the flag as a proud symbol of Southern culture and entirely devoid of racial overtones. Thus, the members of Lynyrd Skynyrd expressed pride and reverence for the flag, and did not see their use of the flag as racist in any manner (Brant 2002: 81–102). In opposition, other bands, most notably Hootie and the Blowfish, have denounced the flag as racist. Hailing from Columbia, South Carolina, the interracial band blasted the South Carolina legislature for continuing to fly the rebel flag at the South Carolina state capitol building in its 1995 song, 'Drowning'. Similarly, Southern Rap pioneer MJG's 1998 album 'No More Glory' pictures the artist in front of a burning Confederate battle flag.

While some African American rap artists have tried to reappropriate the Confederate battle flag, other musicians have tried to problematize both heritage and hate readings of the flag. The Charleston, South Carolina rap group, Da Phlayva, released a 1993 album, 'phlayva 4 dem all', the cover of which featured the Confederate battle flag drawn in red, green and black instead of red, white and blue. Red, green and black are the colours of Marcus Garvey's pan-African flag, also known as the black liberation or black nationalist flag. Two African American entrepreneurs in Charleston started their own clothing line featuring this 'new' battle flag, with sales being brisk to both blacks and whites. They marketed this flag as a unifying force, targeting sales 'to the sons and daughters of former slaves and former slave owners' (quoted in Leib and Webster 2002: 229).

The battle flag has also been associated with college American football and stock car automobile racing, two spectator sports with long histories in the South. The flag was first waved by Southern football fans at the University of Virginia in 1940, its use being most common when Virginia played Northern colleges (Coski 2005). However, the university most associated with the battle flag is the University of Mississippi. By the late 1940s, the flag had become an unofficial symbol of the school and was traditionally waved by thousands of fans during Ole Miss Rebels football games (Coski 2005; Eubanks 2003; Walton 1996). In 1982, controversy erupted when the university's first African American cheerleader refused to carry a large battle flag into the Ole Miss football stadium prior to a game (Cohodas 1997). The controversy over the role of the battle flag at Ole Miss was not resolved until the late 1990s, when the University's president took the lead in an effort to ban battle flags at the football stadium (Leib 1998; Morrello 1997). In 2005, African American students at Louisiana State University launched protests over the flying of Confederate battle flags at outdoor pre-football game parties on the LSU campus. Notably, the LSU battle flags were in the University's colours of purple and gold. While LSU officials stated that they could not ban battle flags from campus on constitutional grounds, they did urge local shopkeepers not to sell the flags (Associated Press 2006).

The national organization that oversees most college athletics in the United States, the National Collegiate Athletic Association (NCAA), has used its influence to try to remove Confederate flags from the South's public spaces. In 2001, the NCAA issued a policy that banned the awarding of 'predetermined' NCAA championship sites to any arena or stadium in South Carolina or Mississippi, because both states still fly the Confederate battle flag (NCAA 2001a, 2001b, 2003). The bans have impacted on South Carolina cities seeking to host lucrative college sporting events. Bids from Columbia and Greenville to host early rounds of the NCAA men's basketball tournament were rejected, as were Charleston's efforts to host an end-of-the-season college football bowl game (Brack 2004; Iacobelli 2006; Person 2006). In late 2006, the Sons of Confederate Veterans announced they intended to file a lawsuit challenging the NCAA's authority to ban sporting events in South Carolina because of the flag issue (Davenport 2006).

The flag has also become an increasingly larger issue in stock car racing. While stock car racing did not originate solely in the South, it is now closely associated with the region and has been dubbed the 'most Southern sport on earth' (Pierce 2001). By the 1950s and 1960s stock car racing was largely confined to the region, with most well-known drivers being Southerners and a majority of the sport's races being held in the region. The sport is most popular among white Southerners, and there are few black drivers or black spectators at stock car races. Battle flags have become a common sight at racing venues (Alderman *et al.* 2003; Hurt 2005; Marcoplos 2006; Pillsbury 1995). Stock car racing has grown tremendously in popularity in the U.S. during the past decade, and its fan base and race locations are now nationwide. However, in spite of the sport's nationalization, it is still an overwhelmingly white sport, and battle flags remain common at the racing events. In 2005, Brian France, Chief Executive Officer of NASCAR, the sport's governing body, told a nationwide television audience on the CBS news magazine show '60 Minutes' that the flag was an inappropriate symbol for the sport and that he discouraged fans from flying the battle flag at races. France, the grandson of the organization's founder, was asked by the interviewer how he could convince African Americans that stock car racing was not 'a good ole boy southern, Confederate flag sport'. He responded that he believed that that image of NASCAR was fading, and that 'I can't tell people what flag to fly'. But he also noted 'It's not a flag I look at with anything favorable. That's for sure' (quoted in CBS News 2005). In 2006, the Sons of Confederate Veterans protested NASCAR's efforts to distance the organization from the battle flag at one of the organization's most important races. It is also the case that France's comments have done little to reduce the number of flags flown at NASCAR races in the South (Southern Poverty Law Center 2006; Wetzel 2006).

Contrasting the meanings of the different Confederate flags

The past two decades has thus seen a series of debates throughout the American South over the meaning of the Confederate battle flag. However, the battle flag is only one of four flags most associated with the Confederacy. Do all four flags carry the same meaning(s)? After the 1993 U.S. Senate floor fight to reject renewal of the design patent for the insignia of the United Daughters of the Confederacy, Senator Carol Moseley-Braun argued that the first national flag, the Stars and Bars, was more offensive to her than the battle flag. Her office suggested that the 'Confederate national flag . . . is to Moseley-Braun a symbol of a defeated nation whose "cornerstone" was slavery. But the Senator sees the battle flag . . . as a symbol for the common soldier of the South, the vast majority of whom did not own slaves' (as quoted in Webster and Webster 1994: 132).

Senator Moseley-Braun's view on which Confederate flag is more offensive, however, is not widely shared by other Confederate flag opponents. In several of the debates over whether states should sanction flying Confederate flags, proposals have been developed to replace the battle flag with the first national flag of the Confederacy (which does not contain the battle emblem). In at least two cases, African Americans supported replacing the battle emblem flag with the first national flag, despite the fact that both are Confederate flags. Thus, not all Confederate flags necessarily carry the same meanings, even to members of the same demographic group.

The visibility of the battle emblem and the way in which it has been used during the past 150 years, most particularly during the Civil Rights Movement of the 1950s and 1960s, has led to passionate and polarized interpretations of its meaning. But the association of the three national flags of the Confederacy with either 'heritage' or 'hate' is far less clear. For example, in 1999, African American legislators unanimously supported replacing the battle flag in the Alabama State House chambers with the Stars and Bars. In spite of the historical fact that the first national flag of the Confederacy had flown over the Alabama state capitol when it served briefly as the Confederate national capitol at the beginning of the Civil War, the switch was rejected by a majority of the body's white members (Leib and Webster 2006; Webster and Leib 2002). For African American State Representative Alvin Holmes, who had failed on previous attempts to get the battle flag removed from the House chambers, striking a compromise to switch one Confederate flag for another was seen as the only way to rid the chamber of what he viewed as the more offensive battle flag.

In 2001, Georgia Governor Roy Barnes, black lawmakers and state business leaders replaced the 1956 battle emblem state flag with a new state flag which minimized the size of the battle emblem and placed it in a historic context with other flags that had flown over the state during its history. In 2003, the state legislature approved a new state flag explicitly patterned after the first national flag of the Confederacy. On its first passage, all 38 black lawmakers in the state House of Representatives unanimously voted against the legislation creating the 2003 flag, not necessarily because it authorized a state flag patterned closely after the Stars and Bars, but rather because the bill set up a state-wide referendum that would present voters with the 1956 battle emblem-dominated flag as an alternative choice. Black lawmakers refused to endorse any bill that had to potential to restore the battle emblem-dominated flag as the state flag. However, subsequently the bill's language was changed to provide for a state-wide referendum on the new Stars and Bars flag that would not include the 1956 battle emblem flag as an option. With the battle emblem option eliminated, all thirty-eight black lawmakers voted for the bill. Thus, black members of the House unanimously agreed that the 2003 Stars and Bars flag was a preferable alternative to the 1956 flag that incorporated the battle emblem (Leib and Webster 2004, 2006).

In 2004, Georgia held the state-wide referendum pitting the 2001 interim state flag and the 2003 Stars and Bars flag. The NAACP supported the 2001 interim flag, arguing that the 2003 Stars and Bars option too closely resembled the first national flag of the Confederacy. But many prominent black Georgians (including former Atlanta Mayor Andrew Young and Joseph Lowery, former head of the Southern Christian Leadership Conference) endorsed the 2003 Stars and Bars option. Battle flag opponents reasoned that while still a Confederate flag, the 2003 Stars and Bars option carried far less baggage than the state's 1956 flag, which incorporated the battle emblem. In addition, they argued that a victory for the 2003 flag would likely end the flag debate and bury any chance of the 1956 battle emblem flag becoming a viable option again. Business leaders in the state also supported the Stars and Bars flag, fearing a win by the interim flag would reopen the debate on the battle flag and have a devastating impact on Georgia's economy. In the March 2004 referendum the Stars and Bars flag won by a three to one margin, receiving significant support from both white and black Georgians (Leib and Webster 2004).

The first national flag of the Confederacy flew over a short-lived country established to preserve slavery and protect Antebellum Southern social structures. This being so, it is fascinating that both black and white Georgians would support a flag based upon its design as their state flag in the twenty-first century. Most clearly this outcome underscores the power of the battle emblem to displace all other Confederate symbols as being strongly associated with hatred and racism in the minds of Georgia voters. Indeed, the *Atlanta Journal-Constitution* (2004), long an advocate of eliminating the battle emblem from the state flag, suggested in an editorial, only days before the referendum, that either the 2001 interim flag or the 2003 Stars and Bars flag symbolized 'inclusion'. Arguably, for flag-weary Georgians any flag but the battle flag had become an improvement.

Conclusions

Different Confederate flags condense different sets of meanings, depending on the context in which the flag is presented and the perspective of the observer. Most clear is the divisive nature of the Confederate battle flag, which is cherished by some and reviled by others. Polls confirm a majority of traditional white Southerners view the battle flag as a symbol of their proud heritage and emblematic of all that it means to be a 'Southerner'. While viewing themselves as no less 'Southern' than the region's white citizens, the vast majority of African American Southerners see the battle flag as representing the South's efforts to preserve slavery during the Civil War in the 1860s and racial segregation a century later. Many traditional white Southerners view Southern culture exclusively through the lens of the white Southern experience in the region, and thus implicitly question the legitimacy of African American claims to be citizens of the South. Many of the region's African Americans have worked to highlight and decentre this white-centred definition of Southern culture by promoting an alternative meaning of the flag. Arguably, this division will continue until white Southern culture becomes more accepting of alternative definitions of what it means to be a Southerner.

Given the vitriolic debates over Confederate flags in the American South during the 1990s and the first part of this decade, it seems unlikely such accommodations will be forthcoming in the near future. However, the level of vitriol has abated somewhat during the past three years. This has been the result of several factors, including, first, the success of flag opponents in highlighting an alternate reading the flag, as a symbol of hatred, racism and shame, rather than the dominant reading of the flag as a symbol of heritage, innocent hell-raising and regional pride; second, the shrillness of some of the most passionate battle flag defenders, which has offended some flag supporters; and third, a 'flag fatigue' that has been felt throughout the region after a decade of unending high-profile battles over the flag. However, despite the victories won by flag opponents in the most high-profile flag debates in the region, the flag's prominence on the Southern landscape has altered little. The battle flag has been removed from the top of the state capitol domes in Alabama and South Carolina, but it continues to be displayed on the grounds of their state capitols. The state flag of Mississippi continues to prominently incorporate the battle emblem, and one Confederate flag has been exchanged for another in the state flag of Georgia. This suggests that while the heated debates over the Confederate flag have cooled in recent years, they are unlikely to be extinguished completely in the near future.

Notes

1   In the end, the ultimate 'winner' in the battle over the Eight Flags display was 'Mother Nature', as the storm surge from Hurricane Katrina in August 2005

washed the display from the beach (or as reported by the *Biloxi Sun-Herald* newspaper, as a result of the storm the 'concrete Eight Flags display marking the Gulfport-Biloxi boundary – a signature of both coastal communities – was gone' [Lee *et al.* 2005]).

2   For good introductions to the literature on critical race and theory and whiteness, see Bonnett 2000; Delgado and Stefancic 2001; Frankenberg 1997b; Rothenberg 2005; and Wray and Newitz 1997.

3   In 2000, a compromise was reached that moved the flag from on top of the capitol to behind the Confederate soldier's monument in front of the capitol building on the statehouse grounds. Some flag opponents who several years earlier had supported this proposal were unhappy with the 2000 compromise as they had concluded that the flag should be removed entirely from the statehouse grounds. For a fuller discussion of the microgeographies of the Alabama and South Carolina flag cases, see Leib and Webster 2004a.

Court cases cited

Brown v. Board of Education of Topeka, Kansas, 347 U.S. 483 (1954).
Mississippi Division of the United Sons of Confederate Veterans v. Mississippi State Conference of NAACP Branches, 774 So. 2d 388 (Miss. 2000).

4 The Star-Spangled Banner and 'whiteness' in American national identity

Manuel Madriaga

Understanding American national identity as an ethnic identity is the theoretical foundation for arguing, in this chapter, that an axiomatic relationship between American-ness and 'whiteness'[1] informs diverse interpretations of collective symbols and ideals, such as the Flag. What makes American identity an ethnic identity is that it is established and maintained in the transactional process of social identification between the boundaries of 'us' and 'them' (Barth 1969; Jenkins 1997). As long as there is a 'them', or Others, to identify against, there will always be a sense of American community. Depending on space and time, this 'them' can reside outside the territorial borders of the US, as in the Soviet Union during the Cold War. However, a sense of Otherness can reside within America itself. Cohen's (1985) notion of community, which is drawn from Turner's (1969) work, is significant here. Community is a multifaceted concept sheltering, like an umbrella, *differences* and a sense of *similarity* simultaneously. Individuals are aware that their lives are structured by caste, class, or 'race'; however there remains a sense of 'communitas', an undifferentiated unstructured sense of 'we-ness' (Handelman 1990; Jenkins 2004: 151; Sturken 1998; Turner 1969: 96).

This chapter attempts to examine the 'us' and 'them' dichotomy that is dramatised by 'whiteness' within the American national collective. Some have already touched on an association between American-ness and 'whiteness' (Du Bois 1903 [1989]; hooks 1990; Morrison 1998; Omi and Winant 1994; Ringer 1983; Roediger 1998). 'Whiteness' as understood here is a process (Frankenberg 1993, 1997a; Madriaga 2005; Ware and Back 2001; Wellman 1977) demarcating those who are included from those who are excluded. As some have argued (Allen 1994; Ignatiev 1995; Jacobson 1998; Roediger 1991, 1998), the category of 'whiteness' helped European immigrants to shed easily their ethnic differences and become American. What will be examined here, using Cohen's (1985) model of community, is how 'whiteness' is represented in the collective symbolism of the Flag.

To explore the axiomatic relationship between the category of 'whiteness' and American-ness, this chapter argues there is an *official* interpretation (Bodnar 1992), or a *public face* (Cohen 1985), of the Flag that in principle binds together all Americans providing that sense of 'us', regardless of ethnic and racial differences.[2] It is this interpretation of the Flag that leaves 'whiteness' unmarked and *invisible* in notions of American-ness. It is the axiomatic relationship between 'whiteness' and American-ness that makes it difficult for people of colour to participate meaningfully within the American collective. Their subjectivities are restrained and hidden *in private* (Cohen 1985) behind 'white masks' (Du Bois 1903 [1989]; Fanon 1967). Being racialised and having to wear a 'white mask' in public (Cohen 1985) can skew one's attachment to the symbolic ideal of the Flag.

The symbolic significance of the United States flag

The Star-Spangled Banner is the most recognisable and holiest of all American national symbols (Leepson 2005; Warner 1962). It holds much symbolic significance and has been compared to artefacts such as the Christian cross (Craige 1996: 11) or a totem necessitating human sacrifice (Marvin and Ingle 1999). To preserve reverence and a sense of the sanctity of the Flag, legislation has often been proposed to prevent the symbol from desecration (Goldstein 1996b; O'Leary 1999). Currently, the flag desecration debate revolves around the issue of flag burning. Should it be legal or illegal? Because of recent U.S. Supreme Court rulings, such as *Texas v. Johnson* (1989), that declared flag burning to be warranted under the Constitutional right of freedom of speech, many Americans have expressed anger and lobbied for an amendment outlawing flag desecration. A national veterans' organisation, the American Legion, and a citizens' organisation, the Citizens Flag Alliance (CFA), have been two major interest groups that continue to advocate this legislation. For Bodnar (1992), these interest groups would be categorised as promoting official interests in a sacred, nationalistic, patriotic culture. Juxtaposed to official interests would be a vernacular interest in favour of flag desecration, as warranted under freedom of speech. Goldstein (2000) has suggested that the proposed legislation is less about the act of desecrating the Flag and more about ideological deviation from the official interpretation of American patriotism. In other words, the issue has more to do with notions of community and silencing deviant, vernacular interests within it. The continual conflict between the many divergent interests is a process that defines the meanings attached to collective symbols such as the Flag. Thus, meanings attached to it are always changing, dictated by varying interests within the collective.

Within the confines of the collective, an 'us' and 'them' dichotomy is conjured up and perpetuated through debate over the meanings of national symbols. As observed by Marvin and Ingle (1999) and Goldstein (2000), the issue of flag burning has not only been a conflict between flag worshippers and free-speech advocates. It has been just one aspect of continuous conflict between a variety of groups in a pluralistic society, to define and legitimate their own interpretations of national symbolism.

There is relatively little literature that examines the relationship between notions of 'race' and interpretations of the Flag. O'Leary's work (1999) is exceptional here. Her overall study presents an historical account of how patriotism and notions of American-ness were racialised. She argued that American patriotism is paradoxical, in that in order to have a sense of 'us', racial inequality is necessary. Other than O'Leary's work, most of the literature already cited here (Craige 1996; Goldstein 2000; Marvin and Ingle 1999) highlights the spectacular, such as the issue of flag burning, in defining the interests of competing groups. With this in mind, not much is said about the ordinariness of the Flag in everyday life, such as when it is hoisted up in front of post offices, or placed in front of school classrooms. Billig (1995) has argued that the ordinariness, the banality, of the Flag is just as significant in determining who is included and excluded within the community as flags waved in parades, military funerals, or in war protests. The point made by Billig takes attention away from the spectacular and places the focus on the impact of national symbols constantly flagged in our everyday lives. This frequent flagging reminds members of a collectivity of the boundaries between 'us' and 'them'. Who comprises 'us'? Who comprises 'them'? These questions of identity have racial dimensions (Chatterjee 1999; Fanon 1967; Jenkins 1997, 2004; McCrone 1998; Memmi 1990; Said 1978 [1995], 1993). This means that *differences* of people of colour could stand out as un-American.[3]

Research into American identity

One objective of the research was to identify commonalities binding the nation together, and the ways in which they are implicated in, and shaped by, 'race'. Americans have varying interpretations as to what binds them into a national community. Although respondents' meanings of, and attachments to, the 'cultural stuff' (Jenkins 1997) are sometimes contradictory and divergent, they still identify themselves as being American. In addition to exploring commonalities, I also considered how the symbol of the American Flag serves as a both a homogenising and an alienating agent, unifying and dividing the nation. Data were gathered about how respondents from different ethnic and racial backgrounds attach themselves to the central, imposing national symbol of the American Flag.

This research was sparked by my own life experience. Depending upon time, place, context, I find myself either at the centre or at the margins of American society. Being a son of Filipino immigrant parents in the US, I have always been racialised. However, when the opportunity arises, I am eager to make known, to anyone who questions my American authenticity, that I do belong. This constant negotiation between my attachment to all things American and my awareness of my racialised identity has been an ongoing daily exercise. I knew going into the field that my racial position was going to be a factor. I understood that, due to my *difference*, I had a 'standpoint' from which to explore the effects of 'whiteness' (Hartsock 1987; Memmi 1990). However, I was also aware that this 'standpoint' offers limited insights into commonalities between the researched and the researcher (Ware and Back 2001; Wellman 1977)

Fieldwork was conducted in the US from July 2000 to August 2001, centred in a particular place along the California central coast. This place was a prime spot to gather veteran respondents for the study because it contained the largest military installation on the west coast of the US. The research revolved around life-history interviews conducted with military veterans. Military veterans have social standing (O'Leary 1999) in determining what is and what is not patriotic. Having social standing, they help to define the boundaries of national identity and what it entails (Marvin and Ingle 1999; O'Leary 1999).

Twenty-five veterans were interviewed. Other than settling in the California central coast and being male,[4] there were not many commonalities between them. Ten respondents were white, nine were black, and six were Latino. They varied in age, from 28 to 85 years old. In order to maintain the anonymity of the interviewees, in what follows I identify them only by their age (in parentheses).

Respondents were not aware of my central interest in 'race' in the study. This indirectness was deliberate. The research was designed to examine the implication of 'whiteness' in *taken-for-granted* notions of American identity. In order to acquire data on how American nationalism and racism may intertwine, I decided it was necessary to be less than completely open about my intentions. I tried to avoid asking questions *directly* related to 'race'. I did not want respondents to have any suspicions that I was interested in issues of 'race'. My desire was not to contaminate or influence the everyday. It was in the everyday perceptions of American-ness that 'whiteness' was sought. This is the sole reason for choosing an indirect research approach. Although not completely open about research intentions, I do not consider that my approach was along the same lines as covert research. A distinction has to be made. Covert research usually involves a researcher hiding the truth about her/his self from those being researched (Bulmer 1982; Burgess 1984: 186–9; Holdaway 1982). In contrast, the indirect approach I chose did not give me the opportunity to conceal my identity or my research. All respondents were aware I was a research student. They all knew of my research interest in American identity and patriotism. The only thing they did not know was of my interest in examining 'race', which was researched indirectly.

White respondents

Despite the diverse range of interpretations, many white respondents upheld official, public conceptions of the Flag. Their interpretations were 'race'-neutral, leaving 'whiteness' unmarked.

One major commonality that was shared between respondents was their attachment to a past in which the Flag was praised and its symbolic significance was not questioned. For them, the present-day is an unpredictable age where individuals do not honour the Flag like generations past. When they observe the present, they see young people burning the Flag. As one veteran (69) stated, 'Some of the things that happens today just makes my blood boil. One thing, for example, is when they start burning the Flag.' [*sic*] The issue of flag burning was perceived as a contemporary issue rather than an issue that has been a mainstay in the flag desecration debate throughout the nation's history (Goldstein 1996b). The past was upheld as an age where the idea of community was firmly established: 'the poor [young] guys just don't know. They never have been exposed to what we were exposed to. We grew up where Memorial Day celebrations really meant something to a little town' (85).

Another common strand shared by some respondents was how the American Legion impacted on attitudes towards the Flag. This national organisation conducts flag worship at each monthly general membership meeting. Not only does it begin each meeting with the Pledge of Allegiance, it also asks members to recite the preamble of the American Legion Constitution. This preamble includes such statements as 'to foster and perpetuate a spirit of Americanism, to preserve the memories of our former members and the association of our members and our forefathers in the Great Wars'. Perhaps, participating in these rituals every month may explain American Legionnaires' fondness for the Flag:

> I was a part of the American Legion for a while and we honoured the Flag in the American Legion. (85)

> When my Dad died, the American Legion played a big part in his funeral service. I got the Flag from when he died. We always fly the Flag on the Fourth [of July] and on different times. (45)

From the evidence given, one does not, however, have to be a member of the American Legion to have a strong attachment to the Flag. Whether they are American Legionnaires or not, a majority of white respondents did not like the idea of the Flag being burned:

> A lot of people say it is just a flag. But, it does stand for something. It stands for everything that we have been through in this country. (69)

> I have no sympathy for them [flag burners] at all. It just irritates me that they could consider something like this. (75)

Although the American Legion has aligned itself with an official interpretation of the Flag, it had members who were not in agreement with the pursuit of legislation against flag desecration. They saw flag desecration as an act of free speech:

> I would rather see the American Legion spend more time helping out Veterans than worry about the Flag. The Flag will take care of itself. The Flag represents the Nation. It is not the Nation. (55)

> Well, they [flag burners] are expressing their patriotism in a way. I am glad that we live in a country where you are free to express your . . . loyalty. I do not consider the individual as disloyal to the country . . . I think that is a very unreasonable type of freedom. I wouldn't encourage it but it's part of freedom . . . (84)

These American Legion members have been highlighted because the organisation is perhaps the biggest interest group in the U.S. that is rallying politicians and the general public to consider flag desecration legislation. As the evidence indicates, there were some members who do not believe it should be pursued. They represented a vernacular view within the American Legion, whose opinions were inconsistent with official, 'dogmatic' meanings (Bodnar 1996).

Talking with members from the Veterans for Peace group, whose views on the military and armed conflict were contrary to the American Legion, I assumed that they would not have a favourable view of the Flag. I thought the following comment would be representative of this particular group:

> Well, it represents a lot of things to me. It represents a lie. It represents a deep, terrible lie. The Red represents the blood of the Indians, the Vietnamese, and Nicaraguans. The White represents the bones. (59)

However, another member of the peace organisation did not share this sentiment towards the Flag. Asked if he had the Flag posted in front of his home, this respondent (58) stated: 'I put it out on holidays.' Asked if he thought it was unique, to hold an anti-military stance and have a fondness for the Flag, he replied,

> Well, I know . . . I know what soldiers go through . . . You can look at a war either way you know. And, the Army looks at it on the one track and I look at it at another track.

He explained that combat soldiers are caught in a dichotomy when looking at the costs of war. One way was to observe the broken, blooded, ugly, dead bodies. The other way of seeing the dead was as fallen heroes. By having this understanding, he straddled the vernacular and the official. This straddling was expressed in his membership of the Veterans for Peace and in his friendships with those he served with during his time in the Vietnam War. Most of his friends did not join in anti-war peace parades as he did.

This straddling that the last respondent describes, between the official and the vernacular, resembles the dichotomy of *public* and *private* faces of community derived from Cohen's (1985) notion of community. This particular respondent was aware of a duality in his allegiance to the Veterans for Peace and his loyalty to friends he served with in Vietnam. This duality can also be stretched to include a minority of American Legion respondents, who understood that their veteran organisation applies pressure on government to draw up legislation against flag desecration. However, they do not believe it is worthwhile to do so.

What is key throughout all white responses about the Flag was the absence of a discussion of 'race'. For these white respondents, there was no parallel between the Flag and 'whiteness'. A desire to maintain 'whiteness' as a norm could perhaps be inferred from their embrace of a glorified past, where communities were close-knit and everybody rallied around the Flag. In any event, 'race' was a non-issue in their interpretations of the Flag. 'Whiteness' was left unmarked.

Black respondents

In contrast to white responses about the Flag, many black respondents, when discussing their connection to the symbol, addressed issues of 'race' as well. By touching on 'race', these respondents simultaneously marked 'whiteness' in symbolic notions of American identity. Whether or not they were aware of a link between 'whiteness' and American-ness, they were committed to the Flag and nation. Their responses indicated that they straddle the public and private faces of the American Flag, where senses of similarity (us) and difference (them) go hand-in-hand. For instance, responding to a question on his thoughts about the Flag, one respondent (66) clarified that he is a patriot and knows the value of the Flag, having fought for it twice, in Korea from 1951 to 1953 and in Vietnam. In the same breath he acknowledged that there is a problem with race relations within the nation:

> ... to me, the American Flag means freedom, freedom of expression even though it has a lot of flaws in race relations and stuff like that ... So, I think as far as being an American patriot, things that you have been exposed to. You should appreciate those things. It has its faults but this is by far the greatest country I ever lived in.

What was interesting about his response was that he positioned himself as a 'patriot' before criticising the racism prevalent within the nation. He did this by emphasising his combat experience and his affinity with the Flag. Perhaps, by listing his military achievements, he was declaring his authority to criticise. It did not appear sufficient that living out the black experience gave him standing to point out that there are 'flaws in race relations'. Nevertheless, he acknowledged that racism and ethnic intolerance exists but remains firm in his adoration of the Flag.

Unlike the previous respondent, another black respondent (43) did not position himself to criticise the nation while expressing his thoughts on the Flag. However, he did address racial discrimination in the same breath:

Regardless of the obstacles a lot of minorities faced, they still went into the military when they got drafted. They still went. You know what I am saying? That is something I look at. Well, things are bad on the outside. There are still some prejudices and discrimination in the military but it is not on the scale as it is out here in the civilian world. I think about it. I don't agree with everything the government do. But, I believe we have the best form of government, you know what I am saying? I believe the American Flag is an institution. It symbolises stuff because a lot of people have died because of the Flag.

Both of these black respondents upheld the Flag as a sacred object. One stated that America was the best country he ever lived in. The other stated that the country has the best form of government. In their reverence towards the collective symbol, however, they both expressed hesitation by acknowledging that racial discrimination persists.

Another black veteran (45) also discussed the issue of race relations while praising the Flag. Contrary to the previous respondents, he does not embrace the Flag wholeheartedly:

When the Flag comes by, I have to salute it because that is military courtesy and that is tradition. You have to do it. You get into trouble for not doing it. I look at it in that context. I am obligated to do it. If I didn't want to do it, I should not have joined the military. And that was a difficult thing to resolve. And, the reason why it was a difficult thing to resolve was because we used to go to baseball games and at athletic events and they would play the national anthem and we wouldn't stand up when I was in college. We wouldn't stand up. We just sit down. And, people would say, 'Why are you not standing?' We say that 'we are not free. When we are free, we will go ahead and respect your Flag.' So, we sat down at the national anthem.

This respondent testified that he is not as confrontational now as he was during college. He does admit that he currently does stand and place his hand over his heart when he is in a situation that calls for a recitation of the Pledge of Allegiance. Asked if he did this out of respect for other people, he replied, 'Yeah, pretty much.' He was the only black respondent who was not very fond of the Flag. As a member of the American Civil Liberties Union (ACLU), which is an interest group committed to keeping flag desecration as a method of free speech, he does not mind burning the Flag. As he stated, 'Burning it is a good thing as a tool of protest because it is such a readily recognisable thing. It just rattles people's cages.' Regardless of his opinion, he shared with other black respondents a commonality. They cannot discuss the Flag without recognising that 'race' continues to divide the national collective.

As discussed above with respect to the white respondents, being a member of veteran organisations, such as the American Legion, was something of an indicator of one's allegiance to the Flag. However, this relationship was challenged because some white respondents who were members of the American Legion demonstrated varying degrees of attachment to the symbol and believed it was acceptable for individuals to desecrate the Flag. The same can be said about the Veterans of Foreign Wars (VFW) organisation, of which the majority of black respondents were members. The VFW also has monthly membership meetings which begin with flag worship. There was a reverence for the Flag comparable to that of white respondents:

> The American Flag, to me, means that I live in a free country and stay within the boundaries of the law, based on what they put out there for us to live under. But, we also have the freedom to contest it. (60)

> I am proud to be an American. Me, I would die for the American Flag. That's how I feel about that. That's my country and that's what I love. (48)

It was not surprising that a majority of the black respondents who were members of the VFW abhor the idea of flag burning, considering that they participated in flag worship every month. As one respondent (49) stated, 'I love [the Flag]. Should it be burned? I was always taught it was a living thing so you don't desecrate it.' Since it held much symbolic significance, the Flag being desecrated was not taken lightly. By investing a large amount of meaning in this symbol, these respondents were quick to defend the Flag. Some of them even said they would commit violence against those who burn the Flag. Their extreme views were perhaps more intense than the views uttered by some of the white respondents. For instance, asked about his opinion of people who burn the Flag, one respondent (70) stated, 'I think they are cowards. I don't feel that much for them. I treat them like the enemy. I'll destroy them, that's what I do . . . If you destroy somebody, they can't come back and bother you.' Another (48) declared that it would be 'wartime' if someone were to burn the Flag in front of him: 'They wouldn't do it in front of me because I wouldn't let them. You got to light the match first.'

As evidenced here, there was much diversity within the black responses towards the Flag. Despite the diversity, some commonalities were clear. The majority of black respondents exalted the Flag. This affirming attitude towards the Flag was much more apparent within the membership of the VFW. These findings reflected an official, public outlook on the Flag that was consistent with the views of many white respondents, where 'whiteness' was unmarked. However, at the same time, many black respondents in describing their attachment to the collective symbol took into account how racism continued to divide the nation. By doing this, they marked 'whiteness'.

Latino respondents

The responses given by this group of respondents were more varied than those of the other two groups. An explanation for this was that some respondents were aware of their recent immigrant past. This recognition impacted on their understanding of the Flag. Despite diverse interpretations of the Flag, all Latino respondents upheld an official, race-neutral interpretation. As one respondent (68), who was a Flag bearer in the VFW colour guard, explained:

> The American Flag is the symbol of our country . . . I believe in the Flag. It stands for a lot of things. To me, it is about courage and sacrifice. Like, we talk about love of country. I always say that without sacrifice there is no love. If you really love somebody, you sacrifice. (68)

Another respondent (66), chairman of a local American Legion post, also held a similar opinion of the Flag. Like the previous respondent, he touched on the term 'sacrifice' in explaining his thoughts on the Flag:

> The American Flag is the only Flag I know and I think it is the greatest flag there is. And, there were a lot of people who made a lot of sacrifices. But, also it has paid off in the end. We have a free nation, a big nation, and it is because of the people who made the sacrifices.

It was interesting that this respondent stated the American Flag was the only flag he knew considering that he was born and raised in Puerto Rico. His strong Puerto Rican accent was still noticeable after serving in the military for 24 years and working at a local clothing chain for another 24 years. He does not think that Puerto Rico was much different than the US:

> And, we are all Americans in Puerto Rico. And, since we were little children going to school when we are six-years-old, one of things we learned, we didn't learn about the Puerto Rican Flag, we learned about the American Flag as soon as we go to school. We had to learn English, which was mandatory. We had the Pledge of Allegiance, the same thing they have in this country.

This respondent was conscious of his Puerto Rican-ness but contends that his native land is America. He does not see a divergence between what he experienced as a child in terms of learning American Flag worship and what children are taught on the US mainland. Thus, in explaining his attachment to the Flag, he downplayed his Puerto Rican-ness, or his Otherness.

Being members of veteran organisations may have had some influence on these respondents' perception of the Flag and of themselves. However, as also evidenced in the white and black responses, Latino Veterans not affiliated with any veteran organisation still invested in an official conception of the Flag. As one respondent (64) stated, 'No flag in the world is as powerful in what it represents as the American Flag.' Whether or not they were members of veteran organisations, these Latino respondents tied the Flag to notions of the Melting Pot and the American Dream. This association with the Flag differed from the responses made by both black and white respondents. Latino respondents reflected upon how their parents or themselves were able to migrate from Latin American countries into the US and were able to achieve the American Dream. One respondent (71), for instance, linked 'the story of the American Flag' with his immigrant past:

> You can take my story. My story is typical for a lot of people. Like my folks came as immigrants from Mexico . . . [The Flag] is a big symbol and sometimes we take it for granted. I bring it out on everyday holiday that I could remember. Yeah. My folks came over here for the Dream. And, as far as I am concerned, since I was little, we always owned a house.

Owning property and worshipping the Flag went hand-in-hand for these respondents. Asked what he thought the American Flag represented, another respondent (28) stated, 'If not for that Flag and this country, I wouldn't have what I have now . . . I am not going to brag that I have two homes and that I have a house that is worth this much.' This respondent's reply to the Flag question does not end here. Later in the interview, he discussed his ignorance of the Flag while growing up in a poor, predominantly Latino community. He also claimed that this ignorance extended into his time in the military:

> Once you serve in the military, it is kind of funny because you don't really think you are serving your country. You are serving your Marine Corps. If anything, you are putting the Marine Corps Flag before the American Flag . . . If you do something good for the country you did it because of the Marine Corps . . . To me, when I am in the service, the Marine Corps Flag means more to me than the American Flag.

He knows that he was not supposed to place more prestige on the Marines Corps Flag than the American Flag. However, he does confess that he does not really know how to define the Flag, given his isolation in a Latino *barrio*. He explained that he and his wife were becoming more aware of the official symbolism of the Flag since they recently bought a home in a white middle-class neighbourhood, where he sees 'about ten American Flags up' posted in front of homes. By purchasing property in this exclusive community, he and his wife also appear to be buying into official rituals of the Flag.

As he engages in flag worship practices, such as posting the Flag in front of his home, this Latino respondent has found himself in heated arguments with his Mexican workmates. Aware of his Mexican descent, his colleagues argue that he should place a Mexican Flag in front of his home:

> They would tell me that I should have a Mexican one. I would say that I am not from Mexico you know. I am not going to rip on Mexico but

I am an American, simple as that. You get an argument big time over that. If there were a soccer game between Mexico and America, I would root for America, you know.

He readily positions himself as an American. He does not see himself as an outsider or an Other. He believes he does what other Americans do. He worships the Flag, cheers for America in a soccer match, and cries whenever he hears the national anthem.

This respondent's interpretation of the Flag was not unique. It echoed the thoughts of many Latino respondents in the study. In contrast to the majority of Latino respondents, who praised the American Flag and de-emphasised their Latino-ness, one Latino respondent (70) embraced the symbol while highlighting his ethnic distinctiveness. This respondent was similar to many of the black respondents. He affirmed his adoration of the Flag, stating, 'I will fly the American Flag on special occasions. This is my country.' In the same breath, he was also aware of Latino accomplishments in the US military that go unrecognised because of racial discrimination:

> . . . if you look at the service, with the preponderant amount of Congressional Medal of Honour winners, they were Latinos. Give me a break. When these guys came home, they couldn't be buried in cemeteries in their cities because Mexicans were not allowed to be buried there, whether in Texas or California.

He understood that a dichotomy existed between his enthusiasm for the Flag and his observation of racial injustice within the nation:

> When I recite an oath to this country with liberty and justice for all and I see how blacks and Latinos are treated without justice, when I see so many of them incarcerated, where is the 'liberty and justice for all?'

Acknowledging that he was torn between what the Flag represented officially and what he feels is just, he was still committed to holding 'this country's feet to the fire to promote justice'. If this means burning the Flag, he would do it out of desperation to get his community's attention in order to address the ills of racial inequality.

The previous respondent's uniqueness extends to him being the only Latino respondent who admitted a willingness to burn the Flag. The majority of Latinos had similar attitudes to both white and black respondents on the issue of flag desecration. They did not take too kindly to those who commit the act. As one respondent (64) warned, if he saw someone burning the Flag he would 'take him to a fight and punch him'. He could not care less if the act was protected under the freedom of speech, because men have fought and died for the flag. Another respondent (28) considered flag desecration un-American. Addressing how he felt about those who burn the

Flag, he comprehended how the nation was divided by differences in religion and 'race'. However, he believed that, if 'you are in this country you should be an American. You should act and behave like one. You should serve like an American. You should set an example of an American.' Does this mean de-emphasising one's ethnic difference? A majority of the Latinos respondents, in interpreting their outlook on the Flag, did de-emphasise their Latino-ness. Their distinctiveness was cast aside. It became insignificant in terms of praising and worshipping the Flag.

Flagging 'whiteness'

The American Flag, like any collective symbol, is multifaceted in meaning. This versatility allows Americans to have different conceptions of the Flag, knowing that the cohesiveness of the nation will still be maintained (Cohen 1985; Turner 1969). For instance, a number of respondents remarked on the significance of the colours (red, white, and blue) of the Flag. One Latino respondent equated red, white, and blue to blood, truth, and purity, respectively. A black respondent believed the red stands for the blood spilled for the fight of democracy, the white stands for purity in truth, and the blue stands for patriotism. A white respondent in associating the Flag with US military aggression perceived the red to be representative of the blood of the Indians, Vietnamese, and Nicaraguans and the white represents their bones. Although these respondents held different views, they all still identified themselves as American. The same can be said about the respondents who identified themselves as either flag worshippers or willing flag burners. They are still Americans at the end of the day. As Ohta (1998) recognised, while observing Americans attending a controversial flag exhibition at a Phoenix, Arizona museum, an individual's interpretation of each symbolic representation affirmed her/himself as a member of the collective as well as confirmed her/his outlook on the symbol.

As a result of the versatility of meanings in *private*, an official interpretation of the Flag predominates in *public* where sacredness is bestowed. Having a recognised federal day to honour it, establishing a Flag Code to maintain its holiness, and having many Americans who worship it in their everyday lives, has legitimated this interpretation. A problem that O'Leary (1999) has already alluded to, in detailing the history of the legitimation of flag worship, was how racism has been intermingled with it. She has argued that racism was fused into notions of patriotism because many of the national veteran organisations, who were already participating in flag rituals before gaining federal recognition after the Civil War (such as the Grand Army, which eventually evolved into the contemporary American Legion), emphasised 'whiteness' in order to attract membership from former Confederate soldiers who were nostalgic for an antebellum South.

From the responses gathered in my study, 'whiteness' still has a foothold in symbolic representations of patriotism such as the Flag. 'Whiteness' was negotiated differently according to each ethnic group. What differentiates the responses made by each ethnic group was the association between how they comprehended the Flag and how they were aware of their own ethnicity or 'race'.

For white respondents, a link between the Flag and notions of ethnic and racial differentiation was not made. It was not taken into account in their thoughts on the Flag. Thus, 'whiteness' was left unmarked and invisible in interpreting the national symbol.

In contrast, a majority of black respondents marked 'whiteness' while discussing their attachments to the Flag. Whether or not they were conscious of an association between 'whiteness' and the Flag, they identified it by distinguishing their blackness. This was significant because these respondents voluntarily spoke about their racial distinctiveness in the same breath as they elaborated upon their feelings towards the Flag. They were not asked questions about how their racial difference might affect their views. This duality, having an allegiance to the Flag and signifying the importance of the black experience, was the dichotomy that Du Bois (1903 [1989]) referred to in his concept of 'double-consciousness'. This double consciousness was the result of American-ness being taken for granted as 'whiteness'. Because they are black, they will forever be marked as Other. These respondents may have understood this. Perhaps, this explains why they discussed their blackness at the same time as discussing their devotion to the Flag.

While blacks affirmed their distinctiveness in their interpretations of the Flag, a majority of Latinos downplayed theirs. These Latinos respondents, like the black respondents, did not have to mention anything about their ethnicity by virtue of the nature of the interview question. By marking their Latino-ness unenthusiastically, they at least identified an association between 'whiteness' and the Flag, whether they were aware of it or not. Why did they frown upon their Latino-ness? There could be a number of explanations. Perhaps, in responding to a question regarding how they felt about the Flag, they wanted to delineate their commitment and allegiance to American-ness by deriding their Otherness.

All Latino respondents praised the Flag. Even a respondent who associated the Flag with racial inequality still praised it and believed it has positive value to symbolise change. This respondent (70) was one of a few Latino respondents who had fair skin. He understood the privileges of having white skin and was aware of his ability to straddle the racial divide. By passing as white, he recalled, as a young Boy Scout, being assigned to always carry the Flag in public ceremonies:

> I saw a person with my look had entrance into other areas. I saw that as a Boy Scout, where I was given preference over an African-American boy scout to carry the Flag. And, I said to myself, why are they selecting me? . . . So, I saw that it was a privilege given to me because of what I looked like because they couldn't tell then that my name is [Spanish surname].

There was nothing visible about my name. There was nothing visible like my ability to speak Spanish. So, white privilege gave me entrance into areas that I normally would not have been afforded.

I end this chapter with this quote because it is indicative of an association between the category of 'whiteness', the Flag and ideas of American-ness. It also shows the pervasiveness of this relationship. It was due to this taken-for-granted relationship between 'whiteness' and American-ness, as the respondent described, that a black Boy Scout carrying the Flag in some public spaces was perceived as out of the ordinary. This chapter shows that this racial dichotomy, between what is ordinary and deviant, continues to haunt the nation, even more so after 9/11. It compels non-white respondents to discuss their racial and ethnic distinctiveness while discussing their allegiance to the Flag. By doing so, they not only flag their Otherness. They also flag 'whiteness' in notions of American-ness.

Notes

1 Inverted commas are used for 'whiteness' to stress, like 'race', that it is a *social category*. Social categorisation is a process of being identified, defined and delineated by others (Jenkins 1997).
2 It is understood that ethnicity and 'race' are of a similar vein in that they both mark difference (Fenton 2003). However, these two concepts can be distinguished, with Jenkins' (1997) idea that ethnicity is a first-order social identity while 'race' is second-order identity. This ordering is based on the notion that ethnicity, the social interaction between 'us' and 'them', has been around since humans have lived in social groups. In contrast, 'race', being an 'allotrope' of ethnicity, is a product of a specific historical circumstance (Jenkins 1997: 59). 'Whiteness', as understood here, is a category derived from American colonialism (Allen 1994). Throughout the chapter, the terms 'race' and 'whiteness' are used interchangeably.
3 The same can be said of the United Kingdom, where people of colour stand out as not being British. Miles (1993), Hall (1996) and Gilroy (2002) have all argued that racism and nationalism intertwine in the context of the United Kingdom, marking people of colour as Other.
4 I did not envision, before the study, that recruiting respondents to discuss American patriotism would produce a gendered effect. I was surprised to find that when women were approached to be interviewed they usually referred me to someone male, such as their husbands or male friends, who at one time or another were in the military. This is a reflection upon the literature intermingling gender and patriotism. Men sacrifice their lives to refresh the borders of a sense of nationhood while women remain at home biologically reproducing members within the borders (Macdonald 1987; Marvin and Ingle 1999; Yuval-Davis 1997). However, there is literature (Enloe 2000) that stresses women that do participate in warfare.

5   Union Jacks and Union Jills

Nick Groom

The end of the Second World War in Europe was signalled by raising the Union Jack over Berlin, described as a 'symbolic unfurling'.[1] Victory crowds surrounded Buckingham Palace and Westminster, which were bathed in light, but one image seemed to float in the air: 'a striking and, to many people, most moving sight in that direction was the great spotlit Union Jack that floated serenely over the lofty Victoria Tower.'[2] There had been some debate over the national flag and the constitutional right of private citizens to fly it before the outbreak of war. On 27 June 1933, replying to a question about whether private citizens were forbidden to fly the Union Jack for the forthcoming silver jubilee of George V in 1935, Sir John Gilmour, the Home Secretary, commented, 'No, Sir, the Union Flag is the national flag and may properly be flown by any British subject on land.'[3] This is the last official pronouncement on the Union Jack. No single government department or public body has overall jurisdiction over the Union Jack or for any policy concerning it. The Union Jack may be flown at any time.

Despite the tremendous outburst of flag-waving at the end of the war, patriotism was not sustained. The American poet T.S. Eliot warned that Britain faced losing its identity in its victory and argued that it was crucial to continue promote cultural diversity within the union by maintaining national identities: 'it would be no gain whatever for English culture, for the Welsh, Scots and Irish to become indistinguishable from Englishmen – what *would* happen, of course, is that we would all become indistinguishable featureless "Britons"' (Eliot 1973: 55). What actually happened is that these national identities began to corrode the integrity of Britain. Although the 1948 Nationality Act extended the definition of British identity to all citizens of the Commonwealth, the Irish were at best semi-detached from Great Britain and Éire became a republic in 1949, and Scottish (and to a lesser degree, Welsh) nationalism was emerging as a powerful post-war phenomenon.

In response to this dissolution, the Festival of Britain (1951) was run as an elaborate attempt to promote cultural and national homogeneity. It was, though, a profoundly insular affair, which did nothing of the sort. There was no international co-operation in this event to emphasize the place of Britain in the world: none from Europe, but, more surprisingly, none from the

Commonwealth. The British Empire Exhibition of 1924–5 ('Walk Up, Walk Up and Hear the Lion Roar') had featured a West Indian cocktail bar, had seen the launch of the Gold Coast Cocoa campaign that boosted the sales of chocolate, displayed the Prince of Wales sculptured in Canadian butter, and also included a miniature history of the Empire in flags (Samuel 1998: 88–9; Wood 1999: plate 15). Not so in 1951. Instead, the Festival celebrated Christian Britain's continuous history as 'the fight for religious and civil freedom [and] the idea of Parliamentary government; the love of sport and the home; the love of nature and travel; pride in craftsmanship and British eccentricity and humour' (Weight 2002: 1999).

Britannia was there, combined with the points of the compass to create the Festival's logo. She had been deployed in both world wars in a minor way. During the First World War, for example, Britannia had endorsed national savings stamps and mourned on memorial plaques. The heraldic beasts, the lion and the unicorn, were also there – indeed, they had their own pavilion at the Festival, for, according to Laurie Lee, these two creatures had for centuries symbolized the British character – as opposed to being heraldic supporters identifying England and Scotland:

> We are the Lion and the Unicorn
> Twin symbols of the Briton's character
> As a Lion I give him solidarity and strength
> With the Unicorn he lets himself go.

And Noël Coward was there, waving his little workers' flag in his wryly enthusiastic song 'Don't Make Fun of the Fair':

> Peace and dignity we may lack
> But wave a jolly Trades Union Jack,
> Hurrah for the festival,
> We'll pray for the festival
> Hurrah for the Festival of Britain![4]

Two years later, the country was celebrating what was essentially another festival of Britain, and one that was rather more successful in uniting the country: the coronation of Elizabeth II in 1953, following what was in essence the same ritual as that used to crown Edgar the Peacemaker in Bath almost a thousand years before. Against the background of increasing American influence, the erosion of the Empire, black and Asian immigration, Scottish and Welsh separatism, and reluctant European integration, the coronation provided a focus for British identity. The event stimulated what was to become the largest domestic market of the 1950s: television sets. Britain was second only to the United States in its use of the television, and by 1953 there were almost two million sets in the country (Hobsbawm 1999: 222n). As the coronation approached, another 526,000 sets were sold, and on the day, 20 million people – 56 per cent of the country's population – crowded around TVs across the country to watch the new queen being crowned; another 12 million tuned in on the radio. It was by far the biggest event in television history.

One of Lord Reith's plans for the BBC before the war had been 'The Projection of Britain' via the Empire Service (begun in 1932), including such broadcasts as the King's Christmas Day speech. The first major BBC television coverage after the war was of the Victory Parade in June 1946, and the continual reaffirmation of Britain on both public and commercial television continued after the war in coverage of the laying of wreaths at the Cenotaph on Remembrance Sunday. Indeed, the Second World War, in both its history and pageantry, proved to be hugely popular televisual entertainment. Over a hundred war films were screened at British cinemas in the 1950s and 1960s, often promoted by local premières involving Territorial Army soldiers, cadets, bunting and Union Jacks; they were then broadcast by terrestrial channels, and the 1970s saw major documentary series such as *The World at War* as well as popular drama such as *Colditz* (Paris 2000: 226). This enthusiasm also reached children's comics, much as it did in the nineteenth century: *Warlord* had, from its inception in 1974, a British Marine who found himself with the American Rangers in Burma: as Sgt Jackson, he was inevitably known as 'Union Jack' Jackson.

The coronation – and indeed television – proved to be a coming of age of sorts for the Union Jack. Despite fripperies such as Union Jack handkerchiefs and the popularity of red, white and blue borders of geraniums planted for patriotic national events, the mood towards the flag was still reverential in the 1950s, and less than a week before the coronation it had been one of the flags solemnly placed on top of Mount Everest by Edmund Hillary and Sherpa Tenzing. But among coronation souvenirs were certain garments bearing the Union Jack design. These was greeted with outrage by Tory MPs, the member for Buckingham asking Churchill to outlaw 'entirely objectionable' items such as 'Coronation ladies underwear, ornamented with the Union Jack at the rear' (Weight 2002: 230). As the 1950s drew to a close, the critic Kenneth Allsop said:

> The collapse of our old image of imperial splendour did give a spur to the idea that our national vigour and imaginativeness no longer lay in the field of panoply or splendour. Suez *was* a spur: a very palpable spur. Suddenly there was a violent swing to the culture of the great, gritty, youthful *lumpenproletariat*. . . . Every generation of kids since has been swayed by the sort of scepticism and derision that produces Carnaby Street knickers with Union Jacks on them.
>
> (quoted in Weight 2002: 300)

The Sixties had begun, and bands such as The Beatles were seen as national exports, cultural colonialists, ambassadors for a new Britishness.

This was an entirely different way of flying the flag, and informal and ironic patriotic gestures became the norm. When the lovable moptops collected their MBEs in 1965, the *New Musical Express* exclaimed:

> Did the Beatles deserve to be honoured by the Queen? The answer must be irrevocably and unquestioningly – Yeah! Yeah! Yeah! . . . Where the Beatles deserve their awards is in the field of prestige. Their efforts to keep the Union Jack fluttering proudly have been far more successful than a regiment of diplomats and statesmen. We may be regarded as a second class power in terms of politics, but at any rate we now lead the world in pop music!
>
> (quoted in Weight 2002: 359)

After centuries of military and imperial grandeur, the Union Jack changed almost overnight into an ultra-fashionable design icon. The Union Jack became a touchstone of the new generation, and the pop scene emphatically embraced the colours and style of the Union Jack. The flag not only appeared adorning girls' bums, it became the commercial trademark of British cool, and it became one of the defining commodities of the 1960s.

Pop music was, as the *NME*'s comment on The Beatles' MBEs suggests, a vibrant reinvention of British cultural identity. Teenage fashion did not begin and end in Carnaby Street, just as the Mersey Sound did not restrict its appeal to Liverpool. As the fashion bible *The Mod* warned, the movement was not confined to trendy Soho clubs:

> We're always inclined to think that the girls and guys up there [Scotland] walk about in kilts saying 'haggis' or 'och' with every other word. It's not true. Seeing the photographs that they have been sending . . . I'd say that in some parts they are in fact just as much fashion mad go-ahead as we are in London.
>
> (quoted in Weight 2002: 392)

Pop television shows, which spread these fashions over the United Kingdom, learned to favour large bold designs for their sets: '*Ready Steady Go!* was targets, chevrons, bright colours, crisp hard edges' (Green 1998: 63, quoting Pearce Marchbank, graphic designer). The quality of black-and-white TV pictures in the mid-1960s meant that they lacked the definition to capture much subtlety or over-elaboration in the graphic design of television studios, so the medium itself encouraged the use of Pop Art motifs, for dressing both the studios and the stars themselves. Jeff Nuttall describes 1960s fashions in *Bomb Culture* as 'applied art':

> As much inventiveness and creativity was employed there as in action paintings, the collages and assemblages. The colours were delirious. England had stopped being grey.
>
> (Nuttall 1970: 121–2)

The Who's drummer Keith Moon, for example, wore trendy roundel t-shirts, which encouraged their manager to market the band as ultra-Mods. They were 'Modernists' – cool, smart, arty, sophisticated, and up-to-the-minute – in contrast to Rockers, the leather-clad bikers who had evolved out of Teddy Boys. The sense of a shared and driving identity among Mods was so powerful that Pete Townshend, guitarist with The Who, remembers that:

> Everybody looked the same, acted the same, and wanted to be the same. It was the first move I have ever seen in the history of youth towards unity: unity of thought, unity of drive, and unity of motive. It was the closest to pure patriotism I've ever felt.
>
> (quoted in Giuliano 1996: 51–2)

Mod united teenagers across the country – and appropriately enough their favourite Pop Art motif was the Union Jack.

Townshend, who had a 'huge Union Jack' adorning one wall of his tiny bedroom,[5] defined Pop Art in the *Melody Maker*, 3 July 1965, as 'representing something the public is familiar with, in a different form', like clothes:

> Union Jacks are supposed to be flown. We have a jacket made of one. Keith Moon, our drummer, has a jersey with the RAF insignia on it. . . . We stand for pop-art clothes, pop-art music and pop-art behaviour. This is what everybody seems to forget – we don't change off stage. We live pop-art'.
>
> (quoted in Kureishi and Savage 2002: 239)[6]

The Who burst through posters of Union Jacks.[7] They were photographed for an album cover in a massive bed covered with a Union Jack bedspread. Was it Art? Did Mod share the same ethos as the American Pop Artist Jasper Johns, who had famously painted the Stars and Stripes? The singer George Melly thought not, arguing that Carnaby Street, the centre of Swinging London, was in a totally different spirit to that artist's 'plastic researches':

> From shopping bags and china mugs [the Union Jack] soon graduated to bikinis and knickers. Americans, for whom the flag in their century of Imperialism has a great deal more significance, were amazed by our casual acceptance of our flag as a giggle. They might burn their flag in protest but they'd never wear it to cover their genitalia.
>
> (Melly 1989: 148)

Mod culture appealed more to commentators such as George Melly as a popular version of Dadaism, the art movement out of which had Surrealism emerged. The Union Jack was, in Dadaist terms, almost a 'ready-made' object: it could be completely transformed through unlikely juxtapositions, and could be reworked into other items, such as a jacket (Hebdige 1979: 104). The writer Angela Carter wondered whether the young Pete Townshend fully realized what he was doing, stealing traditional signs and objects such as smart suits and Union Jacks and placing them in new contexts:

> In the pursuit of magnificence, nothing is sacred . . . The pursuit of magnificence starts as play and ends as nihilism or metaphysics or a new examination of the nature of goals.
>
> (Kureishi and Savage 2002: 239)

But The Who did have some sense of their impact. Townshend had been a member of the Young Communist League and CND, and had even played banjo on the Aldermaston marches. Like many aspiring pop stars of his generation, he attended art school. In 1964, there was a ten-year retrospective of American art at the Tate (*54/64*), including works by Robert Rauschenberg and Jasper Johns: 'targets and flags and what have you'. Pearce Marchbank, a graphic designer of the period, remarked, 'Then you'd drift off to see The Who and you'd put two and two together. There seemed to be a direct line between what was going on at the Tate Gallery and what was going on at the Marquee' (quoted in Green 1998: 63). The ritual destruction of luxury goods wrapped in a Union Jack was therefore a considered gesture. The Who wore Union Jacks or hung them over their amplifiers and then hurled guitars into them; they were enticingly ambivalent in their attitude towards the flag (Davey 1999: 80). On the other hand, comedy bands such as The Scaffold, famous for *Lily the Pink*, were also using the Union Jack for their own eccentrically patriotic reasons, declaring it to be 'the most democratic flag in the world', and it continued to appear on girls' knickers – girls who had no interest in making radical modernist statements.[8]

The flag was omnipresent in 1960s culture. The 'archetypal 1966 pad' – like that of the actress Julie Christie – was decked out with Victoriana, potted plants, and a Union Jack.[9] This ubiquity may explain the enthusiasm for the Union Jack during the 1966 World Cup, hosted by England. English football fans did not carry banners of St George crosses or even standards of the three lions or the Tudor rose, but, like the event's mascot World Cup Willie, flew the Union Jack: in other words, the competition was for the fans as much a celebration of Swinging London and the Sixties as it was the England football team. Two decades after the defeat of Nazi Germany by the Allies, this was history repeated as farce; VE Day became Cup Final Day, the Union Flag unthinkingly appropriated for another famous victory over the Germans. The *Sunday Express* described how,

> A blaze of union Jacks waved, as people unashamedly gripped by emotion and patriotism danced, wept, and hugged each other . . . What they will tell their grandchildren in the years to come is that it was English nerve and English heart and English stamina which finally

overcame the tenacious resistance of [the Germans] . . . No one who saw
this historic World Cup Final can deny England their 'finest hour'.

(quoted in Weight 2002: 462)

Union Jacks were everywhere: at Wembley, in the streets, at parties, and
festooned around pubs and clubs. Kenneth Wolstenholme, who uttered the
most famous words in English sporting history – 'Some people are on the
pitch, they think it's all over . . . it is now!' – later complained that, 'Sooner
or later I hope it will dawn on all English fans that the Union flag is the flag
of the United Kingdom and that the flag of England is the St George's Cross'
(Wolstenholme 1998: 118). But England had appropriated the Union Jack
to the extent that at Wembley Stadium the Winners' Board for 1966 was
emblazoned with the Union Jack. English football had been in the doldrums
since 1953's shock defeat by Hungary, melodramatically described by *The
Times* as 'Agincourt in reverse'.[10] This was its triumphant return, establishing the English as world leaders in football, as they were in pop music.
Simply by waving the Union Jack on the Wembley terraces, English fans had
turned the Swinging Sixties into an English rather than a British phenomenon. Most Scots, for example, were indifferent to England's success,
although the Scottish Football Association shamelessly congratulated the
English FA on their great 'British' achievement. For others, such as Scottish
international Denis Law, the day that England won the World Cup was 'the
blackest day of my life' (quoted in Weight 2002: 464).

Law's comment indicates the extent to which national rivalries within the
United Kingdom over activities such as sporting fixtures were eroding British
identity. Neither was this factionalism helped by the simultaneous appropriation by the English of the Union Jack and all that went with it. The
evergreen film *The Italian Job* (1969), for instance, takes for granted that the
Union Jack stands for England rather than Britain. The film is set against
Swinging London, and although it mixes social classes and even includes a
black man and a camp homosexual as part of Charlie Croker's – Michael
Caine's – gang, the whole patriotic caper is resolutely Anglocentric, and
there are no Scottish, Irish or Welsh characters. The heist – ostensibly to help
the UK's balance-of-payments crisis and masterminded by the archetypal
aristocratic gangster Mr Bridger (Noël Coward) – is made under the cover
of an England–Italy football match, for which the English supporters are
festooned in Union Jacks. In one of the most famous car chases in British
cinema, the three Minis that make the getaway through a traffic jam are, of
course, painted red, white and blue.

As had already happened in the aftermath of the Second World War, the
only way was down from this peak of supreme confidence. Europe, the far
right, frictions between the constituent nations, and radical popular protest
all contributed, and the following decade saw an inevitable slump and a
decline in the fortunes of both British identity and the Union Jack. Memories
of Britain's isolated stand during 1940 were still reasonably fresh and the

British people had little enthusiasm for a European Union, but on 1 January 1973, the UK became a member of the EEC. In recognition of this historic event, the Union Jack flew over Brussels – upside-down (Weight 2002: 511). Among its more unfortunate effects, membership of the EEC provoked a resurgence of extreme right-wing and neo-fascist politics. Predominantly targeting immigrants who had settled in the country, the skinhead National Front occupied the national identity vacuum left after the 1960s and hijacked the Union Jack. Throughout the 1970s, the flag remained strongly associated with the racist National Front, whose first policy was 'Stop all immigration and start phased repatriation'. The Union Jack appeared in the party's advertising – one image, for instance, showed a Union Jack 'stained' with dreadlocks – it was painted on steel-capped Dr Marten boots, and waved at marches expressly to intimidate immigrant communities (Hebdige 1979: 150, n. 16). Today's liberal and left-wing antipathy towards displays of the Union Jack seems to derive in part from memories of skinhead racist violence being conducted under the banner of the red-white-and-blue.

The discovery and exploitation of North Sea oil, meanwhile, reignited Scottish antipathy to England, and, moreover, Scotland went through a popular cultural renaissance akin to England's in the 1960s. The Scottish singer Rod Stewart (previously 'Rod the Mod') was an international superstar, and the tartan-clad teenybopper pin-ups the Bay City Rollers were enjoying phenomenal worldwide success; even Paul McCartney and Wings jumped on the bandwagon with the bagpipe anthem 'Mull of Kintyre', which spent nine weeks at the top of the charts in 1977. At football matches, Scottish fans booed 'God Save the Queen' and sang 'Flower of Scotland' instead – and have done so ever since.

There were of course positive occasions for the flag. At the same time that it was being brandished by the National Front, the Union Jack continued to deck out British athletics teams, who have always performed under the flag of the United Kingdom rather than as constituent nations, and it featured prominently at Queen Elizabeth's 1977 Silver Jubilee. The jubilee was an attempt to rekindle a sense of a united Britain, the Queen toured extensively, there was much Union Jackery in the shape of souvenirs such as milk bottle-tops and the ubiquitous underwear, and the day itself was characterized by street parties, bunting and a blizzard of flag-waving. And the jubilee also inspired the most pungent reinvention of the flag since the Mods: the cataclysmic arrival of punk rock was under the banner of a slashed Union Jack, raised both in ironic homage to the Swinging Sixties and in outright antagonism to the establishment.

The Union Jack was clearly a highly resonant and contested sign, and so became a favourite design for punks – an appropriation inspired by the Situationist thinking of punk impresario Malcolm McLaren and graphic artist Jamie Reid. The Sex Pistols in particular seem to have had a distinct agenda, making persistent, iconoclastic assaults on the institutions that had become the tourist traditions of British identity – the monarchy, Parliament, the Union Jack – through singles such as *Anarchy in the U.K.* and *God Save the Queen*. Malcolm McLaren, their manager, declared on the BBC's flagship news and opinion programme *Nationwide*, 12 November 1976, 'You have to destroy in order to create, you know that' (quoted in Savage 1991: 255). Situationism was a way of subverting, dismantling and re-assembling the world in order to undermine conventional thinking – which is precisely what Jamie Reid did to the Union Jack on the record covers he put together. For the Pistols' first single, *Anarchy in the U.K.*, Reid cut up a souvenir silver jubilee Union Jack flag and loosely reassembled it with safety pins, paperclips, and bulldog clips. The idea was repeated for the *God Save the Queen* single, when a furling and inverted flag was used behind a treated version of the Queen's head, and the record sleeve was also printed in the jubilee colours, blue and silver. Danny Friedman of the Victoria and Albert Museum said of the institution's purchase of the Jamie Reid archive:

> . . . just as the Sex Pistols were important in democratizing music, the designs democratized art . . . All you need is a newspaper and some scissors and an airbrush if you get a bit flash later. I mean the whole thing about photo collages, xeroxes, polaroids was really bringing Art with a big 'A' right down to where anyone could do it.
>
> (quoted in Vermorel and Vermorel 1987: 205)

The Sex Pistols and The Clash both adapted the design of the Union Jack and there were bands with names such as the UK Subs (originally the UK Subversives, who had seven Top Thirty hits and two Top Ten albums in two years) and UK Decay (whose singer coined the description 'gothic' for another emerging musical genre). Derek Jarman's edgy punk film *Jubilee* (1978) also made ambivalent figures of the flag and national icons such as Britannia, who is 'Amyl Nitrate' in the film, played by a punk ice maiden called Jordan. Punk recognized that despite the Union Jack's institutional status and its wartime and imperial history, the events of the past decade had made the flag wholly ambiguous. It was a sign determined by its context: the red, white and blue design on a bikini sold from a tourist stall on the corner of Oxford Street had a profoundly different meaning to that on the flag raised on Remembrance Sunday, and the Union Jack pinned to the back of a Mod's fish-tail parka was entirely at odds with the Union Jack tattooed on the arm of a Dr-Marten-booted skinhead. In addition to its formal roles, the flag could be a declaration of monarchist patriotism, a tourist souvenir, a neo-fascist banner, or a homage to the Sixties, and by cutting it up and then pinning it back together again, punks could present themselves as symptoms of the degeneration and fragmentation of Great Britain (Sabin 1999: 209–10). Predictably, however, the slipperiness of this symbolism under-mined punk's own position, and the British establishment was able to absorb these attempts to unravel the integrity of the flag. Before long, punks found themselves alongside bobbies, pillar boxes and beefeaters as just another patriotic London tourist attraction – as English, one is tempted to say, as the Union Jack.

The Union Jack has since become a pop fetish, eternally returned to. Freddie Mercury of Queen made the flag a favourite stage prop, and even the chameleon David Bowie had a frock coat based on a Union Jack made for his *Earthling* phase. But it has not always been received with equanimity. Former Smiths singer Morrissey draped himself in the Union Jack in 1992 while performing at Finsbury Park and was vilified. The music press had been happy for others to take the flag: The Who, of course, were considered to be prime exponents of 1960s Pop Art, and more recently the post-punk Mod band The Jam had dressed themselves in 'Union Jackets' as a way of reclaiming the flag from the National Front skinheads. But Morrissey's handling was different. Many commented that Morrissey seemed to be embracing neo-fascist chic: unfurling the flag before a backdrop of harsh black-and-white photos of bovver boys, and performing songs such as *The National Front Disco*. And not only were there skinheads in his audience making Nazi salutes, but outside the venue, National Front and British Movement supporters were confronting left-wing marchers. In such a context, Morrissey appeared to be using the Union Jack as a way of flirting with racism.

For the flag at least, the storm of controversy blew over. Since Morrissey's misconceived antics, the flag has been adopted by Britpop groups as different as the Spice Girls (Geri Halliwell's minidress at the Brit Awards) and Oasis (Noel Gallagher has a Union Jack guitar and was also photographed on a Union Jack bedspread). It was further revived at the opening of the 1998 London Fashion Week by a topless model painted with red, white and blue stripes. All of this has helped to distance the Union Jack from neo-fascist racism, and by 1997, New Labour had spotted its opportunity. The party leadership endorsed the concept of Cool Britannia – a phrase popularized by the press since 1996, and eventually the name of an ice cream, but which actually dates back to a Bonzo Dog Doo Dah Band song from 1967 – and promoted it by the emblem of the Union Jack. Labour politician Peter Mandelson, in a lecture delivered in that year, declared:

> Now, together, we have reclaimed the flag. It is restored as an emblem of national pride and national diversity, restored from years as a symbol of division and intolerance to a symbol of confidence and unity for all the peoples and ethnic communities of a diverse and outward-looking Britain.
>
> (quoted in Davey 1999: 11)

The cult comic *2000AD* was quick to explode Labour's 'Cool Britannia Myth' in a special 'True Brit' issue, festooned with ironic Union Jacks.[11] The music collective Asian Dub Foundation subsequently criticized new Labour's opportunism with *Real Great Britain* (2000):

> Union Jack and Union Jill
> Back up and down the same old hill
> Sell the flag to the youths
> But who swallows the bill
> Murdoch she wrote
> Him have his hand in the till.

Mercifully, Cool Britannia had by then fizzled out.

Attempts to rebrand the United Kingdom have always proved problematic. In 1996, the Chief Executive of British Airways, Bob Ayling, had been publicly criticized by Margaret Thatcher for replacing the stylized Union Jack on the tail-fins of BA's fleet with world art liveries: she covered up a model of a 747, saying 'We fly the British flag, not these awful things'. Versions of the Union Jack had appeared in British civil aviation since at least 1931, when Imperial Airways had requested the adoption of the Civil Air Ensign, and the design was later adapted for aircraft livery. British Airways, 'the world's favourite airline', eventually returned to the traditional red, white and blue in 2001. By this time, Virgin had taken up the initiative, adding Union Jacks to their own planes' winglets and to their figurehead in 1999.

Other national icons were also redesigned. Interest in the imperial figure of Britannia has declined since the war, and indeed Cool Britannia's adherents seemed wholly ignorant of the figure. Britannia was, however, recently restyled, for the 1993 £10 postage-stamp, by having her figure moulded to the nation's average women's chest measurement of 36B.[12] Her transformation perhaps recalls that of Mrs John Bull, who in the nineteenth century was represented literally as a domestic goddess (as Britannia at home, armour neatly stowed away), but by 1928 had become Joan Bull, representing recently enfranchised women. Joan Bull could be recognized by her top hat and Union Jack dress, rather than a coal-scuttle helmet hanging on a hat-stand, and she later stripped off down to her Union Jack brassière (1946).[13] Her husband John Bull's Union Jack waistcoat, meanwhile, was sported by everyone from comedians (Tim Brooke-Taylor in *The Goodies*) to the royal family (as a prefect at Eton College, Prince William was permitted to customize his uniform – he did so with a Union Jack waistcoat), to dogs (in 2005, Tory MP Andrew Rosindell campaigned with his bulldog, Spike, so attired; Rosindell was elected), to proud fathers (Shajaad Khan, the father of the British Muslim boxer Amir Khan, attended all of his son's 2004 Olympic bouts wearing a Union Jack waistcoat).

The flag has, in the face of its fashionable popularity, necessarily maintained its military bearings. In 1955, for example, HMS *Vidal* was sent to Rockall, 300 miles from Scotland, a tiny island in the North Atlantic, 25 metres long, 30 wide, and 19 high. Commander Richard Connell's orders from the Queen were as follows:

On arrival at Rockall you will effect a landing and hoist the Union flag on whatever spot appears the most suitable or practicable, and you will then take possession of the island on Our behalf . . . When the landing has been effected and the flag has been hoisted you will cement a commemorative plaque to the rock.

(Cawthorne 2004: 259)

All this was accomplished and the *Vidal*, named after Admiral T.E. Vidal, who had discovered Rockall in 1831, gave a twenty-one-gun salute. The importance of Rockall lay in the possibility of discovering oil or gas, and it later became strategic during the Cod War with Iceland (1975–6). Rockall's status as part of Invernesshire is currently contested by Denmark, Iceland and Ireland.

In a more gung-ho mood, a Task Force was sent to the South Atlantic in 1982 with the express purpose of raising the Union Jack again over the Falkland Islands; appropriately, the warships were seen off from Portsmouth quay by bevvies of girls with Union Jacks painted on their breasts, waving and blowing kisses. Similar scenes accompanied the departure of troops to the First Gulf War (1991), and the *Daily Star* promoted red, white and blue t-shirts displaying the Union Jack and Old Glory, with the motto 'These Colours Don't Run'. During the Second Gulf War (2004), the *Sun* newspaper produced a grotesque coalition flag, made up of the Stars and Stripes diagonally joined with the Union Jack; this travesty was apparently waved solely by Page Three models.[14]

The other 'British' flags

If the postwar life of the Union Jack has been restless, so too have been the recent histories of the crosses of Saints George, Andrew and Patrick, and also that of the Welsh dragon – indeed, the Welsh have acquired an admirable degree of recognition for their once unofficial standard. The Welsh flag had, of course, been a standard of Henry Tudor, and was based on the medieval Welsh dragon. As Henry VII, the king introduced it into the Royal Standard as a supporter, but it was later replaced by the Scottish unicorn of the Stuarts, and Wales was not included in any of the Union Flag designs by heralds from the time of James I to that of Queen Anne and George III.[15] Traditionally, Welsh patriotism has not been expressed antagonistically – 'Land of My Fathers', for example, the Welsh national anthem written in 1856, celebrates 'poets and minstrels', 'brave warriors', and even 'the ancient language', but makes no mention of Welsh separatism, or even of St David, who fades from the cultural record from this point on. But the arrival of the twentieth century encouraged Wales to begin to assert its identity within Britain and to reconsider its heraldic invisibility. An acknowledgement of the Welsh contribution to the Union was long overdue: Wales needed a more prominent position in the iconography of the United Kingdom.

Consequently, in an attempt to achieve greater national recognition, the Welsh petitioned the government in 1897, 1901, 1910, 1935 and 1945 to request that the Welsh dragon ('Y Ddraig Goch') be included in the Royal Arms. Each time they were refused because, in the words of the College of Arms, Wales had never been a kingdom: 'There is no such thing as a Welsh national flag.' The Garter Knight of Arms told the Home Office that, 'There is no more reason to add Wales to the King's style than there would be to add Mercia, Wessex or Northumbria or any other parts of England' (Weight 2002: 283, 284). Eventually, in 1953 – the coronation year – the palace offered a compromise in the shape of a new royal badge. The traditional dragon was redesigned, a crown was added, and the motto 'Y DDRAIG GOCH DDYRY CYCHWYN' ('The red dragon leads the way'). The badge was for use in periods when there was no Prince of Wales; it was, however, ridiculed. The depiction of the dragon was derided for having its tail pointing downwards, and it was claimed that the motto was an unintentional *double entendre*, originating from a verse in which a peasant farmer petitioned a neighbour for his bull, which he wanted for stud; the bull simply had to follow the way of his '*ddraig goch*'.

Official permission was still, in any case, required to fly this new Welsh standard, even on St David's Day, and so the popular Welsh dragon continued to be seen at rugby matches and in trinket shops. By 1958, a campaign had been launched to save it. The Gorsedd, a traditional gathering of Welsh bards, announced:

> We proclaim that the Red Dragon banner, as borne by Henry Tudor on Bosworth Field and as flown by Prince Cadwalador centuries earlier, is the only banner adopted by the Welsh people themselves over many years now as our national flag and that there is therefore no need to seek permission from any heraldic authority outside the Principality for the continuance of this usage. We entirely reject the badge granted in 1952–3 [as] too puny to signify anything.
>
> (Weight 2002: 285)

Wisely, the authorities conceded. Henry Brooke (Minister for Housing and Local Government, and Minister for Welsh Affairs) said in Parliament,

> I now have it in command from the Queen to say that Her Majesty has been pleased to direct that in future only the Red Dragon on a green and white flag and not the flag carrying the augmented Royal Badge shall be flown on Government buildings in Wales and, where appropriate, in London.
>
> (Boutell 1978: 259)

The Red Dragon became official on 1 January 1960. In 1999, at the opening of the Welsh National Assembly by the Queen and Prince Charles, Buckingham Palace was persuaded to fly the Prince of Wales's flag (the four lions) alongside the Royal Standard of the Queen, which, as the most senior standard, should have been the sole flag flying.

As for the components of the Union Jack, the Scots have never balked at flying St Andrew's cross, which even appeared on the Black Watch's armoured vehicles during the Second Gulf War. The saint's feast day, however, has been overshadowed by Hogmanay celebrations and Burns Night (25 January), although it is popular among Scots in America, Australia, India and New Zealand. As for the ruddy lion, King George V issued a Royal Warrant in 1934 that allowed the standard to be used during the Silver Jubilee celebrations of 1935 in Scotland 'as a mark of loyalty to the Sovereign', but not to be flown from flagpoles or public buildings – it was solely for 'decorative ebullition', comparable today to its being displayed at football matches. By an Act of 1679, the misuse of the Royal Arms actually remains a capital offence – as Denis Pamphilon, a St Albans linen merchant, discovered in 1978. Pamphilon was threatened with the death penalty by Scotland's Lyon Court for 'usurping' the red lion, which he had been printing on souvenir bedspreads and selling to Scottish football fans. He was fined £100 daily until he desisted. The Lyon Court then went on to admonish the Scottish National Party and Glasgow Rangers for using the St Andrew's cross with the red lion (Cawthorne 2004: 11–12).

The cross of St Patrick has become increasingly significant throughout the twentieth century as an emblem that might be able to steer a course between political and religious factions. It has appeared in St Patrick's Day parades as a neutral Irish banner, and now forms part of the insignia of the reformed Police Service of Northern Ireland. It has also been adopted by the General Synod of the Church of Ireland, and churches may fly it on 'Holy Days and during the Octaves of Christmas, Easter, the Ascension of Our Lord and Pentecost, and on any other such day as may be recognised locally as the Dedication Day of the particular church building', thus avoiding the sectarian implications of raising the Union Flag, which is known to some republicans as the 'Butcher's Apron'.

The status of the Union Jack in Northern Ireland is, of course, particularly fraught. The Government of Northern Ireland had introduced its own flag in 1924. This was an Anglicized version of the Ulster Flag, an ancient standard of the O'Neills that alluded to a widespread Irish legend that Ulster had been promised to the first man to lay his hand on the ground of the province – whereupon one warrior hacked off his hand and hurled it onto the land, throwing it over the heads of his comrades as they raced to claim the territory. The standard of the O'Neills, which dates from at least the sixteenth century, was yellow with a red cross surmounted by a white shield bearing the bloody hand. Following the declaration of the Irish Free State and partition in 1922, this design was reworked into a cross of St George, on which beneath a crown the red hand appeared on a six-pointed star, signifying the six counties. No use was made of the cross of St Patrick.

This Ulster flag was abandoned in 1973 when the Belfast Stormont parliament was dissolved, and, since then, the Union Jack has been the only official flag in Northern Ireland. There have, however, been plenty of unofficial flags, among them the alternative Ulster flag (a British White Ensign bearing a central white shield and red hand), Orange Order flags (orange with purple stars, sometimes with St George's cross in the canton), UVF flags (Ulster Volunteer Force: blue with St George's cross in the canton), the Starry Plough (a pale blue flag bearing the constellation, borne by republican paramilitary groups), and the flag of Fianna na hÉireann, the IRA youth wing (blue with a rising yellow sun in the bottom left). In Belfast, Protestant streets display Union Jacks, St Andrew's crosses, and Israeli flags, whereas the Catholic areas have elaborate murals and fly Irish tricolours and Palestinian flags (Miles 2005: 446).

Despite (or perhaps because of) its incorporation of St Patrick, the Union Jack is perceived by republicans as partisan, and in the meantime the red hand has been appropriated by ultra-loyalist paramilitaries, much as the Union Jack itself was by neo-fascists in the 1970s. Indeed, in 2005 the BBC children's TV programme *Blue Peter* (itself named after a flag and characterized by badges) was embroiled in a row for suggesting the red hand be used as an emblem for aircraft livery representing 'the best of British'. The BBC immediately apologized for promoting sectarianism, but perhaps they apologized too soon. The iconography of the red hand is, in fact, subtle and complex, as both loyalists and nationalists identify with the symbol: loyalists see it representing the six counties of Northern Ireland, whereas nationalists perceive the nine counties of Old Ulster (three of which are now in the Republic). The red hand is also used as a symbol of a united Ireland, sometimes with a severed thumb to indicate the split between the north and the south. So this may actually be an emblem over which different factions agree. In any case, it remains in widespread use in Northern Ireland: the badge is worn by sports teams and the fire brigade and since 1951 has even been used in the Republic by Na Piarsaigh, a hurling team from County Cork.

Throughout this period there were also sporadic calls for St George's Day to be recognized, and for the cross of St George to be flown, but St George has not had the same success as his fellow saints have, nor indeed as has the dragon, and celebrating St George's Day has suffered from fears of rising English neo-fascism. The observance of his feast day declined seriously after the war, although the flag continued to be flown from parish churches on particular occasions.[16] Aside from these glimpses, the flag of St George for many years fell from view (Fox-Davies 1949: 362n), until the extreme right appropriated St George much as it did the Union Jack. In 1975, the neo-fascist League of St George was formed to revive Oswald Mosley's plan for a united Europe. It was a tiny and ineffective group, but as an ultra-right organization that adopted the cross of St George, the League of St George has to some extent tarnished the emblem.

The name of the group, the League of St George, has since been taken by a football website, and it is, indeed, to football that St Georgism owes its most recent revival. At Euro 96, English football supporters finally began to wear the colours of St George as opposed to the red-white-and-blue of the Union Jack, and a popular sense of Englishness, as distinct from Britishness, emerged. English nationalism had for too long overlapped with British patriotism; at last some attempt was being made to distinguish the two. The English fans also realized that the Scots hated the English team with a rare vehemence – 75 per cent of Scottish football fans would not support an English team; 40 per cent would prefer any other team to win – and they reluctantly began to reciprocate (Weight 2002: 711). Coincidentally, a few weeks after Euro 96, the Church of England restored St George's Day to the status of a compulsory feast.

All of this led to a revival of St Georgism. The first St George's Day greetings cards were mass-produced in 1995 and currently sell about 50,000 every April. The Sun printed a cross of St George poster in April 1997, and the next year launched a campaign to revive the celebration of St George's Day. In 1998, the English Tourist Board ran a programme of events with the title 'St George Invades Britain'. At the 1998 World Cup, English football fans were again identified by the cross of St George. In 1999, the Royal Society of St George reversed its sixty-year decline in membership and the English Tourist Council (formerly Board) changed its logo to a flag of St George. Even the Christian name 'George' became almost five times as popular as it had been in the previous decade, and it is the name under which Prince Charles intends to rule (Paxman 1999: 21; Weight 2002: 713). The revival has since continued, and by 2005 the English Folk Dance and Song Society was sponsoring St George pageants across the country by offering a £600 award for the celebration receiving the most coverage.

United Kingdom?

At the beginning of the twenty-first century, the different nations of the United Kingdom are all developing a sense of their respective identities, and of the symbolism that expresses those identities and how it can be combined into more elaborate devices such as flags and coats of arms. Interestingly, it is just at this point that some radical redesigns have been proposed for the Union Jack itself.

In 2003, a group calling itself 'reFLAG' launched a campaign to 'modernize' the Union Jack. The suggestion was to add diagonal black stripes to the current design. The reason given was that this would represent black Britons: reFLAG's logic derived, somewhat paradoxically, from the neo-fascist chant, 'There ain't no black in the Union Jack', and aimed to rectify this apparent oversight – which of course completely misses the point.[17] The white in the Union Jack does not represent white people any more than the blue represents blue people or the red, red people: the colours are there to draw together three territories into a United Kingdom. To add black lines would infringe the laws of heraldry (perhaps a minor misdemeanour, but these laws did develop for very good reasons). It would destroy any sense of territorial integrity – which is, quite literally, the one thing that unites British citizens. And it would obliterate the saltire of St Andrew – and therefore Scotland – from the flag completely. It would also, incidentally, produce a flag that looked as if it had unsuccessfully tried to incorporate the cross of St Piran, patron of Cornwall – a white cross on black.[18] The reFLAG campaign was ridiculed – why not add pink for homosexuals, grey for the third age, and a variety of other hues? – and has since foundered.[19]

It is, however, striking that at precisely the same time, the Turner Prize-winning artist Chris Ofili redesigned the flag in a very similar way to create the *Union Black*, a piece inspired by the symbolic colours of the pan-African flag proposed by Marcus Garvey, civil rights campaigner and founder of UNIA (Universal Negro Improvement and Conservation Association and African Communities League), that was first unveiled in 1920. This consisted of a horizontal tricolour in red, black and green, in which red stood for blood, black for skin and green for the fertile land of Africa. Hence Ofili, declaring that he 'wanted to make a flag for the African British people', replaced the white and blue of the Union Jack with black and green. The idea of tampering with the colours in this way was, it transpired, nothing new. In 1997, fellow artist Mark Wallinger flew a Union Jack in the colours of the Irish tricolour over Brixton; the piece was titled *Oxymoron* – literally, 'pointedly stupid' – and the writer and polemicist Stewart Home reported that Kenny Murphy-Roud had done the same thing with a piece called *Flag* in the 1980s in his decidedly more sectarian home town of Glasgow.

The design of the Union Jack obviously lends itself to recolouring for more commercial purposes as well. The cover of the Asian style magazine *Second Generation* displayed the pattern of the Union Jack in browns and yellows; Harrods advertised an Anglo-Italian festival with the flag in the colours of the Italian tricolour; Marmite celebrated its hundredth anniversary with a Vivienne Westwood Union Jack in red, black, and yellow; and the logo of Karrimor, suppliers of outdoor clothing and equipment, is based on the Union Jack, as if the emblem is a traveller's talisman, carried to the least hospitable places on the globe in imitation of the flags planted by pioneering explorers and mountaineers to claim territory and stake their conquests. In contrast, in 2002 the National Union of Students and Union of Jewish Students had an advertising firm tastelessly redesign the Union Jack into a swastika for an otherwise laudable poster campaign to stamp out campus racism.

The only justifiable argument for the redesign of the Union Jack is if the territories it represents change. And yet the flag remained the same, even with Irish independence. In 1937, the Irish Free State, established in 1922, became Éire, and in 1949 it became a full republic, wholly independent of both the United Kingdom and the Commonwealth. Northern Ireland remained a union province, but could no longer consider itself a separate kingdom. Technically, it should not therefore be afforded a separate status on the flag, any more than the principality of Wales is separately recognized. In other words, the red saltire of St Patrick should have been removed from the Union Jack back in 1937, and the flag should have reverted to the first Union design.[20] Perhaps if Éire had adopted St Patrick's cross as its own national flag, the red saltire would have been removed from the Union Jack. But that was never likely. The republicans continue to hoist the tricolour – indeed, this banner had such significance that, in the 1960s, the Irish government petitioned British Prime Minister Harold Wilson for the return of the original tricolour that had flown over the Post Office during the Easter Rising of 1916, and which had since been kept in London's Imperial War Museum. It was eventually returned.

In direct contrast, the Ulster Independence Movement has proposed the Ulster National Flag, since adopted by Ulster Nation. This party seeks Northern Irish independence from both Dublin and London, yet stresses the mix of Irish and Scots in Ulster. Its flag is effectively derived from a Union Jack from which the cross of St George has been removed, leaving the combined saltires of St Patrick and St Andrew: the flag is therefore a fimbriated diagonal red cross on blue, featuring a yellow star and the ubiquitous red hand.

These attempts to rethink the Union Jack show the flag's profound relevance in the current political climate and national culture. It is, therefore, all the more surprising that there is so little legislation concerning the flying and administration of the flag, except in the armed forces and at sea. The Ministry of Defence offers guidance for the military use of flags in *Flags of All Nations* (known as *BR20*), and there are garrulous instructions in Navy manuals. Similarly, from the seventeenth century onwards, maritime laws governing what ensigns may be flown at sea have been scrupulously maintained, in order to ensure that merchant and civil vessels are not confused with Her Majesty's ships. Under the 1995 Merchant Shipping Act, it is an offence for a private citizen to fly the Union Jack afloat. But no such regulations exist for citizens on land. Indeed, there are still no stipulations on the design and proportions of the Union Jack, or on correct flying regulations, and no specific administration by the government. Even the flag's name remains in doubt. 'Rules for Hoisting Flags on Government Buildings' are administered by the Department of Culture, Media, and Sport, and there is a list of nineteen official Union Flag days, from Remembrance Sunday to the Countess of Wessex's birthday, but there is no active discouragement – or encouragement, for that matter – to fly the flag at other times.[21] Indeed, public demand can lead to quite unconstitutional displays. To mourn the death of Diana, Princess of Wales, the Union Jack flew at half-mast over Buckingham Palace, despite Diana being a commoner who therefore had no right to a half-mast salute.[22]

This attitude – a familiar combination of avid reinterpretation and apathetic indifference – has characterized the history of the Union Jack for four hundred years. In times of national confidence, the government was content to let the flag fly on land, but since the Second World War, Britain has been in a perpetual, if leisurely, decline, and the deep reluctance to engage seriously with displays of public patriotism today, symbolized by the ambiguous status of the Union Jack, suggests a refusal to acknowledge the very real possibility that the Union might disintegrate.

Acknowledgements

The following online resources have been used: The Flag Institute and The Oxford Dictionary of National Biography.

Notes

1 'Union Jack flies over Berlin', *The Times*, 7 July 1945: 4. Raising the Hammer and Sickle over the Reichstag on 2 May is the more familiar image.
2 *The Times*, 16 August 1945: 1.
3 *Hansard* (1933), cclxxix: 1324.
4 Weight 2002: 199, 195.
5 *Disc Weekly*, 17 July 1965: 6.
6 Kureishi and Savage 2002: 239. See also, 'It is re-representing something the public is familiar with, in a different form. Like clothes. Union Jacks are supposed to be flown, we have a jacket made of one' (*Melody Maker*, 3 July 1965: 11).
7 *Disc Weekly*, 1 October 1966: 20.
8 *Fabulous 208* (1969): 38.
9 *Telegraph Magazine*, April 1966 (Sheila Macivor); *Telegraph Magazine* (4 September 2004): 15
10 *The Times*, 26 November 1953; Weight 2002: 259.
11 *2000AD* 1084, 25 Feb–10 March 1998.
12 In 1955, separate stamps were proposed for Scotland (thistle), Wales (leek), and Northern Ireland (red hand), the flora accompanied by the Queen's head; no English rose issue was even suggested. The stamps went into production in 1956. In July 2004, a Rule Britannia set of stamps and first-day covers issued by the Post Office featured Union Jack stamps and Great British icons such as milk bottles on a doorstep, a red pillar box, a deckchair, a red double-decker bus, a red telephone box, tea, a Union Jack umbrella, and a stick of rock.
13 Joan Bull was created by cartoonist David Low, most famous for Colonel Blimp.
14 In 2004, the artist and anti-war campaigner Peter Kennard produced *Decoration*, an exhibition profoundly influenced by the invasion of Iraq. Kennard produced photo-montages of medals in which the ribbons were frayed strips of the Stars and Stripes and the Union Jack, while the medallions were human faces.
15 This leads Richard Weight to note, somewhat archly, that 'in a sense, therefore, it was the Scots and Germans, and not the English, who erased the Welsh from the British mind' (2002: 281).
16 An Earl Marshal's Warrant of 9 February 1938 stipulates that the flag proper to be flown by any church in the Provinces of Canterbury and York is, 'The Cross of St George and in the first quarter an escutcheon of the Arms of the See in which such Church is ecclesiastically situate [the diocesan arms]' (http://www.church care.co.uk/atoz_flags.php). The expense attendant on this, however, means that

the cross of St George is usually flown instead. The flying of such flags is not compulsory.

17 The line 'Ain't no Black in de Union Jack' also appears in Benjamin Zephaniah's poem 'Self Defence' (Zephania, 1996).

18 St Piran (Pirrin), the patron saint of miners, was adopted by the Cornish in the 1950s.

19 This campaign was parodied by Mick Hume in *The Times*, 16 June 2003, who discussed adding green, orange, pink, grey, and so forth (*T2*: 2).

20 Capt. Malcolm Farrow, RN, recommends setting up a Union Flag Committee to investigate this and other anomalies.

21 The flag days have recently been questioned by Labour MP Tom Watson (West Bromwich East); see *Independent on Sunday*, 9 May 2004: 10. Among his proposals are making 6 June, the anniversary of D-Day, a flag day. Currently in England secular public buildings are only permitted to fly the English flag alongside the Union Jack on St George's Day.

22 The Union Jack was also flown at half-mast from royal residences after the terrorist attacks of 11 September 2001, and 7 July 2005.

6 Pride and possession, display and destruction

Neil Jarman

Each year, from mid-June onwards, many Protestant working-class areas of Northern Ireland are bedecked with a variety of flags that display the population's sense of a British identity and their political association with the United Kingdom (Jarman 1997). Many people have flag-pole holders as a permanent fixture on their houses or shop fronts from which personal displays are made, while in many staunch Loyalist[1] areas flags are flown from almost every lamppost and other public sites. Many of the main thoroughfares in Loyalist housing estates and in predominately Protestant towns and villages will also be decorated with bunting strung across the road, often in the form of alternating red, white and blue pennants or as miniature Union Flag designs. The most recognisable of the flags are the Union Jack of the United Kingdom and the flag of Northern Ireland, the cross of St George with the Red Hand of Ulster on a shield in the centre, which appears in a variety of forms. Some areas also display flags that are associated with the various Loyalist paramilitary organisations such as the Ulster Volunteer Force, the Young Citizen Volunteers, the Ulster Defence Association and the Ulster Freedom Fighters, each of which has designed or adapted their own formal flags. These include a variety of designs: the purple flag of the UVF with the Red Hand of Ulster in a gold oval surrounded by the word 'For God and Ulster' and the blue and white YCV flags, with references to the battles of the First World War, are based on historical emblems carried by the original UVF in their opposition to Home Rule in the 1912–16 period. But the sky blue UDA flags and black UFF flags with a clenched Red Hand in the centre are of more recent design, despite their use of Latin mottoes 'Quis Separabit' and 'Feriens Tego'. The UDA also sometimes fly the French Tricolour in Loyalist areas, but this appears to be due to the colour scheme matching the Union Flag, in a design that replicates the Irish Tricolour, rather than representing any allegiance to France.

In some areas other flags associated with recent Loyalist history can be seen, such as the flag of the Vanguard movement from the 1970s, or the Independent Ulster flag designed in the 1980s, and which includes elements of the Scottish and Irish saltires along with the Red Hand of Ulster. This was one part of a consciously created national repertoire of symbols which also included a female icon, an anthem and an origin myth, but is the only element that has achieved any sense of public recognition, although the idea of an Independent Ulster, which it conveys, has not generated any significant support. Other flags associated with Britain are also flown, the most prominent of these being the St Andrew's cross of Scotland, which acknowledges the close historical, social and cultural ties between Ulster and Scotland. Occasionally one may also see the Welsh Dragon and more recently some areas have taken to flying a selection of flags associated with the British Empire including the flags of Australia, Canada, Gibraltar and South Africa. Finally, in the recent past some communities have also displayed the Israeli flag, primarily in response to displays of the Palestinian flag in neighbouring Catholic areas. This brief review of the diversity of flags that can be seen across Northern Ireland provides an indication of the importance of flags as an element of the Protestant ritual calendar and in conveying a sense of the identity of the Protestant community and its place within wider international contexts.

Flags are a much less prominent feature of Catholic symbolic displays. The Irish Tricolour is the most significant flag associated with Nationalist political culture, although the flags of the four provinces of Ireland, the Papal flag and various flags associated with Gaelic sports teams are all flown at some public events and in some locations. As noted earlier, flags are also sometimes used as more overt political emblems, as was the case when Palestinian flags appeared in many Nationalist areas of Belfast shortly after the beginning of the second Intifada in 2002. Sometimes unlikely flags appear, as was the case during the 2002 European Championships when a number of Catholic areas flew the Swedish flag, with a portrait of Henrik Larsson, who played for the Scottish football club Celtic at the time, in the centre. In the period following partition of Ireland in 1921 displays of Nationalist symbols were not welcomed by Unionists in Northern Ireland. Legal restrictions and forceful policing methods ensured that any such displays were effectively limited to Catholic areas and were kept well away from any shared or neutral spaces (Bryan 2000; Jarman and Bryan 2000). Displays of the Irish Tricolour are still regarded by many Unionists as 'offensive' and provocative, and despite the Belfast/Good Friday Agreement acknowledging the equality of the British and Irish national identities, this has not been translated to equality of flag-flying.

The promiscuous flying of these various flags is a prominent aspect of a rich visual culture that has developed in Northern Ireland over the past two centuries (Bryson and McCartney 1994; Buckley 1998; Hayes McCoy 1979). The flags are part of a wide variety of visual displays that are erected by Protestants as part of the marching season, the annual cycle of parades held to commemorate the most important victories of the Williamite wars of the seventeenth century – the Siege of Derry and the Battle of the Boyne – but which also now includes commemorations of the first day of the Battle of the Somme in 1916. This cultural repertoire includes the carrying of elaborately painted banners at parades, the erection of colourful arches decorated with symbols of the Orange Order and one of the oldest traditions of painting political murals in the world (Buckley 1985–6; Jarman 1997, 2001). The Nationalist repertoire has been more limited but the main anniversaries, including the 1916 Easter Rising and the 1981 Republican Hunger Strikes, include many of the same visual elements (Loftus 1990, 1994; Jarman 1997; Rolston 1991). Flags are one element of the material culture through which the two competing collective identities are asserted, defined and renewed, through which territorial claims are enforced and social and spatial boundaries are marked out. Flags are also an important element of the ongoing tensions and conflict and have increasingly been a means by which the opposing political aspirations have been sustained throughout the duration of the peace process since 1994. They are used to give and take offence, they are flaunted and derided, and their presence on many public buildings and at parades is frequently challenged. However, this essay does not intend to explore the history or meaning of the various flags (Hayes McCoy 1979) nor will it specifically focus on their role in defining cultural and political identity (Bryson and McCartney 1994). Nor will it consider the ways in which flags have been used sustain hostility or the attempts that are being made to limit such conflict through management of the displays or their temporal limitations (Bryan and Gillespie 2005; McCormick and Jarman forthcoming). Instead the chapter focuses on one curious aspect of the use of flags, their destruction. Or rather the way in which these erstwhile symbols of nationality, identity, pride and defiance are allowed to rot and decay, rather than being treated with the respect one might more readily expect of such revered national and factional symbols.

The flying of flags is part of a wide range of visual displays that are erected for the 'marching season', the annual cycle of anniversary, celebratory and social parades that dominates the summer from late June onwards. The final event of the marching season takes place at the end of August and many of the visual displays, for example the bunting, the Orange arches and Orange pennants, are removed soon afterwards. However, although the flags that have been flown from private residential property will also generally be removed at this time, many of the flags that have been erected informally in public spaces, in particular those on the streets, are allowed to remain. They remain fixed to the lampposts, while they gradually fade in the sun, are dirtied by the rain and are shredded by the wind. This casual attitude prompts many questions. Why is it that people who are prepared to risk confrontation to assert their right to fly the flag, who insist on the importance of the flag to their national identity and who might well physically assault someone from the other community if they tried to remove or destroy 'our flag', appear to be quite happy to allow its slow decay and destruction? This phenomenon has been noted in conversation and in passing, often in an ironically questioning way, but it has never been considered in a serious manner before. Rather it has been accepted as something that happens, in the same way that the destruction of the flags themselves just happens. This chapter draws upon over 15 years research in Northern Ireland in beginning to explore this issue. My initial anthropological work focused on the relationships between the diversity of symbolic and ritual displays associated with the parades and the demonstrations of collective identity (Jarman 1992), while more recent work has addressed issues of ongoing conflict and violence associated with the period of the peace process, from 1994 to date. This chapter draws on both of these strands of work. It represents some initial thoughts on the place of flags within Protestant material culture and some further consideration of the fragile physicality of the various visual displays (McCormick and Jarman 2005, forthcoming).

Destroying flags

Individuals, communities and nations are often fiercely proud of their flags. But, it is because of the importance that flags have, the emotions that they can generate and because they are widely recognised to have such significance and power, that the destruction of flags is not such an unusual occurrence. Flags may be destroyed for a variety of reasons as a result of their symbolic importance, although such destruction takes place usually, but not exclusively, for reasons of hostility. One of the most prominent forms of flags destruction is when they are physically destroyed as a surrogate for a political enemy, as for example when Irish Tricolours are burnt by Protestants on the Eleventh Night bonfires or when American flags have been burnt in a wide range of countries, and often in front of TV cameras.[2] In such contexts the flags act as a metonym for the country, while destroying the flag allows both for a real expression of anger and is also a symbolic act of revenge or aggression against the particular enemy nation. Flags may also be considered as being symbolically destroyed when an opponent's flag is captured in battle. In such cases they may either be displayed as a trophy or they may be physically destroyed as a surrogate for the enemy. Consequently for many armed forces or military units the loss of their flag to the enemy may be considered as an act of extreme dishonour. Flags may also be destroyed in an act of protest, as in the case of American citizens burning the Stars and Stripes to demonstrate their opposition to government policies. This issue continues to generate considerable debate in the USA and despite hostility by conservatives has been established as an element of freedom of speech that is protected by the American Constitution (Curtis 1993; Goldstein 1996a). However, such are the passions that are aroused that the debate over the right to destroy the Stars and Stripes remains a live issue (Welch 2000).

While the hostile burning of flags may be the most prominent form of destruction, flags may also be destroyed in an act of reverence or respect. For example, Section 8 of the US Flag Code, entitled 'Respect for the flag', notes that: 'The flag, when it is in such condition that it is no longer a fitting emblem for display, should be destroyed in a dignified way, preferably by burning' (4 US Code 1, Section 8 (k)).[3] This seems to be a case where the destruction of a flag is undertaken to avoid the possibility of causing it to be disrespected or of disrespecting the nation through displaying a damaged emblem. However, in an interesting contrast to this perspective, a regulation from 1914 recommended that old British naval flags should be 'torn up into small pieces and disposed of as rags'.[4] It is unclear what would happen to the rags, whether they would be used or simply disposed of in some other manner, but the British case does perhaps imply that the actual fabric of the flag, its very materiality, was considered to have no great value compared to the importance given to the symbolic display. Flags may also be symbolically destroyed by their association with the death of an individual and an act of burial. Although in some cases an individual may be buried with or even in their national flag, in many cases the flags are removed before the actual burial rite but are allowed to retain a function as a *memento mori* for the living. The physical fabric can no longer be used as a flag but rather exists as a symbolic device that serves to represent the individual as the conjunction of nationality and person. These differing attitudes to flag destruction illustrate the different attitudes that exist to the physical presence of a flag. In the American example the power of the flag is embodied, at least in part, in its physical existence, its materiality, whereas the British naval example suggests that the material status of the flag as an object or artefact can be separate and distinct from its symbolic status and power and indicates that one can respect the symbol without fetishising the object.

This diversity of wilful and/or considered acts of destruction is in stark contrast to the casual manner in which many flags are allowed to be destroyed in Northern Ireland. Although any instance of the deliberate destruction of a Union or a Northern Ireland flag by an individual Nationalist or a Nationalist organisation would be virulently criticised and cited as an example of a lack of respect for the culture of the other community, the numerous examples of the casual destruction of the same symbols by Unionists has largely been ignored. The remainder of this chapter explores some of the possible factors that can help us understand this apparently casual attitude towards material representations of some of the most important symbols of the Ulster Protestant community. I will not argue for a singular or definitive explanation but rather seek to understand this activity through the intersection of diverse and varied interpretations, activities and contextualisations, which mutually reinforce each other in practice, over time and in different social and geographical spaces. I want therefore to consider processes that involve changes in the meaning and values of these symbolic devices, in which meaning is related to, and generated from temporal and spatial context, rather than being fixed and constant or embodied in a physical status. This involves both a conceptualisation of control, ownership and possession, and a sense in which value emerges from a process of opposition and confrontation.

Figure 6.1 Loyalists flying the Irish Tricolour, prior to consigning it to the bonfire's flames on the 'Eleventh Night'. Note also the Sinn Féin leadership, bound for the same fate.

Over the course of a relatively short period of time and through their use the various flags erected for public display change from being considered as the material embodiment of the Ulster Protestant identity and as important and valuable symbolic artefacts to being disregarded and even valueless rags. Their status thus shifts from being an artefact full of meaning and significance, to apparently becoming an essentially meaningless object. They change from being an emblem of pride to something that is ignored, unseen and disregarded. Whilst one can argue that a common-sense assumption would expect important national symbols to retain their basic meaning and value amongst the adherents, at least over a short- to medium-term time period, we also have to acknowledge that the value of symbols is in part due to their ability to represent multiple meanings (Ortner 1973). If not 'all things to all men', then certainly a diversity of meanings to diverse sections of society, while meaning not only varies among different individuals and groups but also within different temporal and spatial contexts. Furthermore, this chapter argues that the meaning of a symbolic artefact can and does change according to context, even to its devotees and adherents, and such symbols may be considered as more important in some contexts and less important in others. The use of national, regional and organisational flags in Northern Ireland suggests that the process of holding meaning may be a more episodic and variable one. Although the value and the meaning of the flags are always contextual, outside of a specific context the solidity and singularity of meaning begins to dissolve and the value is eroded. In some contexts of commemoration, contest and antagonism, key symbols may in fact lose their meaning, only to regain it and lose it again, in a recurrent cyclical process.

Flags in time

The Northern Ireland and Union flags obtain much of their contemporary significance in Northern Ireland from their temporal and spatial use, from the episodic nature of the displays rather than from the continuous presence. Flags are erected as part of the build up to the marching season, a period that is used to reconstruct a sense of Protestant unity and solidarity in the face of the Catholic enemy. The meaning and value of the flags are inflated by the temporal context, which is a period of contemporary tension but also a time when social memories of violence, threat, siege and confrontation are reinvigorated. The build up to the marching season is not only a time for remembering the victories of the Williamite Wars of the 1680s and 1690s, which consolidated Protestant power and authority in Britain and Ireland, but also a time for recalling more recent conflicts. These include the Battle of the Somme, regarded as a blood sacrifice for Britain, the violence of the Troubles, or the ongoing challenges to the right to parade. The displays of flags are one of many visible means of reaffirming the collective British identity of the Protestant community. Many of the other displays are predominantly focused on the ritual celebration of collective self. They are internally directed, to focus on bringing people together through events such as bonfires and parades, and thereby practically and symbolically unify the otherwise fragmented and dispersed Protestant community. In contrast many of the displays of flags are more intently focused outwards and towards the 'Other'.

The positioning of flags in many residential areas is designed to make them visible to the outsider. They are flown from high on lampposts, they are raised above the interface barriers or 'peacelines' that segregate Protestant and Catholic working-class residential areas, they are placed atop the bonfires built for the Eleventh Night, although they will be replaced by Irish Tricolours before the bonfires are lit. One of the uses of the flags is to remind the 'Other' of the continued presence and existence of the Protestant population. Their meaning is thus in part created and sustained from a context of heightened inter-communal opposition. The meaning and value of the flags is therefore linked as much to their capacity to annoy, humiliate and antagonise the 'Other', as it is to demonstrate pride and unity. The use of flags is part of the widely invoked and always denied practice of 'coat-

Figure 6.2 From the bottom: an Ulster flag, a Union Jack and two loyalist
paramilitary flags.

trailing', a means of displaying one's presence that is in reality designed to
provoke the other. The flags are therefore erected to flaunt and taunt the
other as much as they are erected as acts of chest-puffing pride.

But this phase of heightened inter-communal tension and posturing is a
relatively short period of time. Once the main parades have passed off things
beginning to return to 'normal'. This sense of the marching season as a

liminal period, a time when neighbourly relations between people from different ethno-religious communities break down only to be reinstated once the parades have passed, has been widely recognised by anthropologists working on Ireland (Harris 1972; Larsen 1982; McFarlane 1986). It is also largely cited as a feature of life before the Troubles. However, even though there is a greater degree of communal segregation and polarisation than in the past, the quality of relations between the two communities still ebbs and flows, tensions rise in late June and early July only to subside through August. Normative patterns of engagement tend to be re-established through the autumn and winter months, only for tensions to rise again in the spring. The meaning of the flags, the rationale for flying the flags and the potential for the flags to inflame tensions and arouse passions is thus greater in the early summer period, when they are at their most meaningful for both sides. By the autumn their meaning and importance is considerably reduced. The two communities are then less focused on activities that create tensions, they try to move on from hostilities, and consequently flag-flying drops down the political agenda. One can suggest that the steady physical decay of the flags is a physical representation of the decline in tensions between the two communities, while the continued presence of the tattered flags remains as a reminder that inter-communal relationships are still ultimately antagonistic, if currently not overtly confrontational.

Flags in place

Temporal meaning is also enhanced by spatial meaning. Flags are flown in a variety of locations, in both urban and rural areas, at official and unofficial sites. But as noted earlier, their meaning increases when they are flown in a way that can be seen by the other side. Thus flags are frequently flown at the numerous interfaces between the two communities where they are used to mark the boundaries and define the limits to territory. Many of these interfaces are marked by walls or fences, which are designed to provide both a physical and a visual barrier between neighbouring communities. But the flying of flags above the walls provides a constant reminder that the neighbouring 'Other' hasn't gone away, even if they cannot readily be seen.

Conflict over flags frequently occurs when a flag is placed in a way that is deemed to challenge the normative order of segregation and control. This may involve flying flags in places they have not previously been flown, or on longer stretches of a road than before, or outside buildings that have been considered as neutral or shared resources. It also may involve flying a larger number of flags, or a wider range of flags, or more controversial flags. The spatialisation of flags is generally, but not exclusively, linked to the marching season, but flags are also used as an element of confrontation and challenge in response to localised tensions and disputes. Flags may be erected in response to a physical attack from the other side, but they may also be erected in response to lesser affronts, verbal challenges or symbolic displays by the other side. Flags are thus used to assert control over place and space, to reinforce a sense of social segregation and difference, but also as a constant reminder of the other and therefore of the potential for hostility and violence.

Furthermore, the demarcation of territories and the challenging of the permanence of communal boundaries is an important element of the process of marching. From a Protestant perspective most of the current cycle of conflicts over parades is related to challenging the reality of territorial divisions, attempting to reassert their historical power and authority over space and to deny the reality of demographic and political change. One of the more prominent issues that is subject to negotiation, regulation and control is the display of flags on controversial marches, where flags are often cited as artefacts that cause affront and thereby raise tension. For some the marches are thus an opportunity to display the flag in enemy territory, to challenge the reality of demographic shifts and to reassert the historical patterns of dominance and subservience. The physical presence of flags at boundaries and interfaces is thus a constant reminder of the presence of the Unionist community, while the presence of Orangemen marching behind those same flags is a reminder of the differences of the power and authority of the Unionist and Nationalist communities.

The importance of artefacts

This discussion has focused on the importance of flags as a means of displaying collective identity, of marking territory and of asserting power over the other. How do we move from a focus on the importance of flags to one where the flags appear to have less meaning and value? I have argued that the meaning of the flags in part comes from their role in speaking to the 'Other', as much as it comes from speaking to the converted. The importance of the flags is as much in the messages it sends to the 'Other' as in what it says to us. Furthermore, this role is heightened at the beginning of the marching season and at times of localised tension and conflict. Much of the meaning given to the flags as symbolic emblems comes from the process of confrontation, contest and conflict. Once this situation is ended, or reduced, the value and significance of the flags is also reduced. Flags that are not required to define or reaffirm boundaries have less meaning than flags that are. Once the flags have done their job, they begin to lose their value and meaning. One might assume then that at the end of the marching season the flags would either be removed and carefully stored away, to be brought out again the next year, or, if they were too damaged or faded, disposed of in the manner of sacred relics. This does happen in some situations, and increasingly attempts to manage the display of flags has focused upon having a clearly defined period when flags would be erected and when they would be taken down. But in many situations the flags are not removed, they are simply left to fade and decay.

The expectation that the flags should be treated with dignity and removed, rather than being allowed to decay *in situ*, is based on an assumption that the flags have some intrinsic value as symbolic artefacts: that is, that their physical objectiveness is itself valued, rather than the meaning that they are able to convey. But this is not necessarily the case. The Ulster Protestant community has a very rich and vibrant material culture that is used to define and display its social and political identity. This culture includes the use of elaborately painted silken banners that are carried on the parades, the erection of Orange arches, made of wood or steel, in towns and villages across the North, the painting of brightly coloured murals which depict a variety of historical images, symbols and paramilitary displays and an increasingly varied range of colourful uniforms that are worn by each of the six hundred or so marching bands (Jarman 2000). But while considerable care is paid in the design and creation of such artefacts, less than appropriate attention is often paid to maintaining them. Banners, which can cost over £2,500 to have painted, are frequently left lying casually on the ground when the parades break for lunch. They may be draped over musical instruments to protect them from the rain or left sprawled on wet grass. The banners can last 40 years or more if they are treated with care, but many are carried in the wind and rain and get torn and damaged; at the end of a parade they may be rolled up while still damp and put away until the next parade (Jarman 1998, 1999). Furthermore, the loyal orders have made virtually no attempt to record or preserve any of their banners and many old banners have been left to rot in attics or Orange halls, while very few are in the possession of any local museums.

Murals have become an increasingly elaborate feature of the political displays, but again little attention is given to preserving the longevity of the images. While considerable time and energy may go into preparing a wall and then painting an image, the completed murals are often allowed to fade and decay (McCormick and Jarman 2005). Some of the more important memorial murals may well be looked after for a while and graffiti will be removed from them, while others may be repainted and restored in the run up to the parades. But most are treated much more casually and are simply allowed to disappear. One street corner in Belfast was maintained as the site of a painting of King William III from the 1920s until the 1990s. Numerous versions of the image were recorded over the years (mostly by journalists or academics) as King Billy was repainted in various styles (Rolston 1991, 1992). However, in the mid-1990s an Eleventh Night bonfire was built immediately adjacent to the painting and the wall was badly damaged. The render was subsequently removed and the image disappeared, never to be replaced. A similar casual attitude is portrayed towards other aspects of the material culture. Objects, artefacts and images are created, are subject to great ceremony and ritual at their first use or display and they are given meaning and value through use. But they are also readily discarded with little concern, emotion or sentiment. Few attempts have been made to record, document, archive, preserve or display old and used artefacts by members of the loyal orders or by the wider Protestant community. For a community that values and exalts the notion of tradition, as the marching orders do, this is perhaps surprising.

There is therefore a cultural pattern underpinning the attitude towards flags, whereby great store is placed in the ability to display symbols and to perform rituals, but relatively little importance is placed on the artefacts themselves. The value and meaning of the numerous symbols is in their display and in the use-value of the artefacts, rather than there being any intrinsic value in the artefacts themselves. Flags are perhaps the most prominent example of this, as they are also usually cheaply made and therefore extremely disposable, and it is as easy to replace them with new flags next year as it is to care for them. Protestant political culture is a culture that is based upon the active performance, enactment and display of its members, rather than a culture based around the maintenance and display of ritually important relics and artefacts. This is not to say that the artefacts have no meaning or significance, rather that they obtain their meaning within the context of performance and display rather than having value that transcends the process of the ritual. Orange banners and arches are put away each year until the next marching season, they are not objects to be viewed and venerated outside of the process of the parade or the marching season. The murals clearly are visible throughout the year, but they are rarely looked after outside of a particular anniversary, they are allowed to decay and degrade slowly. They merge into the local landscape and while they remain notable to outsiders they may be virtually invisible to local residents. Similarly, once the marching season is over the flags are left to fly in the wind, they are no longer given any particular respect or prominence, they are disposable as objects, even while their fragmenting presence serves as a reminder of the enduring presence of the Protestant people.

Possession and permanence

There is, however, a difference between the status of the various artefacts, which also has some influence on how they are treated. The banners and arches belong to individual lodges, which have responsibility for their maintenance and the times when they are on display. The banners are important symbolic devices and they are also the visible representations of a specific group of men. The banners serve to identify the lodge by their geographical location and offer something of their history. Similarly an arch is a symbolic representation of a larger body of men, usually an Orange district, while a mural is frequently associated with a particular organisation, which in recent years will have been one of the various paramilitary organisations. In each case a group or an individual has some sense of ownership and responsibility for the artefact or display, to choose to erect, display, preserve, remove or maintain the object.

The flags are less readily associated with a specific group or individual within the community than with the community as an entity. Although an individual or a group has to take responsibility to purchase and erect the flags, this is not particularly expensive or time-consuming compared with commissioning a new banner or painting a new mural. In most cases the flags are also not visibly associated with any particular section of the community, rather the symbols of the Union and of Northern Ireland which transcend the fractionalism of Unionist culture and politics. They belong to everyone in general and no one in particular. While it can be considered to be part of a social duty to help with the displays and show one's allegiance to the Union by erecting flags in the run up to the marching season, it is less obviously a social responsibility to decide to take them down again. The logic of inter-communal tension and conflict demands that displays are made, but does not expect that symbols be actively removed. It is easier to leave them flying up above the heads of the pedestrians walking by below.

The flags may also be left in place because, despite their state, they remain as a reminder of the identity of the area and to remove them might be considered as undermining this. Historically the use of symbolic displays to mark and define a sense of place has changed from event-focused displays to increasingly permanent markers. Through the nineteenth-century sectarian displays were mostly of short duration, erected a few days before a parade and removed soon after. The adoption of mural painting in the years before the First World War, when the Home Rule crisis was at its peak, was one example of a cultural shift from temporary to more permanent displays. Recurrently over the past two centuries symbolic displays and ritual events have taken on greater prominence at times of constitutional debate and political uncertainty. It seems that yet again during a period of political tension, resort is once more made to extend the longevity of symbolic displays. Finally, the continued presence of the flags implies a sense of control and possession towards the flag as a symbol. It is a symbol that is owned and belongs to all within the community and as such can be used and treated as seems appropriate. The flags are erected not because someone authorises their display or provides them, they are erected because they can be. The flags are erected and flown because people feel an affinity for them and value their role both as a means of defining their identity and asserting a right to place. This also gives people a right to treat them as they think is appropriate. In practice this means that they are not fetishised as objects, but rather quite the opposite. They will be left to decay and when the time is right they will be replaced with new ones. The logic and rationale of the consumer society, which is heavily ritualised and full of symbolism, has been extended to include elements of the ritual and symbolic culture, which is otherwise rooted in the notion of the traditional. The transitory and the traditional become perfectly merged in the fragments of flags.

Conclusions

In conclusion, I would suggest that flags, and other material artefacts, do not have any great value or meaning within Protestant culture as objects in and of themselves. But, they do clearly function as carriers of symbolic meaning in certain contexts and they do retain a symbolic presence even if they are in a frayed, dirty or shabby physical state. The presence of the flags through the winter months remains as evidence of the collective identity of the area. In summer the issue of identity is everything and the flags are new and pristine. In winter identity issues are less prominent, but the flags remain as a mnemonic trace of the tensions of the marching season, of collective resolve and of a sense of identity. They thus provide a thread of continuity between one season and the next and they provide a visible reminder of boundaries, territories and identities.

The decaying flags are a symbolic reminder of the Protestant identity of the area, a reminder that is sustained throughout the year. They serve to reaffirm a sense of the collision of identity and place that might otherwise be undermined by the lack of any visual displays. The decaying flags maintain an affirming presence through the winter and spring until the approach of the marching season once again demands that new flags are erected and new displays are made. The presence of the flags outside of the marching season helps to provide the sense of reassurance and certainty that the Protestant community in Northern Ireland is claimed to lack. The fragile traces of the Union never disappear, even though they may fade, their trace remains and they will be renewed again when spring and the marching season returns.

Notes

1   Northern Ireland contains two major ethno-national groups: Protestants and Catholics. The Protestant population traces its ancestry from settlers from Britain in the seventeenth century while the Catholic population is associated with the indigenous population of Ireland. Most Protestants identify themselves as British and politically as Unionists, while Loyalists are the hardline element of Unionism. Most Catholics identify as Irish and politically as Nationalists, while Republicans are the hardline element of Nationalism.
2   http://www.theodora.com/flags/new8/flag_burning_1.html
3   http://www.usflag.org
4   http://www.crwflags.com/fotw/flags/gb.html#disposal

7 Between the national and the civic

Flagging peace in, or a piece of, Northern Ireland?

Dominic Bryan

On Saturday mornings I take my son up to play football at the Valley Leisure Centre in Newtownabbey, County Antrim, a large suburb at the northern end of Belfast in Northern Ireland. Outside the leisure centre is a set of six flagpoles that seem to suggest the building might be somewhat more important than it is. On one of those poles flies a Union (Jack) flag. There is of course nothing unusual about a national flag flying on a civic amenity or a public building. Travel through other parts of the United Kingdom and you might find the same sort of symbolic display. Not every local council and facility would fly the flag every day but some would (Bryan and Gillespie 2005: 82–9). Similarly, cross the border from Northern Ireland into the Republic of Ireland and you will find some civic buildings flying the Irish Tricolour every day of the year (Bryan and Gillespie 2005: 87–8). But in Northern Ireland the context is different.

After my son has finished football, I take my daughter up for dance classes in Carnmoney, a suburban village less than five minutes from the leisure centre. On every lamp-post running the length of the village are a range of Union flags and Northern Ireland (or Ulster) flags (the Cross of St George on a white background, with a red hand within a white six-pointed star, with a crown above it, and sometimes a Union flag in the top left corner). Depending upon our route home through north Belfast we might go through the major junction of Glengormley, which has a display of Union flags and flags commemorating the Battle of the Somme, flying shabbily and tattered from lamp-posts, although the 1 July anniversary of the battle was three months earlier. Alternatively, we could go via Whiteabbey, around the back of the large Tesco supermarket, where some equally shabby Irish Tricolours, the flag of the Republic of Ireland, fly from a couple of lamp-posts. In Northern Ireland national flags mark territory in a much more specific and direct way than the civic markers common in most countries.

Flags and war in Northern Ireland

Northern Ireland has a long history of conflict over rituals and symbols, with particular intensity being reserved for parades and flags (Brown and

MacGinty 2003; Bryan 2000; Bryan and Gillespie 2005; Bryan and
McIntosh 2005; Bryson and McCartney 1994; Buckley and Kenny 1995;
Feldman 1991; Jarman 1993, 1997; Loftus 1990, 1994; McCormick and
Jarman 2004; MacGinty and Darby 2002; Nic Craith 2002; Rolston 1991,
1992, 1995, 1999; Santino 2001; Wilson 2000). A series of commemorative
events take place throughout the summer months, marked by parades and
demonstrations, which lead to symbolic displays such as flags being placed
on private houses, lamp-posts and almost any vantage point that can be
used, murals being painted on gable wall ends and kerbstones being painted
either red, white and blue for the Union flag or green, white, and orange for
the Tricolour. At Easter Irish Republicans remember the Easter Rising of
1916; in May they commemorate the 1981 Hunger Strike by Republican
prisoners; on 1 July Unionists remember the Battle of the Somme; on the
Twelfth of July they remember the Battle of the Boyne, when Protestant King
William defeated Catholic King James in 1690; in August Republicans
remember Internment without trial (1972 onwards); and on the 'Last
Saturday of August' a series of parades take place within the Protestant community. This collective period is commonly known as 'the marching season'
(Bryan 2000: 118–36).

It is important to point out, however, that the two ethno-political communities in Northern Ireland are not equivalents of each other. The Protestant community, Unionist and loyal to the British monarchy, are
supportive of Northern Ireland being part of the United Kingdom. As the
majority population in Northern Ireland they dominated politics from 1921,
when the quasi-state of Northern Ireland was set up and the Ulster Unionist
Party (UUP) took power, until 1972, when the British government pro-
rogued the Northern Ireland Parliament. Consequently Unionism dominated
public space. As such, public buildings carried the symbols of Unionism, the
centre of cities, towns and villages contained war memorials reflecting the
British Empire, and parades organised by the Orange Order, the Royal Black
Preceptories and the Apprentice Boys of Derry, collectively known as the
'loyal orders', were free to hold parades marking 'the Somme', 'the Twelfth',
'the Last Saturday' and many other events.

Indeed, the Twelfth and Thirteenth of July were made public holidays
from 1926 onwards, and the two-week period around the Twelfth of July is
still viewed as the holiday season, with schools closing in the last week of
June, significantly earlier than in the rest of the United Kingdom. The Union
flag flying on government buildings, local council buildings and other public
buildings must be seen therefore within a broader context of the historical
control of public space – political, physical and symbolic – by Unionism.

In contrast, the Catholic community broadly supports a united Ireland,
meaning that the six Irish counties that comprise Northern Ireland leave the
United Kingdom and become part of the Republic of Ireland. The Irish
Tricolour has never been displayed in Northern Ireland at any official
occasions of which I am aware. Nor was the Tricolour greatly tolerated by

the police when it was used on popular occasions. Nor were those popular events within the Irish Nationalist community, such as St Patrick's Day (17 March) or Lady's Day (15 August), ever allowed to take place anywhere except in villages dominated by a Catholic population (Jarman and Bryan 1998, 2000). Infamously, in September 1964 the Rev. Ian Paisley, a staunch Unionist, threatened to walk up the Falls Road, a predominantly Catholic area of Belfast, and remove the Irish Tricolour from the front window of the offices of the Republican Party. The attempt by the police to deal with the flag, and not Ian Paisley, led to serious riots. The police were enforcing the 1954 Flags and Emblems (Display) Act (Northern Ireland). This Act gave the police powers to deal with any flag the display of which was likely to cause a breach of public order, except the Union flag which was excluded from the Act. As such, the legislation, enforced by the Royal Ulster Constabulary (RUC), a predominantly Protestant police force, was most frequently used to stop displays of the Irish Tricolour.

To put this situation another way, into the 1960s civic space was domi- nated by the politics of Unionism, the symbols of Britishness and empire, and the rituals of loyalism. There were moments of opposition, limited forms of resistance, and certain spaces when alternative identities made appearances, but in the main the Union flag dominated. It is within this context that the development of the Civil Rights movement from 1967 onwards needs to be seen. As a diverse political grouping, comprising Catholics and Protestants and including left-wing activists and liberals as well as Irish Republicans (English 2003: 89–108; Hennessey 2005: 129), they sought an end to discrimination in housing and jobs, and an end to gerrymandering at elections. Practically, however, they developed their campaign through attempting to hold demonstrations in town and city centres in Northern Ireland. The immediate reaction within Unionism was the development of demonstrations opposing the marches by standing in the centre of the towns holding Union flags. This effectively vetoed the chances of the Civil Rights demonstrators rallying in the central civic spaces, since the RUC were unlikely to remove people waving Union flags. As such, it was the supporters of the Civil Rights movement that were deemed likely to cause a breach of the peace and who were then stopped, which often led to violent clashes.

In this context loyal order parades and other expressions of Britishness became increasingly unacceptable to those living in predominantly Catholic areas, so events like the annual Apprentice Boys' parade, held in Derry on the nearest Saturday to 12 August, became problematic. Indeed, rioting after the 1969 parades led to the introduction of British soldiers to undertake policing duties in Northern Ireland and started what is now commonly termed the Troubles. In working-class Nationalist areas the Irish Republican Army (IRA) grew in popularity and their campaign of violent opposition to the state gained support. In working-class Unionist areas 'loyalist' para- military groups, the Ulster Volunteer Force (UVF) and, after 1972, the Ulster Defence Association (UDA) also developed violent sectarian campaigns. The territorial boundaries, always a feature of the Northern Ireland landscape, now became more marked through violent acts, through the erection of check points and eventually physical barriers, leaving a range of what are now called interfaces (Shirlow and Murtagh 2006: 59–66). Territories also became marked symbolically, by graffiti, kerbstone-painting and flags.

Once the UK government introduced direct rule in 1972, buildings within their remit most often flew flags on official days, which was, in effect, a reduction from the practice under the pre-1972 Unionist regimes. However, the Union flag still flew over police stations and law courts and, significantly, popular flying of flags over the Twelfth of July increased, as space in Northern Ireland become more territorial. Unionist-controlled local councils flew the Union flag every day and on all of their buildings. In contrast a number of Nationalist councils stopped flying the Union flag, and either flew a council flag or no flag at all. The controversial 1954 Flags and Emblems Act was repealed in 1987, with the introduction of the 1987 Public Order (NI) Order.

Contests over symbols were secondary to the violence throughout the 1970s, 1980s and into the 1990s. Nevertheless, debates over the use and abuse of symbols would still form a constant diet for the media, and the symbols used as territorial markers became associated with the presence of violence. Just as significantly, as political circumstances changed the range of symbols used also changed, with new flags, emblems and images being used, whilst other fell out of use. It may only be anecdotal, but after the introduction of direct rule from Westminster in 1972 the Northern Ireland or Ulster flag grew in popular use amongst Unionists and was particularly widely used in 1974 during the Ulster Workers Council strike, when a power-sharing agreement was brought down by loyalists. This is a flag never used in official circumstances by the British government. In addition, the loyalist paramilitary groups developed their own symbolic repertoire, with distinctive flags flying alongside the Union flag and Northern Ireland flag on lamp-posts and carried by some of the marching bands in Orange parades. This is in spite of the Orange Order, officially at least, banning such paramilitary flags in their parades.

Similarly, as the forces of the state were less able to control many working-class Catholic areas, the Tricolour was more often and more prominently displayed. Its most frequent appearances have been at the funerals of dead members of the IRA, despite attempts by the authorities to stop the practice. Indeed, its connection with areas controlled by the IRA almost certainly means that, to this day, for many Protestants the Tricolour is associated as much with physical force in Irish Republicanism – the IRA, its political wing Sinn Féin and leaders Gerry Adams and Martin McGuinness – as it is with the state and government of the Republic of Ireland. It is interesting that whilst in the past the bonfires set ablaze by loyalists on the Eleventh Night (ushering in the Twelfth of July) used to burn effigies of the Pope, they now more often burn the Irish Tricolour.

Flags and peace in Northern Ireland

Given the historical, political and physical context in which the meaning of flags in Northern Ireland was constructed, it is not surprising that the peace process in the 1990s led to an increase in the profile of the struggle over the use of symbols. Sinn Féin had entered into local politics in a more determined way after 1981, standing for local and national elections in the UK and Republic of Ireland. However, it was only in 1992 that a Republican Internment parade was allowed past City Hall in the centre of Belfast and in 1993 that, in spite of protests from Unionists, Gerry Adams was allowed to make a speech in front of the statue of Queen Victoria in front of City Hall in Belfast (Jarman and Bryan 1998: 78). In the context of nearly two centuries of Irish Nationalist and Republican symbols being excluded from Belfast City Centre, the decision by an RUC police officer to allow the event was momentous. A year later, in 1994, the IRA called a ceasefire, closely followed by the UDA and UVF. Since then Irish Republican events in central Belfast have become routine, with the Irish Tricolour often being placed in the hands of Victoria's statue.

In retrospect these changes in the use of public space can be seen as part of the developing peace process. In 1998 a Multi-Party Agreement (also known as the Good Friday or Belfast Agreement) was signed in Northern Ireland, which, it was hoped, would lay the basis for a political settlement in Northern Ireland. It was done against a backdrop of 30 years of political violence resulting in around 3,500 deaths. In the rest of this chapter I would like to explore issues over the use of symbols after the Agreement, particularly official flags, in what might be described as civic space. I will look at how elements of the Agreement have been interpreted, in terms of legislation and policy. I then want to look specifically at the ramifications for the flying of official flags over government buildings and local councils.

The Agreement set a new political context, affirming the current position of Northern Ireland within the UK. Whilst it is unambiguous over the status of the six counties that make up Northern Ireland it also acknowledges the aspirations of many Catholics to be part of the Republic of Ireland. It is a consociational-type agreement, recognising the existence of two (and effectively only two) political communities, Ulster Unionism and Irish Nationalism. It did this by creating a unique set of political institutions governing power-sharing and the relationship between the United Kingdom and the Republic of Ireland. Within the Agreement are provisions for an Assembly to be run using a system of weighted voting, which leaves a requirement of consent from 'both communities' for the passing of legislation. The Agreement uses the language of plurality and diversity:

> The participants endorse the commitment made by the British and Irish Governments that, in a new British–Irish Agreement replacing the Anglo-Irish Agreement, they will:

...

(v) affirm that whatever choice is freely exercised by a majority of the people of Northern Ireland, the power of the sovereign government with jurisdiction there shall be exercised with rigorous impartiality on behalf of *all the people in the diversity of their identities and traditions* and shall be founded on the principles of full respect for, and equality of, civil, political, social and cultural rights, of freedom from discrimination for all citizens, and of parity of esteem and of just and equal treatment for the identity, ethos, and aspirations of *both communities*; ...

(Multi-Party Agreement 1998: 2, my italics)

So, whilst there remains a commitment to Northern Ireland remaining in the United Kingdom so long as the majority wish it, and that commitment is accepted by the government of the Republic of Ireland, the Nationalist political party, the Social and Democratic Labour Party (SDLP), and, in theory at least, Sinn Féin, there is also an attempt to define a civic space which is somewhat different from the one which was controlled by Unionists prior to 1972 (see above). This new space could not exclude Irish Nationalists, as had previously been the case. But, like so many other things in the Agreement, there was no detail as to how this would be reflected in official symbolic terms, although participants at the talks were well aware of the potential for rituals and symbols to be a source of conflict. The Agreement recognised this with the following words:

All participants acknowledge the sensitivity of the use of symbols and emblems for public purposes, and the need in particular in creating new institutions to ensure that such symbols and emblems are used in a manner which promotes mutual respect rather than division. Arrangements will be made to monitor this issue and consider what action might be required.

(Multi-Party Agreement 1998: 20)

Under the Agreement a range of agencies were also set up: the Equality Commission of Northern Ireland, the Northern Ireland Human Rights Commission and the Independent Commission on Policing in Northern Ireland, which joined existing agencies such as the Community Relations Council and the Parades Commission, all with duties more or less designed to effectively define citizenship and attempt to interpret the broad thrust of the Agreement through policy.

The key piece of legislation, Section 75 of the 1998 Northern Ireland Act, which was introduced to enact the UK's obligations under the Agreement, is of importance here. Section 75 imposes statutory duties upon public authorities:

75. –

(1) A public authority shall in carrying out its functions relating to Northern Ireland have due regard to the need to promote equality of opportunity –

   (a) between persons of different religious belief, political opinion, racial group, age, marital status or sexual orientation;
   (b) between men and women generally;
   (c) between persons with a disability and persons without; and
   (d) between persons with dependents and persons without.

(2) Without prejudice to its obligations under subsection (1), a public authority shall in carrying out its functions relating to Northern Ireland have regard to the desirability of promoting good relations between persons of different religious belief, political opinion or racial groups.

Government policy on community relations has also been revised with the publication of *A Shared Future* (2005), by the Community Relations Unit of the Office of the First Minister and Deputy First Minister (OFMDFM). It provides an overarching aspiration for the future of Northern Ireland:

> The establishment over time of a normal, civic society, in which all individuals are considered as equals, where differences are resolved through dialogue in the public sphere, and where all people are treated impartially. A society where there is equality, respect for diversity and a recognition of our interdependence.
>
> (OFMDFM 2005: 7)

Within the policy there are specific suggestions aimed at flags used to mark territory thus 'freeing the public realm (including public property) from sectarian aggression' (*ibid.*: 18, para. 2.1) and 'creating safe and shared space for meeting, sharing, playing, working and living' (*ibid.*: 21, para. 2.2).

Therefore, there exists a legal and policy framework within which judgement about what constitutes a 'normal, civic society' in Northern Ireland must be developed. However, in this context the symbolic depiction of government becomes problematic. Should the Union flag be used to represent its constitutional status, or should the Tricolour also be used to represent the aspirations of Catholics? Or maybe no flag should be used, or perhaps a new flag should be created (Wilson 2000)?

Flags in a 'new' Northern Ireland

There was some difficulty in setting up the new Northern Ireland government, but eventually devolution took place on 2 December 1999, when formal power was handed over to the Office of the First Minister and Deputy

First Minister and ten government departments (three run by the Ulster Unionist Party, three by the SDLP, two by Sinn Féin, and two by Rev. Ian Paisley's Democratic Unionist Party). And on that first day, up in the grounds of Stormont, where many of the government buildings are sited, officials had to decide which flagpoles belonged to which government departmental building. Ministers of both Unionist parties ordered the Union flag to be put up, whilst the SDLP and Sinn Féin asked for no flags to be flown. The headquarters of the Department of Education, run by Sinn Féin's Martin McGuinness, sits in the Unionist-dominated town of Bangor, in north County Down. Consequently the lamp-posts surrounding the building were soon all displaying Union flags, as some local 'loyalist' citizens sought to make their point of the lack of an official flag.

The flying of official flags may not have seemed the most important issue to be tackled by the new government but it was actually at the heart of how the new Agreement was to be interpreted and thus at the heart of the political debates taking place. Indeed, so contentious was it that Peter Mandelson, the Secretary of State for Northern Ireland, introduced the Flags Regulations (Northern Ireland) 2000. Regulation 2 designates particular days on which the Union Flag should fly, on seven, and only seven, designated government buildings:

Flying of flags at government buildings on specified days

2. –
(1) The Union flag shall be flown at the government buildings specified in Part I of the Schedule to these Regulations on the days specified in Part II of the Schedule.

(2) The Union flag shall be flown on the days specified in Part II of the Schedule at any other government building at which it was the practice to fly the Union flag on notified days in the period of 12 months ending with 30th November 1999.

The notified days, in the main, represented birthdays of members of the British royal family and included Remembrance Day. However, of great significance given the previous history of Northern Ireland, the list did not include the Twelfth of July or the commemoration of the Battle of the Somme, commemorative dates beloved by Unionists (see Figure 7.1). Interestingly, it did include St Patrick's Day, which had once before, in the nineteenth century, replaced the Twelfth commemorations as the day recognised by the British state, then in Dublin, governing all of Ireland (Hill 1984).

In October 2001, this legislation was challenged in the High Court by Sinn Féin MLA (Member of the Legislative Assembly) Conor Murphy, on the basis that the Regulations were used for political purposes; he contended that they were 'not in keeping with the Good Friday Agreement' and that it breached Section 75 of the Northern Ireland Act since it failed to promote

20th January	Birthday of The Countess of Wessex
6th February	Her Majesty's Accession
19th February	Birthday of The Duke of York
A day in March to be notified by publication in the Belfast Gazette on or before 31st January annually	Commonwealth Day
10th March	Birthday of The Earl of Wessex
17th March	St Patrick's Day
21st April	Birthday of Her Majesty The Queen
9th May	Europe Day
A day in June to be notified by publication in the Belfast Gazette on or before 31st January annually	Official Celebration of Her Majesty's Birthday
2nd June	Coronation Day
10th June	Birthday of The Duke of Edinburgh
4th August	Birthday of Her Majesty Queen Elizabeth The Queen Mother
15th August	Birthday of The Princess Royal
21st August	Birthday of The Princess Margaret
A Sunday in November to be notified by publication in the Belfast Gazette on or before 31st January annually	Remembrance Day
14th November	Birthday of The Prince of Wales
20th November	Her Majesty's Wedding Day

Figure 7.1 Official designated days for flying the Union flag in Northern Ireland, as listed in The Flags Regulations (Northern Ireland) 2000.

equality. Sinn Féin argued that 'parity of esteem' for the two traditions demanded that both national traditions should be reflected in the flying of official flags. For a range of legal reasons the case failed, with the judge arguing that limited flying of the flag 'merely reflects Northern Ireland's constitutional position as part of the UK'. The judge felt that by restricting the flying days to those practised in the rest of the United Kingdom the Secretary of State was striking a balance between acknowledging the constitutional position of Northern Ireland and those who opposed it. Accordingly, the Regulations were not contrary to the Agreement (see Belfast City Council 2004: 25).

This provided a rather unsatisfactory, imposed, solution for government buildings. But, in any event, shortly afterwards, the new executive collapsed, in a dispute over the failure of the IRA to decommission its weapons. For now, government buildings were back in the hands of ministers appointed in London. Northern Ireland's 26 district councils, however, were not included in the legislation so, needless to say, the debates in many of those chambers have been fierce. Policies vary depending on which political party controls the particular council (Bryan and Gillespie 2005: 35–43). In councils controlled by Unionist parties, the Union flag is usually flown on council headquarters every day, although in some areas it is just flown on designated days, which more or less conform to the list supplied by the government. Interestingly, a couple of councils have the Twelfth of July on their designated flag-day lists. However, many of these councils also extend the policy on flying the Union flag to other buildings that they run. As such, swimming pools, leisure centres, tourist centres and golf clubs, as well as other administrative buildings, all fly the flag. Newtownabbey Council runs the leisure centre which I mentioned at the start of this chapter. In 2005, 17 of the 26 councils flew the Union flag on one or more of its buildings on all or certain days of the year. In addition, some Unionist council admin-istrations fly the Northern Ireland, or Ulster flag, described above. At other councils, more or less controlled by Sinn Féin and the SDLP, either no flag is flown or a specific council flag, such as the coat of arms, is used. For some councils, such as Newry, a 'no flag policy' has been in existence for many years. In others, the taking down of the Union flag was bitterly opposed by Unionists. Interestingly, although Sinn Féin's policy position is for both Union flag and Tricolour to be flown, this has not been tried in public. However, when Sinn Féin's Alex Maskey was Mayor of Belfast, in 2002/3, he did fly both flags in his office.

Although the councils are left out of the Flags (Northern Ireland) Order 2000, they do fall under Section 75 of the 1998 Northern Ireland Act (see above). This legislation places strong pressure on public authorities, in terms of equality and good relations, and it is possible that flying flags or the display of emblems (such as pictures of the Queen) might contravene the Act. Public authorities are bound to produce what are known as Equality Impact Assessments (EQIA) for all policies, to show that new policies do to not contravene Section 75. A number of councils have undertaken these, leading to heated debates. Unionist-controlled Lisburn Council offers a good example. The council carried out an EQIA in 2002, entitled *Promotion of Equality and Social Inclusion/Civic Leadership*, the outcome of which led to the Union flag being flown only at the civic offices and only for those days set out for government buildings under the Flags Regulations (Northern Ireland) 2000, plus 1 July (commemorating the Battle of the Somme) and the Twelfth of July. However, in May 2005 DUP and UUP councillors voted for the flag to be flown on every day of the year at the six locations within the council's remit that have existing flagpoles. The DUP had done well in the previous council election and councillors claimed that it had been party policy and thus endorsed by the electorate. A complaint that the council thereby disregarded its own equality scheme was registered with the Equality Commission by Sinn Féin councillor Paul Butler (see Equality Commission for Northern Ireland 2006). The Equality Commission, also set up after the 1998 Agreement, has consistently stressed that, in its opinion, displays of the Union flag must be viewed in the context in which the flag is flown. Factors affecting the context include the manner, location and frequency with which the flags are displayed. In this case, the Equality Commission recommended that Lisburn Council should return to the policy that complied with designated days, but also recommended that the two additional days should not be included.

Further legislative pressure on district councils is supplied by strong fair employment legislation. Council buildings are, of course, work places. In the work place there has, for sometime, been pressure on employers to provide an atmosphere militating against intimidation. This has meant that flags and emblems, and items like pictures of the Queen, have been taken down. There have been disputes over employees wearing a Remembrance Day poppy, black ribbons which have been used by Republicans to remember events like Bloody Sunday, or various sports shirts. The Fair Employment and Treatment (Northern Ireland) Order 1998 makes discrimination on the grounds of religious belief and political opinion unlawful, both in the work place and in the provision of goods, facilities and services. The Fair Employment Code of Practice states that employers are required to identify any practices that do not provide equality of opportunity (1.1.2). They should:

> Promote a good and harmonious working environment and atmosphere in which no worker feels under threat or intimidated because of his or her religious belief or political opinion, e.g. prohibit the display of flags, emblems, posters, graffiti, or the circulation of materials, or the deliberate articulation of slogans or songs which are likely to give offence or cause apprehension among particular groups of employees (Fair Employment Code of Practice 5.2.2).

The Code of Practice also suggests that employers might take affirmative action by considering:

> . . . ending displays at the workplace of flags, emblems, posters, graffiti, or the circulation of materials, or the deliberate articulation of slogans or songs which are likely to give offence to, or cause apprehension among, any one section of the population.

Consequently employers in Northern Ireland that might have flown the Union flag over major buildings do not now do so. As such, many employers within the public sector, such as the two universities, have also adopted this approach. This was further underlined by the Independent Commission on

Policing, chaired by Chris Patten, which recommended that the Union flag no longer be flown at police stations (Independent Commission on Policing for Northern Ireland 1999: 98–100).

In relation to the Fair Employment and Treatment (Northern Ireland) Order 1998, which obliges employers to take steps not to discriminate against any person, legal advice given to Belfast City Council suggested that the council would be on safer ground if it restricted the flying of the Union flag to designated flag days, as is the practice in most of the rest of the United Kingdom. Actually, it is clear that the custom for flying the Union flag varies quite widely across the UK. But the legal advisor to the Council suggested that the city council ran the risk that, if challenged, they might be in breach of Article 19, if the flag was flown every day (Belfast City Council 2004: 24). Despite this advice, Belfast City Council's EQIA decided to leave the policy unchanged and that the council would continue to fly the Union flag every day of the year on all three of its civic buildings (Belfast City Council 2004: 7).

Flagging civic 'shared' space

The signing of the 1998 Agreement ushered in the possibility that the political sphere in Northern Ireland could be developed in such a way that fundamental differences over the legitimacy of the state might be overcome, or at least set aside, given sufficient protection offered to the citizenry. Prior to 1972, civic space in Northern Ireland had contained virtually no other symbols than those of Unionism. Indeed, the very appearance of an Irish Tricolour in the centre of Belfast would have been seen as a threat to public order. However, although those involved in the 1998 Agreement recognised the importance of symbols, no specific arrangements were made to deal with them. New symbols were created to represent the new assembly (a flax plant) and the 11 new government departments (a design representing the Giant's Causeway). Under the review of policing the badge of the RUC was replaced by a badge with more inclusive symbolism for the new Police Service of Northern Ireland (Bryan and McIntosh 2005: 130). Even Stormont, the building that had housed the pre-1972 administrations, was opened up, by the holding of popular concerts in the surrounding grounds, in the hope that it would carry broad acceptability as a venue for the new political dispensations (Bryan and McIntosh 2005: 131–6). In theory at least, there was potential for the policy and practice for the flying of official flags to represent the aspirations drawn up in the Agreement (Wilson 2000). However in spite of the broad language of recognition of diverse communities, and an attempt at the politics of a new Northern Ireland, the Agreement is consociational in nature – revolving around equal parity of esteem – and the debates over the flying of official flags have represented this. This is particularly true of arguments emanating from Unionist politics, but also true of arguments coming from Republicans. Neither has argued in a coherent fashion that the symbols used might represent a wider community, or diverse communities, simply that they should represent the Unionist community and/or the Nationalist community.

Part of the problem with both the Union flag and the Tricolour being used to demarcate a shared civic space is that they are already used widely as 'popular' markers of territory throughout Northern Ireland. In this context, both are used in conjunction with symbols representing paramilitary groups and, of course, in the case of the Union flag, identified with the use of physical force by the British state through the RUC and British Army. As such, both flags are viewed with fear by sections of the community. The Northern Ireland Life and Times Survey has contained a series of questions over attitudes towards flags and murals since 2000. One striking statistic from both the 2001 and 2002 surveys is the level of ambivalence in both communities towards both the Union flag and the Tricolour. When asked in 2002 how they feel when they see the Union flag, 43 per cent of Protestants and 77 per cent of Catholics feel neither proud nor hostile towards the flag. The same question asked about the Tricolour produced figures of 42 per cent for Protestants and 70 per cent for Catholics. In 2005, 25 per cent of people said that in the previous year they had felt intimidated by Loyalist murals, kerb-painting or flags, and 23 per cent said they had felt intimidated by Republican murals, kerb painting or flags. All this suggests that whilst we cannot take for granted the meanings associated with Union and Tricolour flags, they do exist within a lexicon of symbols that for some people invokes fear.

To return to where I began; the Union flag flying outside the Valley Leisure Centre in Newtownabbey is an issue. The Union flag carries specific local meanings related to the marking of territory and violence. In this chapter I have looked at the uses of official flags since the Multi-Party Agreement in 1998. The Agreement attempted to set out a new agenda for dealing with the symbolic practices that have frequently played a role in the conflict. But the Agreement has not led to many imaginative approaches to the use of flags, and certainly not to many examples of the rebranding of civic space. Political parties have very much maintained strategies that value the use of the two respective national flags, and 'popular' territorial marking remains prevalent. Any changes that have taken place have tended to be driven by legislation relating to equality and employment issues imposed from Westminster. That said, there are possibilities for change, and in some areas the use of flags by communities has changed. In a quite striking recent event, on Sunday, 6 November 2005, the Union flag and the Irish Tricolour flew together in the centre of the city of Derry, as part of a commemoration of those Irish people who lost their lives in the two world wars.[1] This was a small but significant sign that, even in the contested civic spaces of Northern Ireland, if the right context is created, a range of symbolic strategies are possible.

Note

1   http://news.bbc.co.uk/go/pr/fr/-/1/hi/northern_ireland/4412584.stm

8 Inarticulate speech of the heart
Nation, flag and emotion in Denmark

Richard Jenkins

Given the ubiquity of flags in the modern world, and their multiple uses, there are surprisingly few social science studies of flags. The studies that do exist cluster round two closely related themes: ethnicity, nationalism, patriotism and ethno-national identity (e.g. Billig 1995; Marvin and Ingle 1999; Perryman 2005; Sorek 2004; Weitman 1973) and, more specifically, struggles over symbolic 'heritage' with deep roots in long-standing and unresolved civil conflicts. Examples of the latter – which are, of course, necessarily concerned with identity-related issues, too – include studies of political parading and symbolism in Northern Ireland (Bryan 2000; Bryson and McCartney 1994; Jarman 1997), of the contemporary resonances of the flag of the Confederacy in the southern United States (Leib 1995; Webster and Leib 2001, 2002), and of national flag-burning in the United States (Goldstein 1995, 1996a; Welch 2000). A common thread running through these studies is an assumption, whether tacit or explicit, that flags inspire strong, perhaps even exceptional, emotional responses, which can be positive or negative, in those for whom they are symbols of group affiliation.

Billig's work stands somewhat apart, inasmuch as he argues that, in fact, flags, for example, are most effective as national symbols when they merge into the background, quietly constituting the nation as the axiomatic framework and setting of everyday life (1995: 38–43). In this respect he is allied to other authors who see nationalism as something more than explicit ideology and organised politics: Eriksen (1993), for example, compares the formal nationalism of the state with everyday 'informal nationalism', while Wilk (1993) contrasts official nationalism with the 'visceral' nationalism of things such as beauty pageants and cuisine. On a similar tack, Borneman (1992) distinguishes public nationalist ideologies from 'nationness', the tacit sense of the kind of life that is appropriate to membership of a particular state, a concept that seems to be broadly similar to Cohen's 'belonging' (1982). When Duara (1993) contrasts the 'discursive meaning' of the nation, found in ideology and rhetoric, with its 'symbolic meaning', found in 'rituals, festivals, kinship forms, and culinary habits', he, too, is addressing similar issues. The meaning of a nation for its members is, therefore, to be sought in everyday local relationships between individuals in civil society and between civil society and institutions of the state (Jenkins 1997: 159–61).

In this chapter I will explore and develop these arguments about flags and nationalism in two directions. First, in the case of Denmark at least, the observable realities demand that we look beyond national identity and symbolic heritage if we are to understand the nuances and complexities of what people are actually doing. Second, although Billig is right to point to the background presence of national flags as a significant contribution to their *symbolic* power, the description of this as 'banal' is, perhaps, misleading and does not help us to understand the relationship between taken-for-grantedness and *emotional* power. There is nothing banal – in the senses of 'trite' or 'feeble' that sit alongside 'commonplace' in the dictionary[1] – about the relationship that Danes, the subjects of this chapter, have with their flag.

The general theoretical framework within which I will pursue these two lines of argument has been presented in detail elsewhere (Jenkins 1997, 2004: 109–23). Drawing on Cohen (1985) I argue that collective identification is constituted, *inter alia*, in and through symbols such as flags. This symbolism is a 'social imaginary' (Taylor 2004), and *all* communities or collectivities – not just nations (Anderson 1991) – are in important senses imagined or socially constructed. They are not, however, imaginary. In that communal symbols are emotionally powerful, they *affect* people and they have consequences. Their power to move and to inspire depends in part on their institutionalisation in ritual (Jenkins 2004: 149–52) and in part on the many and varied meanings which have been invested in them, often over a considerable time, and which are still condensed within by that history, waiting to be conjured up (Turner 1974: 48–9).

Shared symbols may thus mean different things to different people, and a measure of contradiction or paradox may be at their heart (Cohen 1985: 11–21). Symbols are not required to be consistent. Because they are abstract and often arbitrary, the range of meanings symbols can convey is not limited to what they 'stand for', pictorially or otherwise (indeed that 'original' meaning may have been forgotten long since). Inasmuch as symbols are abstract and arbitrary, men and women are able to come together under the collective spell of their enchantment without having to explore their individual differences from each other. Symbols allow people to imagine that they have something in common, despite the many things that divide them. As a result, of course, they *do* have – or *come* to have – something in common.

Introducing Dannebrog

The ethnography that follows was collected during field research in the Danish town of Skive, in mid-Jutland, between 1996 and 1998.[2] Having been brought up in Northern Ireland, where flags are provocative symbols of inter-ethnic conflict (Bryan 2000; Bryson and McCartney 1994; Jarman

1997), I probably could not help but be interested in a place where, although extreme nationalism is a minority, not even respectable, political position (perhaps because of its historical association with Germany) the national flag is everywhere to be seen. The more I learned and the more I saw, the more interested I became and the more I realised that Danish 'flagways' have much about them that is quite particular. There are parallels, in different ways, with Norway, Sweden, Switzerland and the United States, for example, but the overall pattern seems to be unique to Denmark.

The Danish national flag is a simple design: a robust white cross on a deep red field. Whether fluttering over the parade ground at Skive garrison, as it does every day, or decorating the town during the special occasion of a royal visit (Jenkins 2002), it symbolises the nation, the history of its people and the place of the royal house at the heart of national life. Whether as a mark of goods made in Denmark or the face painting proudly worn by a Danish football fan, the flag is instantly recognisable. It even has its own name, Dannebrog; and it is simply called Dannebrog, it is not *the* Dannebrog. It also has its own mythology, which insists that it is nothing less than the oldest national flag in the world, having fallen from Heaven in June 1219 during the battle of Lyndanisse, against the heathens of what is now Estonia, to save King Valdemar II, the Conqueror, and his knights from otherwise certain destruction.[3]

Figure 8.1 Danish flags descending from Heaven, in a shopping centre.

Whether or not the story is true is not the point: it's a good, and very visual, story, which adds something special to the flag, a little bit of magic and a great deal of legitimacy. And whatever its actual origins – because a white cross on a red field was a common medieval standard throughout Europe – Dannebrog is, as Elgenius mentions in her chapter in this collection, certainly an old flag. It appears on Valdemar IV's coat of arms in the late fourteenth century, and in the sixteenth-century wall paintings in Skive's Vor Frue Kirke, Duke Knud bears what looks like a Dannebrog (which, given that Knud died in 1131, is artistic mythological licence).

However ancient it may or may not be, for most Danes there is clearly something very special about Dannebrog. In the words of Axel Juel's well-known song of 1916, which children still learn in school: 'There is nothing that means as much as a flag being raised, while it draws our hearts and minds towards Heaven' (*Der er ingenting, der maner som et flag, der går til top, mens det drager vore hjerter og vort sind mod himlen op . . .*). At the other end of the musical spectrum, although their sentiments may not have been precisely the same, even the Danish pop group Shu-Bi-Dua have wrapped themselves in the flag from time to time.[4] Whatever those sentiments are, however, the red and white flag on a white flagstaff, with the deep blue sky as its background, is an image that appears to call up strong and authentic emotions for most Danes.

The popular (*folkelig*) appropriation of, and identification with, the Danish flag has an interesting history (Adriansen 1999; Balle-Petersen 1979; Ringgaard Lauridsen 1995), which should be understood in the context of a century-long, but internally non-violent, struggle to establish democracy and a modern state in the wake of serious Danish military and diplomatic reversals between 1800 and 1865. On the one hand, there was a conservative élite and monarchy, on the other, small farmers, the *petite bourgeoisie* and workers (Borish 1991: 158–206; Jespersen 2004: 58–76). Patriotism and national renewal became fused in rural social movements emphasising 'popular enlightenment' (*folkeoplysning*), co-operation and self-determination. The modern nation-state that emerged in the twentieth century was characterised by consensus politics, institutional decentralisation and partnership between state, capitalism and organised labour in the Nordic social democratic welfare model.

To return to the flag, the Danish common people were apparently using Dannebrog in 'unofficial' ways – to mark weddings, birthdays and solemn occasions – as long ago as the early decades of the nineteenth century, following the disasters of the Napoleonic War. So much so, in fact, that in 1834 King Frederik VI felt moved to issue an edict reserving to the state and royalty the right to fly the national flag. That did not work, however – the prohibition had to be repealed in 1854 – and popular enthusiasm for the flag grew and was further strengthened by subsequent conflicts, defeats and occupations by Prussia, Austria-Hungary and, subsequently, Germany between 1848 and the end of the Second World War.[5] Far from retreating into official and ceremonial use, it seems likely that today the popular everyday use of Dannebrog may be more frequent, in more contexts, than ever.

The flag in everyday life

What is the place of Dannebrog in Danish society and culture today? Let us begin by looking at Princess Benedikte's official visit to Skive in October 1996, only a few days after my arrival in the town to begin my research. The Princess came to town to unveil the new sculpture of Two Jutland Horses (To Jyske Heste) in front of the home for the elderly at Møllergården and to visit the Dantherm factory. But her first port of call was, of course, the Town Hall, where the Mayor and an enthusiastic crowd of townspeople welcomed her. In front of the Town Hall, on The Square, four large Dannebrog were flying and the municipal flag, Dannebrog with the Skive coat of arms in the centre (every *kommune* in Denmark may use its own version of the flag) hung over the main entrance. Before the Princess arrived the local girls' marching band, Skive Pigegard, unfurled and raised their own standard, a Dannebrog with the band's emblem in the corner, and played one of the two Danish national songs, 'There is a Lovely Land' (*Der er et yndigt Land*).

Later, as the official party walked from the Town Hall to Møllergården, the streets along the way, Fredriksgade and Asylgade, were lined with small children – for whom it was an exciting break from the usual routine of kindergarten – enthusiastically waving paper '*hurra* flags'. The shops along the route displayed the flags that they use on other occasions to mark festivities, sales, and special offers. In front of the old people's home several Dannebrog flying against the blue sky made a pretty picture as a girl Scout presented the Princess with flowers. When the formalities were over, and the Princess went in to visit the old people, the Pigegard and the Scouts furled their flags and went home.

What did I learn about the flag from observing this royal visit? First, I was perhaps a little surprised by the absence of royal flags on the official car. More important, however, I began to learn something about the many different kinds of Dannebrog. I even began to wonder whether perhaps Dannebrog is not one flag but many, each with its own particular function or meaning. For example, the state flag is one shape – the swallow-tail *splitflag*[6] – while the *handelsflag*, the flag that is used by ordinary citizens, municipalities, the church and voluntary associations or *foreninger* (each has its Dannebrog standard or *fane*), is the plain rectangular flag. And there are many different version of the *handelsflag*, depending on the badge or symbol of the municipality or association that is displayed. What's more, every *fane* belongs to its *forening*, and every flag on a private flagpole belongs to 'Hansen and Jensen' as well as the state. Harking back to the tussle between Frederik VI and the people over the popular use of the flag, we should remember that the people won.

Watching the care and concentration on the faces of two girls Scouts as they furled their standard outside Møllergården, I also learned something about respect. Whatever else must happen – and the flag rules are in no doubt about this[7] – Dannebrog, the sacred flag that came down from Heaven, should never touch the ground. It is, of course, enough that one should simply do one's *best* to ensure that it doesn't touch the ground, as often happens just before sunset during a long birthday party, after many, many toasts have been drunk: that is still showing respect. The people's flag is still the state's flag, after all, and it is still special, perhaps even a little magical, touched by the same enchantment as the monarch (Jenkins 2002).

In a land where birthdays are taken seriously, I observed another significant occasion the following summer, Dannebrog's 'birthday'. Also known as Valdemar's Day, to celebrate the original battle in the heat of which it was reputedly born, Dannebrog celebrates its official birthday on 15 June, which is also Genforeningdag or Reunification Day, commemorating the Danish recovery of North Slesvig in 1920. This annual event is organised by Danmarks-Samfundet, the organisation whose role is 'to strengthen national solidarity . . . around the national symbol of Dannebrog' (Danmarks-Samfundet 1992: 6). A non-governmental organisation, independent of the state, its main work today is collecting money to spend on the standards that it presents to voluntary associations and other organisations on Valdemar's Day. In 1997, since 15 June fell on a Sunday, the celebrations took place on Monday 16th, when a small procession marched from Skive's Bus Station to the town's park: the Pigegard, a couple of policemen, the Home Guard, the Danish Red Cross, various groups of Scouts, local Civil Defence volunteers, and a small detachment of soldiers from the garrison, all representing organisations that have received *faner* from Danmarks-Samfundet. In the Park, new standards were presented to Scouts from Durup and Skivehus, and to Spøttrup Home Guard company. Then there were some speeches, after which the parade returned to the Bus Station.

Few people in Skive turned out to celebrate Dannebrog's birthday, either in the parade or as spectators. The local Industrial Development Officer, Kai Jørgensen, guest speaker at the 1997 Valdemar's Day meeting, acknowledged during his speech that, despite a lot of public flag-waving, many Danes are not much interested in such matters:

> I don't think that one can find any country in the world with so many flagpoles as Denmark . . . We are perhaps not so clever at remembering the flag days. In Skive, those of us who cross Skive-Karup River in the morning have a good reminder of which days are flag days. DSB [the railway company] has its system in order. What flag day is it today, one asks oneself, as one crosses the bridge over the railway.[8]

He was referring to the national railway company's conscientious observance of its statutory responsibilities on flag days, flying flags on the bridge that carries the main road over the railway.

Dannebrog is officially flown in public on many different occasions, and by many different organisations.[9] Even if on any given day most people aren't sure exactly why, there is always a reason, an evocation of something special. On the official flag days, civil and military state establishments are obliged to hoist their flags, to commemorate key holy days of the national church (Folkekirken), significant royal birthdays, and the anniversaries of important occasions in Denmark's history. In addition, there are some specifically military flag days commemorating battles. In the case of the Skive garrison, for example, where Dannebrog flies as a matter of daily military routine, a particularly large flag is hoisted to mark flag days. Together, official flag days amount to a publicly visible calendar of Danish national identity, nationhood and national history. In addition, every municipality may have its own particular local flag days, such as, in Skive, the agricultural show (*Dyrskuet*) and the local children's charities' festival (*Børnehjælpsdage*).

Whether these uses of the flag are expressions of nationalism depends on which of the many and various definitions of nationalism one chooses to adopt (Hutchinson and Smith 1994: 15–131). National and official flag days are certainly sponsored by the state, and self-consciously invoke patriotism, and national or local identity. In this they are quite different from how the flag is flown and used by ordinary citizens. As an everyday practice of civil society this, while it can be can be described as 'informal' nationalism, is an expression of 'nationness' and 'belonging' which doesn't necessarily have much to do with the grand narratives of the nation.

The distinction between official and popular flag flying is sometimes blurred, however. In Skive, the flag often flies over the municipal offices in Østergade for reasons that have nothing to do with the official flag calendar: to celebrate a local resident's 100th birthday, or at half-mast to mark the death of a municipal employee, for example. This use of Dannebrog to signal and acknowledge special occasions, both sad and happy, is one of the more specific ways in which the Danes use their national flag. Driving through the Danish countryside, where many houses have a flagpole in the yard or garden, it is possible to have some idea of the social events and celebrations that are happening. A flag flying on a Saturday at a farmhouse probably means a wedding or a birthday. On weekdays, it is almost certain to be a birthday; except on a Tuesday, however, when a flag flying may also mean that a silver wedding is being celebrated (allowing for leap years, Tuesday is the 25th anniversary of an original matrimonial Saturday). A flag flying at a church on a Saturday almost certainly means a wedding; on a Sunday, however, it simply indicates that there is a normal service.

A flag flying at half-mast outside a church, of course, means something else, a funeral. It may also be flown at the house of the dead person. In many villages – for example, Oddense, Selde, or Lihme, near Skive – the residents' association will often erect a 'flag avenue' (*flagallé*) along each side of the principal street before the funeral. A line of Dannebrog hanging solemnly at half-mast is a powerful expression and symbol of communal respect for the dead person and support for their family. It also symbolises communal solidarity: as an explicit 'symbolic construction of community' (Cohen 1985) it can have few parallels. I can still remember the first time that I encountered a funereal *flagallé*, while driving through Ørum, east of Viborg. Even though I am not a Dane it made a profound impression on me.

Celebration and joy

The public salute of the *flagallé* is not reserved for royalty or the solemnity of a funeral. Respect, emotion and communal feeling may also be appropriate when there is a wedding, or a silver wedding, or a particularly impressive 'round birthday' – a birthday that ends with a zero – to celebrate. Even if there is not a full avenue of flags, family and neighbours will often hoist their own flags. And the inn or village meeting house where the party is taking place will certainly be flying at least one flag, and often several. How else should visitors know where the party is being held? Nor is it just a matter of 'proper flags' on flagpoles: on greeting cards, gift wrapping paper, and so on, Dannebrog is the ubiquitous symbol of congratulations and good wishes on birthdays, anniversaries, confirmations, graduation, and so on. Hence also its appearance on trees at Christmas, a time of happiness and celebration (and also, let's not forget, a birthday).

Children are not excluded from all the flag-hoisting and waving, either. A child's birthday party can involve *many* flags: paper flags on the table and on the cake, a table cloth with a flag design on it, strings of flags hanging from the lights, larger *hurra* flags planted in the flower beds to let everyone know that the party is *here*. And in the garden these days there may be something like a *flagallé*: paper flags corresponding to the number of years of the birthday – which is why it is a only children's thing – lining the path from the street to the door. A very happy and welcoming sight for small partygoers it is, too.

So Dannebrog is a way of showing respect for others and a symbol of coming together in solidarity and fellowship. It is a symbol of and for community and fellowship at all levels, from the family to the nation. It is also clear that Danes associate the flag with emotion and, particularly, with happiness and joy. In the words of a 9th *klasse* pupil – which would make her about 16 – from a school in the rural Salling *kommune* of Spøttrup: 'Our flag means a lot. But particularly joy. For example, one flies the flag on birthdays or for weddings . . . And I think that it is not ugly either'.

Nor is it is only young people whose words fail them when confronted with the flag. Nils the architect, with whom I was having a beer one afternoon, tried for ten minutes, without much success, to explain why the Danes fly Dannebrog so much. In the end, he said: 'It is simply joy. We are happy about our flag.' He got off his bar stool and stood with his hand on his heart. 'It is the people's flag, it is not the state's flag!'

A matter of the emotions, of happiness and joy, he found it really difficult to explain. As did another 9th *klasse* pupil from Spøttrup, when I asked her the same thing, although for her there were two sides to the question: 'Because we are so self-satisfied, and it is cosy and cheerful to raise the flag . . . I don't know.'

For Danes, Dannebrog is, to borrow an expression from the Northern Irish songwriter Van Morrison, an important part of their 'inarticulate speech of the heart'. Long before language – because for many Danish babies it begins when they are brought home from hospital[10] or with their baptism – this simple, vibrant, visually arresting symbol is experienced in powerful association with good times, good company, pleasure and rewards. There I suspect it stays, reiterated and reinforced every time there is something to celebrate.

Trading on the flag

This strong association with festivities and happiness, and the place of the flag in leisure activities such as sailing and rowing, creates considerable consumer demand for everything from little paper party flags to new flagpoles and full-size flags to fly on them. This has encouraged a veritable Dannebrog industry. In 1994, for example, a journalist estimated that the Danish market in full-size flags and accessories was worth 50 to 60 million *kroner* a year (Boas 1994). It has been suggested to me that this market has expanded since Denmark joined the European Union, expressing a need to assert national identity. In the words of Skive's municipal Director of Education at the time of my research:

> There are many more Danish flags than there used to be now. In the countryside, when you go for a drive, you can see them for birthdays, or weddings, or because a young person has passed their student's exams. Twenty years ago you would not have seen so many flags . . . It is much more important than it used to be, all this nationalism. I think it has something to do with foreigners coming in, and with Europe.

Whether or not this is true, the flag is also involved in commerce in other ways. These are perhaps the most idiosyncratically Danish flag practices, with few or no equivalents elsewhere. To my outsider's eye this was, at first, the most difficult aspect of Danish 'flag culture' to understand: display windows, shop interiors and shopping streets are frequently decked out with Dannebrog. Why? A shop's owner may have a birthday, or it may be the anniversary of the business's foundation; these were the explanations given by most shopkeepers to whom I spoke about this. Some shops, however, seem to have an implausible number of anniversaries and birthdays. Other shops simply display little flags on each side of the door as a matter of everyday routine. It is also obviously the case that many of these flag displays are connected to, if not actually advertisements for, special offers, sales or other marketing events.

It is also clear that, in contrast to the historically earlier use of the flag by the protectionist organisation Dansk Arbejde, which I will discuss below, the modern decorative commercial use of Dannebrog seems to have little to do with the promotion of Danish goods or industry. I have seen Dannebrog mobilised, without any apparent sense of incongruity or irony, in the marketing of Japanese cars, bananas and French cosmetics. To give an extreme example, one day I was shopping in Kvickly, a supermarket in Skive's main indoor shopping centre, when I came across a car on display in the middle of the shop. It was an old, white East German Trabant that had been lovingly restored by an enthusiast in Randers. Two large, paper Dannebrog were sticking out of the back of the car. In the boot and around the car were piles of shampoo bottles. Made in Norway, the shampoo was what the car was advertising. An East German car, Norwegian shampoo, and two small Danish flags: not an obvious set of associations.

The easiest explanation of this is that the flags are a just a way of catching the eye. They are also, perhaps, a way to make people feel happy, by association with parties and other celebrations, as they spend their hard-earned money. However, if this is how it works, it certainly isn't a conscious process. Confronted by a curious anthropologist, many of the people to whom I talked appeared to be reflecting on this matter for perhaps the first time. As an artillery major put it, when I asked him what he thought was going on:

> I don't think that most Danes think much about that. I don't think that the commercial use of Dannebrog ever sold anything. It looks good, we think it's pretty, it makes us feel at home . . . Okay, okay . . . so maybe we buy more things, I don't know.

Similarly, here is an eighth *klasse* schoolboy from Skive, fourteen or fifteen years old:

> I think that the Danes use Dannebrog so often because it is festive and it makes people happy, and in Føtex [a national supermarket chain] it makes people look. I haven't really thought about the flags before, because we have grown up with it.

Having been prompted by me to think about it, not everyone liked what they saw. Here is another lad from the same class:

> I think that it has become a bad habit, using the flag every time something is for sale. Also in the magazines they use the flag as fill up. Maybe the flag symbolises all the good things, so whenever something is good you just put a flag with it.

As we have already seen, although the celebratory use of the flag by communities and families may have waxed and waned over the years, popular flag-flying has a history stretching back into the early nineteenth century. But what of the use of Dannebrog in shops: how long has that been happening, and what has changed and why? These aren't questions that can necessarily be answered with precision, or even imprecision, by local people, if only because it is something that, as we have seen, they do not seem to think much about. It is one thing to tell me that there has been change – as did the Director of Education, quoted above, and many other people – but quite another thing to discern its parameters and direction clearly.

A local answer can be found, however, in Skive's Archive (Skive byhistoriske Arkiv), which houses a photographic collection extending back to the late 1800s. We can, in effect, 'go back in time' and take a look. Hundreds of photographs of the streets, shops and businesses of Skive between the late-nineteenth century and the early 1970s reveal that, excluding flags on municipal buildings, in use as political propaganda, or carried in parades, Dannebrog rarely appears decorating the streets or shops. It is only from the mid-1970s that the photographs of the streets and shops in the Archive begin regularly to include decorative flags. Take as an example Adelgade, one of the main shopping streets: of the 20 photographs which, at the time that I searched the Archive,[11] included examples of Dannebrog in all of its decorative manifestations, only five are earlier than 1970. For Nørregade, the equivalent figures are 26 and nine. Looking at the few photographs of individual shop interiors and exteriors, seven include Dannebrog of various kinds, and only two are from before 1970.

For this to be definitive evidence I would require a larger sample of photographs of these streets. Nor am I wholly confident that these numbers don't simply reflect the increased frequency of photography since 1970. Nonetheless, allowing for these reservations, the archival material suggests some conclusions about the occasions on which Dannebrog decorated the shops and the shopping streets. Before 1970 these were public occasions and celebrations,[12] noteworthy business anniversaries[13] and other unusual commercial events.[14] The one exception, which I have already mentioned, is instructive: from before the First World War until its demise in the 1990s, the organisation 'Danish Work' (Dansk Arbejde), the motto of which was 'Give Hands Work', promoted Danish wares and products. In Skive, Dansk Arbejde was particularly active and visible up to the end of the 1930s, holding regular 'Danish weeks' featuring public meetings, processions and exhibitions of goods and produce. These sometimes included Dannebrog, explicit nationalism overlapping with local commercial interests.[15]

According to the photographs, from the mid-1970s Dannebrog begins to appear in more diverse settings. As before, there are public occasions, special anniversaries and events such as business openings or the pedestrianisation of Adelgade in 1981. In addition, however, we now see 'open-house' receptions marking minor anniversaries and other occasions, and, most strikingly, flag-motif bunting decorating the streets from the mid-1970s into the 1980s, apparently not marking any special occasion. As suggested by the Director of Education, one explanation for this increased use of the national flag at this time is a fear of 'little Denmark' being overwhelmed in the European Community, which it joined in 1973.

With respect to the commercial use of the flag by shopkeepers and as a decoration on the shopping streets this is not, however, convincing. The bunting that brightened up Nørregade in 1972 and Adelgade in 1985, for example, featured the flags of many nations, including the United States, the United Kingdom, Norway, Finland and various tricolours, as well as Dannebrog.[16] This does not suggest defensive nationalism.

A more plausible explanation invokes other changes. During the 1960s Denmark gradually emerged from post-war austerity to become more affluent and more consumerist, the latter a trend that continues today. Shops and businesses were at the heart of this and in the process their advertisements and decorations became more eye-catching. This is all visible in the Archive photographs. During the 1970s, for example, the bunting that waved over Nørregade featured various 'feel good' motifs: red-and-white and blue-and-white anchors and ship's wheels in 1973, and bright flowers and stripes during 1975 and 1976.[17] It is not remarkable that Dannebrog, the Danish symbol of celebration, happiness and good times, colourful and eye-catching in its own right, featured in this gradual transformation. Between 1977 and 1979, for example, the bunting that decorated Adelgade and Nørregade incorporated a Dannebrog motif and the word 'Skive'.[18] In 1981, when the Adelgade shopkeepers' association celebrated pedestrianisation, strings of small Dannebrog fluttered overhead.[19] Similarly, when there was a market on The Square in 1987, the Adelgade side boasted four large Dannebrog.[20] Today, Dannebrog is one of the dominant motifs in Skive's shops, as in every other town in Denmark.

Dannebrog, combining many messages in a simple image, is a powerful symbol. Nor is there any contradiction between nationalism – or at least national identity and pride – and capitalism. As Knud Møller Jensen, Salling Bank's marketing manager and a leading light of the town's business community, explained it to me, the flag both looks and *feels* good:

> The background is that we are Danes. We think that Dannebrog is beautiful and pretty to decorate shops with. We like our flag. We are proud of it.

The combination of Dannebrog and the slogan 'Buy Danish in Skive City Center' (*Køb dansk i Skive City Center*), used by Skive City Centerforening, an association of business folk and shopkeepers, in their advertising campaign, brings together all of these themes. Modern consumerism sees absolutely no incongruity between historically consecrated symbols, appeals to national identity, the manipulation of people's emotions, and the unsentimental pursuit of commercial self-interest.[21] It is all grist to the mill, and all good for business.

Which doesn't, of course, necessarily undermine or diminish the flag's non-commercial meanings. Dannebrog is a rich and many-faceted symbol, and Denmark is a complex and changing society. It is not surprising, therefore, that the meanings of Dannebrog – the state's flag and the people's flag – are not static. In fact this is probably the best indication one could have of its continued vitality as a living symbol. And as it develops it gives some Danes, at least, food for thought. As the last word on this particular facet of Danish flag culture, here is the opinion of another 9th *klasse* school pupil from Spøttrup:

> I think that it has just as much to do with tradition and habit as with national feeling. My family, for example, use Dannebrog on birthdays because we have nearly always done it. But we use it on the 5th May also, to celebrate Denmark's liberation on that date [in 1945] and to show respect for all the fallen, who fought for our freedom. Shops use it almost as an eye-catcher, to celebrate their five birthdays per year. And it is sad that the flag should be misused in that way.

Whether Dannebrog's contributions to advertising and marketing are use or misuse, I'll leave the reader to decide. Whatever the answer, however, it's a good question, both locally and more generally, dramatising as it does awkward issues about who owns collective symbols, and how they should be used. In a way, we have come full circle, back to King Frederik's decree of 1834.

'Det er der bare' . . . It's just how it is

Whether or not Freud got it right in his discovery of something called 'the unconscious' – the dark basement of the human psyche – there is little doubt that we are not fully aware of everything that we do in our everyday lives, or its significance. Anthropologists and sociologists have long recognised the importance of this for the complex ways in which the human world seems to hang together without apparent orchestration (Berger and Luckmann 1967: 70–85; Bourdieu 1977, 1990; Jenkins 2004: 134–7). Reflex, habit, taking things for granted, conditioning, thoughtlessness, preoccupation: call it what you will, we do not always invest much – or even any – time in thinking about what we do. Sometimes this enables us to process trivia without interrupting the important stuff of life. Just as often, however, it is the important stuff, the very marrow of our selfhood, that is habitual or unreflexive.

That this applies to the relationship between Danes and Dannebrog became particularly clear during my research with young people in schools in Skive and the surrounding rural area. I have already used some of this material, above. In all, 122 of the school pupils with whom I worked answered the question, 'Why do Danes use Dannebrog so much?' Most offered several explanations for Danish enthusiasm for the flag. Half of them mentioned pride and national identity – an unsurprising and conventional answer, not in itself particularly revealing – and 26 mentioned the close association between Dannebrog and happiness or joy. It is no less interesting, however, that 44 accounted for their use of the flag simply as 'tradition', 'culture' or 'habit', and a further ten specifically said that they had never noticed this before I raised it and had therefore never thought about it. The following young people who were studying at Skive *gymnasium* – which puts them between 16 and 18 – can perhaps be allowed to exemplify these responses:

> It is a tradition that it is used at birthdays, funerals and many other special occasions.

> Yes ... why do we use Dannebrog so much? Do we really do that? Personally I think that Dannebrog is unbelievably beautiful. I have just grown up with Dannebrog and the use of Dannebrog, so I have never thought much about it.

> It is a tradition. We feel a special connection to Dannebrog – our cultural heritage.

> We don't pay any attention to that – I just think it has become part of our culture. And as I said earlier, it is just our form of fellowship. I don't think we make so much out of it – not something like 'It is for Denmark's sake' – it's just how it is.

Det er der bare ... It's just how it is. For these young people, Dannebrog was so familiar, so deeply woven into the fabric of their lives, that detailed explanation or eloquence were not appropriate. Perhaps not even possible.

One of the most important contributions to our understanding of the human world that anthropology or sociology can offer is to make the familiar and the everyday appear a little less familiar, to cast the routine and the taken-for-granted in a different light. In August 1998, a year after I had finished the main fieldwork, I returned to Skive, this time to work with the local museum to create an exhibition presenting some of the results of the research (Jenkins 1998). Creating the exhibition was an eye-opener for me. It was the first time I had attempted to communicate research largely through pictures, artefacts and installations instead of words. Divided into four sections – 'The state's flag', 'The people's flag', 'Celebration and joy', and 'Use or misuse?' – the exhibition took the visitor from solemn official ceremonies of honour and remembrance, through funerals, weddings and birthdays, to finish with football supporters and the flag as a commodity.

Instead of offering extended commentaries, telling those who visited the exhibition what I thought about the ways in which Dannebrog is used, I hoped to invite them to draw their own conclusions and reflect upon an aspect of Danish life to which they probably didn't usually give much thought. The juxtaposition of things that don't usually occur side-by-side, the cumulative effects of repetition, and the display of material out of its usual context, made it possible for practices, feelings and attitudes that were usually utterly taken for granted to become explicit.

The most consistent response to the exhibition was along the lines of, 'Do we really do this? So much? I had never noticed before.' Not everybody was impressed, however. A conversation I had with one woman – who simply couldn't really see the point of having an exhibition about the flag – puts the matter into perspective:

KATRINE: When I have a birthday I put the flag out, and out in the garden we put little flags out to the street. And we put little flags all over the table. That is just what I learned from my mother, and my children will learn it from me. It's just what we do.

RJ: Is it not interesting, to ask why you do it?

KATRINE: No. I don't think it is interesting at all. We just do it. I would never think about it at all.

I can think of no better tribute to the ubiquitous – and fundamental – presence of the flag in Danish life and Danish identification. More concrete than public debates about the European Union and Danish-ness (*danskhed*), more mundane than royalty or stirring patriotic songs, Dannebrog is so much part of everyday life that, despite its colourful visual presence, it is, for most of the time, if not actually invisible then simply part of the background. It's just there, something which one just *does*. Something one doesn't generally think about. Something one *feels*.

Nation, flag, emotion

This brings me back to the two themes with which I began this exploration of Danish flagways. In the first, I suggested that, in the case of Denmark, focusing only on ethno-national identity is insufficient if we want to understand whatever's going on. In the second, I argued that we need to look at how the taken-for-granted, background presence of a flag might be anything but 'banal' in the emotional sense.

The first thing to say about Dannebrog is that, regardless of the diversity of ways in which it is used popularly, it is a national symbol and a symbol of an established nation-state. It is *the* pre-eminent Danish national symbol: nothing comes close. In this important respect, although the nineteenth-century *folk* won their tussle with the monarch on this point, my architect friend was simply wrong. Dannebrog is the state's flag *as well* as the people's flag. The popular uses of the flag to mark local and family celebrations and events may have a long history, but their emergence and development had more than a little to do with patriotism, if not actually nationalism.[22] Threats to the integrity of the Danish state during the nineteenth century – a succession of national defeats at the hands of Britain and Prussia – encouraged and fuelled popular enthusiasm for the flag. In the twentieth century, the reunification of Jutland in 1920, followed by German occupation of the whole of Denmark between 1940 and 1945, are likely to have had the same effect. Whether historically or in the here-and-now, whether in its official or popular uses, Dannebrog remains a national flag, sanctioned by and symbolising the state and embodying ethno-national identity.

There is, of course, more to the nation than the nation-state, and the directions in which the Danish *folk* took Dannebrog, as they took it to their hearts, have created a complex of flagways in which, in terms of frequency if nothing else, popular uses outweigh the official. Having said that, however, the distinction between the official and the popular is not always clear-cut, and at the heart of the matter is the relationship between the state and civil society in Denmark. Despite creeping rationalisation and centralisation in the last fifteen or so years, in the social democratic welfare state that has developed in Denmark since the end of the nineteenth century many core functions of the state are delivered either by the municipalities and regions (which have recently replaced the counties), or by voluntary associations such as trade unions. The collection of direct taxation and the payment of welfare benefits, are both, for example, devolved. The national church, *Folkekirken*, to which nearly 90 per cent of the population belongs, is another good example of the uncertainty of the boundary between state and civil society: although funded by elective direct taxation and under the oversight of a state Church Ministry, from parish priest to bishop it is independent of the state. Lastly, the fact that Denmark has two national anthems – one, *Kong Christian*, for royal affairs of state, the other, *Der er et yndigt land*, for civil society occasions such as international football matches or a Princess opening a factory – seems to me to make a similar point.[23]

It is, therefore, not surprising that the distinction between official and popular flagways is often unclear. Three examples that have already been mentioned will serve to make the point. First, Dannebrog standards (*faner*) are distributed to voluntary associations and official organisations alike by a non-state organisation, Danmarks-Samfundet, which is funded by public collections. Second, each municipality may have its own official flag days and may also fly the flag – its own *kommune* flag, with its own coat of arms in the corner – to mark other occasions of local significance as they happen. Finally, Dannebrog flies outside churches when there are weddings, christenings, funerals and ordinary Sunday services. In each of these examples, the flagways partake of something of the official and something of the popular. To revisit the earlier discussion of informal nationalism and nationness, a fruitful way to further develop these ideas might be to map them, and the distinction between state and nation, onto the distinction between state and civil society, and to see how that mapping works in any concrete situation.

There are also, however, a mass of flagways that are clearly definitively popular and unofficial, from the birthday party and the welcome home at the airport, to the special offer in the supermarket. While some of these, such as the use of the flag at international sporting occasions, explicitly invoke the nation and identity – and are thus easily described as informal nationalism – the remarkable thing about many of them is the degree to which state and nation effectively become completely invisible. The commercial uses of the flag are particularly notable in this respect. While the complex history of national reconstruction and nineteenth-century nation-building during which the national flag came to be the pre-eminent Danish symbol of *fest og glæde* and *højtidlighed* – celebrations and joy, and solemnity – is lurking somewhere in the very distant background, the modern use of Dannebrog in marketing and other commercial contexts must also be understood within a more recent history, of consumerism. Focusing on the nation and national identity is not enough in the Danish case: once a national symbol acquires connotations that, in principle, have nothing to do with state or nation, this autonomy can take its uses and meanings into other places altogether.

The invisibility of the nation at the birthday party or in the supermarket, if that is indeed what it is, brings us directly to the second theme, which is concerned with Billig's invocation of banality as an adequate description of civil society flagways such as those I have described for Denmark. In the same discussion, he also brings into play notions such as 'forgetting' and 'mindlessness' (1995: 38–43). Before going further it is necessary to emphasise the importance of Billig's work, particularly for its extended theorising of informal nationalism and nationness, the depth and breadth of the detail with which he opened up the discussion, the way in which he places the development of the nation-state at the heart of the matter, and the subtlety of his analysis.

However, the Danish case forces a re-examination and critique of some key aspects of his argument. In the first place, there is nothing trite or feeble – among the meanings of banal, let's remember – about most of the practices that I have been describing. Certainly not if we are talking about emotions. The popular identification of Dannebrog with joy, on the one hand, and solemnity, on the other, is authentic and powerful and rooted in experience, in that they are regularly reproduced and reinforced at festivities, funerals and so on. In that both emotions are as appropriate to occasions of state, and to patriotism, as they are to family, neighbourhood and community, there is a convergence or coincidence of the official and the popular. None of this can sensibly be called trite or feeble (or trivial). We need a better vocabulary for talking about this.

We also need to recognise that 'inarticulate' doesn't mean mindless, or forgotten. In the first place, what might 'mindless' actually mean for humans, if anything? How can we recognise agency and yet talk about mindlessness? Second, there is also a basic epistemological problem, in that what goes on in other people's minds is fundamentally unknowable, so it would be impossible to recognise mindlessness even if it existed. There is a similar problem with forgetting: how can one ever really know that something has been forgotten? Once again, we need a better vocabulary to address the issue than that which Billig offers us. Without falling into the conceptual black hole that is 'the unconscious', whether individual or collective, we need to recognise that something that isn't talked about (much) or thought about (much) can be emotionally and politically powerful.

Put like this, I realise that I'm actually making and agreeing with Billig's major point, his choice of words notwithstanding. Or rather I am making it, and agreeing with it *in part*; because Billig's argument does not allow us to recognise how the inarticulacy of Danish popular flagways, the fact that they are more done than reflected on, actually contributes in no small way to their *affective* power and wider significance. To appropriate a Danish expression, these flagways are something that one 'learns in the body'. To appropriate an expression from Raymond Williams, albeit one that is notoriously difficult to pin down (e.g. Williams 1965: 64–88), they amount to a 'structure of feeling', an established, but tacit, collective way-of-being that is rooted in shared history and experience and independent of formal ideology and institutions: 'it's just how it is'.

Maybe that *is* just how it is, but times do, also, change. And when times change the axiomatic, the tacit and the inarticulate may, perhaps, come into sharper focus. One such moment recently could have been the national and international uproar about the 'Mohammed cartoons', published in the Danish newspaper *Jyllands-Posten* in September 2005. Regardless of the rights or wrongs of that publishing decision, or the newspaper's motives, how have Danes responded to pictures of the Danish flag being burned in protests in the Middle East and elsewhere? The answer is that, in fact, this apparent desecration of the Danes' sacred symbol has not been at the heart of the matter. Explicitly, it has been reported but little commented on at all. While making for graphic images in the newspapers,[24] the real debate has been about other things: the freedom of the press, the responsibility of the press, the uncomfortable reality – for many Danes – that a significant section of the Danish population is now Muslim, and the equally uncomfortable reality – for many other Danes – that their self-image as a tolerant and liberal nation no longer stands up to close inspection (if indeed it ever did). What's more, lots of Danes are struggling, sincerely, to make sense of, and to come to terms with, both uncomfortable realities.

Perhaps the point about the flag here is that its sacredness is neither at issue nor at risk, not for Danes themselves. It is not they who are doing the burning. Nor, as Thomas Hylland Eriksen discusses in the Norwegian context, in the opening chapter of this collection, were *real* flags being burned. Improvised, often apparently made of paper, where was their sacred quality? They were made to be burned, not worshipped. Nor were they made by Danes. What's more, paper Dannebrog are trampled under foot and disposed of as rubbish in the aftermath of Danish parties and celebrations

Figure 8.2 Dannebrog: from the sacred to the profane.

every weekend, so taken-for-granted, axiomatic distinctions between the real and the ersatz, the sacred and the profane, are ready to hand. They do not have to be worried over, or worked out. They do not, really, have to be thought about at all. To return to an earlier point, there are many different Danish flags. Perhaps not all of them *can* be desecrated.

Notes

Abbreviation: SBA = *Skive byhistoriske Arkiv.*

1 *Concise Oxford Dictionary*, ninth edition (1995).
2 The bulk of this fieldwork, between 1996 and 1997, was made possible by generous study granted leave by the University of Sheffield. All translations from Danish in this chapter are mine.
3 This mythical event is famously portrayed in Lorentzen's painting from 1809 (just after Nelson's destruction of Copenhagen), now hanging in the National Art Museum, Statens Museum for Kunst, in Copenhagen.
4 See the cover of *Shu-Bi-Dua 15* from 1995 (CMC 24150–2). The flag also gets an oblique mention in 'Sorgenfri', a humorous tribute to Queen Margrethe (1980). More generally, Shu-Bi-Dua do a good line in patriotic songs, most obviously 'Danmark' from 1978, and their 1980 setting to a new tune of Holger Drachmann's *Midsommersangen* ('We love our country . . .').
5 For example, the Danish popular practice of decorating domestic Christmas trees with Dannebrog seems to have been originally a popular response to the Prussian Wars in 1848 and 1864, and the occupation of Northern Slesvig, or Southern

Jutland, 1864–1920. This is suggested by the appearance of the flag in this context in the illustrated children's poems 'The Christmas Tree' (*Juletræet*, better known today as *Højt fra Træets Grønne Top*, by Peter Faber, 1848) and 'Peter's Christmas' (*Peters Jul*, by Johan Krohn, 1866). The fact that Christmas tree flag garlands are in the shape of the state's *splitflag* also supports this interpretation. Other examples of the high popular visibility of Dannebrog at these times are Hans Christian Andersen's poem, '*Soldatens sang til Dannebrog (Vor gamle fane, vort Dannebrog)*', ('The Soldier's Song to Dannebrog (Our old standard, our Dannebrog)'), first published in the magazine 'The Fatherland' (*Fædrelandet*) in early 1849, and Grundtvig's hymn *Korsbanneret* (The Cross Banner), first published in 1864 in *Psalmer for danske Krigere* (Hymns for Danish warriors).

6   On the varieties of the *splitflag* see: *Den Store Danske Encyclopædi*, vol. 4, (Copenhagen: Gyldendal, 1996), p. 454.

7   For the flag rules, see: Danmarks-Samfundet 1992; Lingren 2000: 49–69.

8   I am very grateful to Kai Jørgensen for supplying me with a copy of his speech. He mentions two local bridges in this passage, however, only one of which, the railway bridge, is routinely decorated with flags on official flag days.

9   For a comprehensive list of the official Danish flag days, with their history and meanings, see Hjermind (1995).

10 American anthropologist Barbara Gallatin Anderson, who gave birth to her daughter Sarah while doing fieldwork on Amager, near Copenhagen, in the 1950s, describes returning from hospital to discover her neighbours flying flags to welcome her home (1990: 57).

11 Since 1997 the photographic archive has expanded considerably. However, most of the new acquisitions date from recent decades and are unlikely to have implications for my conclusions.

12 These included royal occasions (SBA 908 – B.332, King Christian IX and Queen Louise's golden wedding in 1892; SBA 806 – B.742, King Frederik VII's visit in 1908), or Christmas (SBA 908 – B.483, dated 1905–10).

13 For example, the 25th anniversary of the grocers Christensen and Olsen, Østergade 6, 1942 (SBA 806 – B.2150 [81A – 883]).

14 Such as the opening of Skive's first petrol station, Nørregade 42, in 1921 (SBA 427A – 5) or General Motors' exhibition on Østertorv, *c.* 1922 (SBA 806 – B.42, B.345).

15 For example, SBA 806 – B.98, B.1158 (118A – 541), B.1159, B.2382 (81A – 275), B.2766; SBA 81A – 440.

16 For Nørregade in 1972 see SBA 908 – B.203, B.496. For Adelgade in 1985 see SBA 909 – B.901; SBA 1992/26 – B.42.

17 SBA 908 – B.501, B.507, B.514; SBA 910 – B. 1458; SBA 1992/26 – B.47; SBA 994/29 – B.426; SBA 32A – 65, 67 and 68.

18 SBA 806 – B.366, B.368, B.370, B.371, B.384, B.387; SBA 908 B.497, B.505, B.515–6; SBA 910 B.1459.

19 SBA 1918/62 – B.2, B.3, B.10, B.19, B.21, B.22; SBA 909 – B.895.

20 SBA 1988/56 – B.122.

21 Complex relationships between the circulation and consumption of material goods and the production and reproduction of meaning – including, conspicuously, symbolism and identification – are, of course, peculiar neither to Denmark nor to modernity (Davis 1992; Lamont and Fournier 1992; Mackay 1997; Miller 1998, 2001; Sahlins 1974).

22 Social science understandings of the relationship between patriotism and nationalism usually define patriotism as a generic feature of human group membership – in other words a species of ethnicity – and nationalism as a more modern ideology of state formation (Varouxakis 2001).

23 It may also be worth pointing out that Danes are even further specialised in the matter of national songs. At Midsummer, for example, round the bonfires on Saint Hans' Evening, they sing Holger Drachmann's *Midsommersangen*, with its opening line, 'We love our country' (*Vi elsker vort land*), originally written in 1885.

24 See, for example, *Berlingske Tiden*, 16 March 2006, p. 4.

9 A flag for all occasions?

The Swedish experience

Orvar Löfgren

flag (Persian origin) A piece of bunting or other material, usually oblong or square, attachable by one edge to a staff or a halyard, and used as a standard, ensign, or signal, or for decoration or display.

(*Shorter Oxford English Dictionary* 1993)

In 1992 I saw my first Swedish flag inside a taxi. As my youngest son and I climbed into a Stockholm cab, we noticed a small Swedish flag on the dashboard – one of those wooden craftshop variants that I remember from the birthday parties of my childhood. Inside the taxi this little quaint souvenir takes on a new aura. My son asked innocently, 'Why have you got a flag up there with you?' The white-haired taxi-driver turned his head to one side and began to explain, in an amicable manner, that 'the Swedish flag is the finest thing we've got, and it's something to be proud of'. I tried to keep a straight face, remembering newspaper articles about the new habit adopted by some taxi-drivers in Stockholm: sticking the national flag on their back windows serves to point out that they are not immigrants; they don't drive 'kebab taxis'.

What is the true significance of that pretty little flag up by the windscreen? 'Three cheers for Sweden – a great country to live in!', or 'Here comes a real Swede and not some bloody foreigner!' Was this an 'ensign or signal', or just 'decoration or display'? Right then I couldn't be sure.

Two years later there was a heated debate in a Swedish magazine for housing co-operatives, *Vår bostad*. It started with a letter to the editor:

> There can be no doubt about it, to put out a flag is racism. On our housing estate there are many immigrants of different nationalities. One must not create boundaries by putting a Swedish flag on the balcony. It is so provocative. You signal that you are Swedish and best. Don't offend immigrants, never put out a flag![1]

The letter produced a heated debate about the Swedish tradition of flying a small flag from the balcony. What did the Swedish flag actually symbolize? Was it still a festive decoration, or had it been turned into a racist symbol:

'This is the home of a real Swede'? Was the flag in some situations used as a racist symbol of exclusion? The debate continued as skinheads and neo-nazis started to wave the flag. There was a new call for 'taking the flag back' from right-wing populists. Slowly the flag debate ebbed away, but in 2006 a columnist in the national newspaper *Dagens Nyheter* (January 4) complained, 'Why can't I hoist a flag in the garden without being accused of being a racist? Have we become too timid in our use of blue and yellow . . .' The same year a flag producer told a reporter that, 'Back in the 1990s Swedish flags were seen as racist symbols, but that's all over now, we sell more flags than ever . . .' (*Göteborgsposten*, June 5, 2006).

There seem to be more national flags per square mile in the Scandinavian countries than in most other countries. Nevertheless, Scandinavians see themselves as non-flagwaving nations, representing a friendly non-aggressive type of national identity, as several of the other contributions in this book stress (see also Jenkins 1998). Flags are waved in the USA, in France or Britain, but not here. This attitude has a long history. In a critique of the Swedish lack of cultural pride, in 1916, the author Carl G. Laurin hastened to add, 'The idea is of course not that we should become as blue-and-yellow as the Americans are "star-spangled"'(Laurin 1916: 116). Michael Billig is also a bit too quick when he states, in his *Banal Nationalism*, 'Of all countries, the United States is arguably today the home of what Renan called "the cult of the flag"' (Billig 1995: 39). Although he has a discussion of waved and unwaved flags, I think he underestimates the power of nations who have perfected the art of unwaving flags.

My chapter explores some striking changes in Swedish flag use and the emotionality of flags during the last century. When, where, how, for whom and why are flags present in the landscape, and how come they are often invisible to the natives? In some ways we are dealing with another process that Billig talks of, when flags move from symbolic mindfulness to a more mindless existence in everyday life. The point here, however, is, of course, that flags can move swiftly from mindless to mindful as well. In many ways, national flags still work as a seismographic surface that may register even the smallest conscious and unconscious national vibrations.

The flag as a tool

> **flag** *A flag raised, dropped, waved, etc., to indicate the start or finish of a race.*

Elsewhere, I have discussed the global construction of a toolkit for cultural nation-building (see, for example, Löfgren 1993), but what are the specific potentials of the flag as one of these tools? The flag is a symbol, but it is also 'a piece of bunting', cloth or silk. Its textile qualities means that it can be folded, draped, torn, ripped, burned, soiled or used as a wrapping. It is gendered in different ways, from the masculine charge of honour to a product that can be sewn or embroidered by 'women's tender hands'. It can be enlarged into giant size or miniaturised. It can be manufactured in other materials for new uses: paper, wood, plastic. It has a given pattern and a set of colours that can be translated into other kinds of representations. In short, it has a quite different materiality than the national anthem or the national emblem.

The textile form also makes the flag alive. It can flap idly or depressively, or can stretch out proudly in the wind, creating ripples and wave effects. It is this latter condition that makes it such a powerful backdrop for presidential appeals or political statements, as for example in one of the recent Danish election campaigns, in which the populist right-wing 'Danish People's Party' (Dansk Folkeparti) produced a patriotic TV-spot, with its leader standing in front of a flag dramatically waving in the wind. It was a kind of rhetoric rarely seen in Scandinavia since the 1940s.

The very fact that the flag is alive and moving also stresses its emotional impact, its ability to move people. 'This flag does something to me', as a Vietnam veteran said in an TV-interview during the first Gulf War. This combination of micro- and metaphysics is also found in the ways that flags acquire magical power. In October 2005, for example, the newspaper *Sydvenska Dagbladet* reported that two Swedish tourists had been arrested in the holiday resort Antalaya for desecrating the Turkish flag. It was still unclear what had happened. They had taken down a Turkish flag from its pole and then, as the report stated, 'in some way desecrated it . . .'.

The magical and mystical power of military flags could take various forms. In eighteenth-century Denmark, for example, the only way an outcast and unclean vagrant or, as the local term was, 'dishonest' person could be taken into normal society as a soldier was through a dramatic cleansing ritual, in which he was placed naked out in front of the regiment and the flag was waved above his head (Ehn and Löfgren 1982). In her discussion of the American 'trooping of the colors' on television during the First Gulf War, Carolyn Marvin (1991) has pointed out that war not only elaborates a sacred and subliminal use of the flag, as a silent but omnipresent symbol of political leadership, but also a shamanistic use of the flag in everyday life, as protective magic, draped around the house, pictured on a cake, stitched onto clothes, performed as a 'living flag' to protect soldiers or prepare for their homecoming.

As flags were nationalized they acquired new magical powers. Thus when gold medal winners run a lap of honour with the flag wrapped around them, this is a very powerful emotional statement. The flag radiates energy and when it is desecrated by being trailed in the mud, or burned in a demonstration, we again have to remember its specific materialities.

The visibility of flags

flag Inform or communicate (as) by means of a flag or flags

In Sweden the flag was transformed rather slowly from a military and royal symbol. The first Swedish flags were carried by the navy in the late-sixteenth century. The flag's pattern, with the cross, had been borrowed from the arch-enemy, Denmark. As the flag started to be used as a civil symbol during the latter half of the nineteenth century, a lot of complaints were made about the lack of interest shown by 'ordinary citizens'. In 1868 a captain asked his new batch of recruits if they could describe the Swedish flag: only 5 out of 114 succeeded. The first time the flag was hoisted over the Royal Palace in Stockholm in 1873, to signal that the King was in residence, reactions to this 'non-military' use ranged from irritation to ridicule. Why should the Royal Palace be disfigured by this kind of ornament (Biörnstad 1976)?

During the first decades of the twentieth century, flying the national flag privately could still be seen as an élite practice. This is made clear in the answers to a questionnaire on the uses of the Swedish flag that was sent out by the Nordic Museum in 1943. Even from the province of Dalecarlia, which was seen as the rural cradle of Swedishness, a man answers:

> In my childhood towards the end of the 19th century the Swedish flag was an almost unknown thing. It was first later on in the next century I started to see the blue and yellow flag in the gardens of upper class people and in vicarages. Hardly anybody thought of the flag as a symbol for the nation, it was just a symbol for royalty, militarism and the well-to-do. The result was that the flag wasn't very popular among those who were not so well off – and it still isn't because tradition is strong.
>
> (Biörnstad 1976: 48)

Another answer to the questionnaire states that, 'In our locality the flag is only found among some pompous well-to-do farmers'.

The Swedish flag was advocated through a private association for the promotion of the flag, which created the 'Day of the Swedish Flag' in 1916, which later came to be seen as a national day. In public ceremonies all over the country flags were presented to voluntary associations and clubs. During the inter-war years the flag was still often seen as a symbol of the élite and the Right, although the Social Democrats, in their attempt to capture the national initiative, started to carry it in First of May demonstrations from the early 1930s.

The translation of the flag from a military tool to a national symbol also meant that an elaborate code of flag use was institutionalized. There were rules about when the flag could be shown and how it should be treated, as a sacred object. Homeowners were instructed when to hoist or haul the flag, how to take care of it, how to fold it and make sure it never touched the ground, etc. In a popular book for boys, written by the leader of the Swedish Boy Scout Union in the 1920s, there is a moral story about a group of admirable Boy Scouts who give the local *nouveau riche* merchant a thorough beating, to make him pay for having left his newly bought flag flying after sunset.

Flag uses varied widely. The most common use was for celebrating family events, as the answers to the 1943 questionnaire show. Tight-fisted farmers only hoisted it sparingly, not to expose it to too much wear and tear; however, a more enthusiastic farmer was said to fly the flag whenever one of his cows calved.

As the custom of flag-flying spread, it gradually became less official and more festive. During the 1950s flagpoles became common in gardens and the flag became a more intimate and private medium. The flag was hoisted to celebrate a birthday, a Sunday visit, or just fine weather. Flags also became a symbol of summer, flying in 'colony gardens' (allotments) and over summer cottages. In Sweden, as in the other Scandinavian countries, the national flag became domesticated to a much larger extent than in most other countries. Miniaturization also helped to domesticate the flag and to create a more intimate and everyday relationship to it. Miniature flags were draped on the Christmas tree, placed on the birthday cake, or produced in small table models for the dining room.

During the 1960s flags started to become more ideologically charged again. In the spirit of 1968, the Swedish flag came to be a symbol of out-moded, conservative nationalism. A 1968 left-wing activist put it like this:

> We had all kinds of flags, Cuban flags, the flags of certain African countries, which were struggling for freedom, and the Vietnamese flag. But we never had the Swedish flag. Not under any circumstances ... It stood for the conservative, that which was blue in society, the established.
>
> (O'Dell 1997: 147)

As Tom O'Dell also points out, it was the American flag that became the symbol of dark forces. It was constantly attacked or ridiculed by the Swedish Left. It was American, not Swedish, flags that were burned during demon-strations, while rockers who were out to bait the left-wing students carried American flags in their cars or flying from their bikes.

In 1968 a young man was brought to trial for using the Swedish flag as a doormat, but in the heated discussions surrounding this event no one really seemed to notice that Swedish flags were marketed – in very unproblematic ways – for all kinds of menial or trivial tasks. After the fashion of Carnaby Street, where the Union Jack had been turned into a decorative motif (see Groom's chapter in this volume), you could at that time buy Swedish flags on waste paper baskets, towels, sponges; and so on. Displaying the national symbol was here seen as a harmless, fun thing. It is important to notice these two parallel trends in the youth cultures of the 1960s: the national as outmoded and oppressive, versus the national as outmoded and, therefore, a fun and non-political piece of Victoriana.

In the 1980s flag rhetoric slowly started to change again. Was it true, as the Swedish King maintained in his 1985 Christmas speech, that the flag was seen more often now than before? During the early post-war decades, the flag had retreated from the public sphere – it was waved more seldom as a national rallying symbol – but, at the same time, it had colonized the private sphere. The result of this change was that in Sweden, as in Denmark and Norway, the flag was everywhere and nowhere to be seen by the 1980s. The frequency of small flags, and of patterns using the national colours, was higher in these seemingly 'post-national' settings than in most other nations. Nowhere else would you find as many private flagpoles as in Scandinavia. At the same time, most Swedes saw this intensification in flag use as non-political: all these little flags were so much part of everyday life that they had become invisible. For outsiders, however, their appearance was more striking.

After joining the European Union, the use of flags proliferated further in Sweden. Little blue and yellow flags invaded the supermarkets, to signal that these pork chops or apples were truly Swedish products, not inferior continental imports. And as the debates on immigration grew more tense, during the late 1980s and early 1990s, the flag symbolism slowly changed again. In the early 1980s I bought a postcard which showed a whole cluster of little red summer cottages, all flying Swedish flags. This was a fun thing, I thought. Ten years later, I saw the same postcard photograph on a poster of a new right-wing, anti-immigration movement. Underneath was the slogan: 'Keep Sweden Swedish'. By the 1990s, as we have seen, the flag had again become a marker of inclusion and exclusion.

Flags at home – and abroad

flag (prob. Scandinavian origin) A spot where a turf has been cut out

National flags abroad have often been a touchy issue. There are strict rules about the official use of the flags of other countries. In the private sphere, the routines are less clear. I remember a Swiss student asking me, after a seminar in Basel on nationalism back in the 1990s, why Swedish backpackers often had little flags sewn onto their backpacks. 'In Switzerland we would never dream of doing that', he assured me. These flags had been totally invisible to me, of course, but they raised the question when and why you bring your own flag abroad. Together with Scandinavians, Canadian backpackers are well-known for their use of miniature flags: for them they work as an identity marker: We are *not* Americans. In the same manner, German and British holiday-makers may have noted that the only tourists who brought miniature flags to put out on the balcony of their rented holiday apartments on Crete or Tenerife back in the 1990s were Swedes and Norwegians.

Even in a holiday setting a miniature flag can, however, turn into a provocation. There was, for example, a conflict between Denmark and Germany in the early twentieth century, when German tourists started to decorate their beloved sandcastle constructions on Jutland beaches with German miniature flags. When local Danes went out and removed the flags, the German tourists protested, and in the end both governments had to exchange stern diplomatic notes (Löfgren 1999: 232).

For the last decades I have followed the flag use among summer visitors on a Swedish island, close to the Norwegian border. During the summer the resident population of 300 grows to over 3,000 inhabitants. During this period the number of Norwegian caravans at the camp site, as well as summer house owners, has increased rapidly. As vacationers, Norwegians are returning to this region of Bohuslän, which was part of the Danish-Norwegian kingdom before 1658.

All over the place Swedes fly their flag, small ones hanging from the caravans, big ones flying from the flagpoles, and miniature ones standing in the windows, but what if you're a Norwegian? There is a delicate balancing act here. It is still unthinkable, or too provocative, to fly a non-Swedish flag from a flagpole, and it took many years before Norwegian miniature flags appeared in the caravan camp. A German summerhouse owner solved the problem by erecting two flagpoles, combining Swedish and German flags. Another more recent strategy has led to the frequent use of Norwegian flags on even the smallest motor boats, building on the naval tradition of boats showing their colours. The increase in this maritime flag use also signals that it is a more acceptable way of showing of your nationality when abroad. As a result of this proliferation, more Swedes have started to fly their own national flag from their small boats. There is a constant but subtle negotiation about which kinds of flag use are acceptable 'abroad'.

Some Norwegians, for example, fly the local, regional flag of Bohuslän from their flagpoles. To ask them to hoist a Swedish flag would really be too much, but hoisting this regional flag rarely provokes any comments. The same goes for the proliferation of regional flags in most other parts of Sweden, with one exception.

In Scania, another of the Danish provinces that were conquered by Sweden in 1658, a local, regional flag was reinvented in the late-nineteenth century. It carried a yellow cross on a red background and was sporadically and privately used. In the 1960s and 1970s the flag became more popular, as part both of a tourist marketing of the province, but also as a sign of regional pride and 'anti-centralist' sentiments. It was also seen as a symbol of a growing populist movement, demanding either Scanian self-government or a return to Danish rule after '350 years of Swedish occupation'. The new EU focus on regions also fuelled the interest in presenting Scania as a distinct region with its own unique history and culture.

Although such political ideas remained a rather marginal element in local politics, the use of the Scanian flag became problematic. What did it actually signify? Local pride, right-wing politics, racism, a critique of the centralist state? From the answers to a questionnaire sent out in 1992,[2] as well as from letters to the newspapers, it is clear that this regional flag really could stir up the emotions. This was especially so after the creation of 'The Day of the Scanian Flag', by a group of enthusiasts who modelled it on the celebrations of the Swedish flag. Reactions were strong, for or against. One critic threatened to file a complaint for high treason, someone else called the new flag 'such a trashy rag', while others called it 'a rebel flag', drawing parallels with the Confederate flag. Other reactions described it as a childish or stupid initiative, and some non-Scanians saw it as yet another example of Scanian provincial arrogance. Those who insisted on flying it from their flagpoles were defined by the critics as odd, or out to provoke. A common argument was that the Scanian flag challenged the national flag: 'I see the national flag as a bit sacred and we shouldn't start messing it up with new versions.'

Today, much of the debate surrounding the Scanian flag has died down. It is still used, but only as a private statement, a marker of regional pride, or as a tourist symbol. Going through the debate I am struck by the ways in which a moral stance, for or against the flag, was often combined with aesthetic arguments. For many critics the most important characteristic of the Scanian flag was its ugliness: 'How much more beautiful are the Swedish colours of blue and yellow compared to the Scanian red and yellow!' The debate also shows that size mattered. Some of those who argued that they would never fly anything else but the national flag from their private flagpole, added that an indoor miniature Scanian flag was quite OK.

Colouring the nation

flag A small object or device resembling a flag

Flags are not only transformed in size and shape, painted on the faces of soccer fans, or turned into labels on packets of pork chops; their colours can also spill over into new fields. Blue and yellow has colonized many arenas as a minimalistic, but effective, flag marker. The Day of the Swedish Flag was never a popular success, and when it finally was established as an official national day in 2005, many argued that Midsummer's Eve should have been chosen instead. It was seen a 'natural' national day for Swedes. Swedish flags have long been flown on maypoles that evening, but over the last decades shops have marketed more and more Midsummer party props in blue and yellow, or with printed flags on: napkins, decorations, miniature maypoles.

Even stronger orgies of flags, and of blue and yellow patterns, have emerged in the rituals surrounding high school graduation. If you walk into a supermarket during the graduation season you enter a sea of blue and yellow, in all kinds of forms and fashions. If flags seem to be invisible to many Swedes, the use of blue and yellow for festive reasons seems to be even more invisible. Why this outburst of blue and yellow? When asked, many people will say, 'You know, I have never noticed'.

Using the national colours may also be a technique for making unobtrusive or indirect references to 'the national', as in for example marketing or fashion (see, for example, Foster's analysis [2002: 122] of how Shell gasoline used the colours of Papua New Guinea in local television advertisements). National colours produce a language of colour symbolism. In Sweden we may follow how the idea of 'the blue and yellow' slowly expanded, becoming a symbol for Swedishness. It can be used as a nationalizing adjective, as in 'blue and yellow socialism'; as a pejorative for chauvinism, as in 'far too blue and yellow'; or as an identity marker, as in 'our blue and yellow boys out on the soccer field'.

Above all, however, the colours of blue and yellow have been used to link the flag with the ideas of an eternal summer. In photographs and on postcards, the Swedish flag is usually shown against sunny blue skies. It signals the optimistic feelings of summer vacations, of good weather, and of high spirits.

Relocating the national

flag Provide with, decorate or mark out (as) with flags; place a flag on or over. Mark with a small flag or tag so that relevant items may be readily found.

Examples such as the above illustrate the rapidly changing and ambivalent meanings of the Swedish flag, but also the ways in which the national was repoliticized during the 1980s and 1990s. As I have tried to show, the national never disappeared from Sweden: underneath the rhetoric of internationalism and non-patriotism, it was relocated to new arenas and became part of everyday life, as in the case of the flag. The use of national rhetoric became less and less frequent during the 1960s and 1970s, but during precisely the same period we may – in retrospect – observe an unprecedented homogenization of Swedish lifestyles. During this era of internationalism, Sweden became both more cosmopolitan but, also, more distinctly different from the rest of the world (Löfgren 2000). The debate about the European Union brought this up to the surface. The anti-European sentiments on the Left, especially among the Social Democrats, had to do with a feeling that there was a distinctly Swedish and progressive style of life, which was threatened by those European countries, 'down there'.

We need to explore the specific potentials of flags, and the ways in which they can swiftly be recharged with, or drained of, emotional power. Their emotionality spans a spectrum from pride to irony (in itself a strong emotion), from strong commitment to total disinterest. They may produce a lump in the throat or a sneer, a smile or a shrug of the shoulder, and sometimes a mixture of all these things. They can, indeed, be used as a marker, a decoration, a signal, an ornament, or a provocation (sometimes simultaneously), in ways which a polarity of 'mindful' and 'mindless' does not really capture.

Such an analysis needs to continue to explore the ways in which meta- and microphysics are combined. Flags are national symbols that are *handled* in everyday life, pinned to lapels, put on cakes, wrapped around coffins, burned in the streets, hoisted in gardens and outside public buildings. The ways in which flags are shaped, enlarged or miniaturized may also change their message, as we have seen. The magical impact of the regular national flag flying from its pole also has to do with the everyday rituals of hoisting and hauling, folding and unfolding. The body movements of hoisting it into the sky, with the eyes fixed on its slow journey upwards, may create moments of embodied solemnity. In this manner we need to focus on both the specific materiality and the handling of the flag, which set it apart from other national symbols. Flags can do things both to the individual mind and in a collective situation that other symbolic props cannot.

This calls for a comparison between different contexts, in time and space. What can the Swedish flag experience contribute to a more general understanding of the role of flags in national culture-building? As I have pointed out, Swedish flags have been put to work in constantly changing settings. They have been markers of class, of ethnicity, of boundaries, or of connections between public and private, state and nation. What we find in the Scandinavian countries are certain forms of flag domestication, that result in an intimizing or informalizing of 'the national'. Hoisting a flag in a Swedish context often means making an everyday situation more festive; it might make the solemnity of the national more mundane, but it might also either trivialize or nationalize the everyday. There is an interesting cultural dynamic between flag modes and flag moods. The history of Swedish flag use illustrates that, just as flag sales tend to go up and down, there is no unilinear development here. As the flag turned from a martial and official symbol into a 'cute little flag', it signalled that Swedes had turned their back on chauvinism and aggressive patriotism (conveniently forgetting centuries of Swedish aggressive warfare on neighbouring nations). But reality was more complex, as in the opening case of the taxi ride. And what became of those taxi flags? They disappeared after some time. They remind us, however, that, all of a sudden, the flag may invade a new territory and redefine a situation.

Notes

1   *Vår bostad*, 1994: 6.
2   The questionnaire (*Skåneländska flaggan*) was sent out by the Folk Life Archives at the University of Lund, and I have gone through the 45 answers as well as the heated debates documented on the Web.

10 Nationalism and Unionism in nineteenth-century Norwegian flags

Ole Kristian Grimnes

By the end of the year 1814, there was in Norway a nation, a state, and a Union and each of them needed a flag. Norway as a *nation* was old. Or, if you are fussy about this and insist, there did in 1814 exist at least some sense of Norwegianness, some kind of Norwegian national identity dating back to the Middle Ages. Norway as a *state* was new, the outcome of the breath-taking events of 1814. The *Union* between Sweden and Norway was also new, the product of the same events. Until 1814 Norway had been part of a Danish absolutist regime (or again, if you want to be fussy, of the absolutist Oldenburg composite state, in which Denmark was preponderant). After 1814, the newly born Norwegian state found itself in a Union with Sweden which was to last until 1905.

If all three of them needed a flag, what precedents and what opportunities were there for giving them precisely that? In those days there was no formal category by the name of 'national flag'. The formal categories were two: either the military ensign (*orlogsflagg*), flown by the navy and by fortresses on land, or the civil ensign (*koffardiflagg*, *handelsflagg*), flown by merchant ships. By and large, the flag was considered an emblem to be used at sea, not on land, with the exception of military fortresses. This was as far as flags were utilized at all. In other words, we are a far cry from the massive and multifaceted use of flags to which we are accustomed today.

Denmark and Sweden, which were the only Scandinavian states in existence before 1814, had their own internationally recognized flags, the only difference between the military and civil ensign of each country being that the military ensign was swallow-tailed (Denmark) or swallow-tailed with a tongue, *splitt og tunge* (Sweden). Although the formal categories were 'military ensign' and 'civil ensign', the Danish and Swedish flag may be considered national flags for two reasons: (1) their long tradition and the memory of heroic battles fought under the flag at sea, and (2) the fact that the ensign was to such a large extent used by ships sailing abroad, where it was continually confronted with flags of other nations or states, giving the ensign a flavour of being 'national'. Whereas Denmark and Sweden had their own flags steeped in tradition, there was little in the way of a Norwegian flag tradition. Norway had its own time-honoured coat of arms (*riksvåpen*), but no flag, Norwegian ships and fortresses having flown the Danish flag during the Union with Denmark. If Norway, as a nation or state, was to have its own flag, it would have to be created from scratch.

The point of departure for nineteenth-century flag history in Norway was the agreement that was concluded in autumn 1814 between Sweden – or rather the successor to the throne, Carl Johan – and the new Norwegian state. In the process of forming the Swedish–Norwegian Union at this time, the Norwegians primarily advocated a flag of their own, and Carl Johan a flag which would symbolize the new Union. To simplify just a bit, the compromise that the two parties entered into was (1) that there would be a combined military and Union flag (i.e. the military ensign would serve also as a Union flag); this flag was to be the same in both countries; its design was to be decided by the King; and (2) that Norway was to have its own civil ensign, to be decided by the Norwegians themselves.

The flags that were the outcome of this compromise reflected two opposite views of the Union. On the one hand, the King decided that the military/ Union flag was to be the Swedish flag, with a badge marking Norway in the upper left corner of the flag, the badge being a somewhat modified Danish flag. The military/Union flag symbolized Swedish supremacy in the Union, the Union as mainly a military arrangement, and Norway's continued cultural and emotional attachment to Denmark, marked by the badge in the corner. On the other hand, the civil ensign was decided by the Norwegian parliament, Storting, in 1821, which thereby gave shape and form to what was to be, and to this day remains, the Norwegian national flag. The new ensign, when put alongside the already existing Swedish civil ensign, demonstrated that the Union consisted of two separate and supposedly equal states. In sum, Swedish superiority in a common Union flag, Swedish–Norwegian equality in separate civil ensigns.

So how does one create a completely new symbol, in this case the Norwegian civil ensign to which the Storting agreed in 1821? Well, you stuff into it as much existing symbolic material and as many honourable references as you possibly can, in order to charge the new symbol emotionally and to confer on it maximum authority from the very start. In the Norwegian flag of 1821 there was an abundance of old and well-established symbolic material. There was the cross, a Christian symbol, though Norway's representatives at the time, being men of the Enlightenment, argued for it only in historical terms, referring to the use of the cross by Norwegian kings in the Middle Ages. The cross is the so-called Scandinavian cross, that is a cross with its centre being set a bit to the left of the centre of the flag (or, in more technical terms, the vertical arms of the flag are set nearer the hoist than the fly). In other cross-bearing flags the centre of the cross coincides with the centre of the flag. In introducing the Scandinavian cross, the Norwegians copied the Danish and Swedish flags, thus putting a Scandinavian stamp on their flag and perpetuating a tradition which Finland, Iceland, the Faroe

Islands and the Åland Islands adhered to later, a tradition broken only in recent times by the Inuit and the Sami, when they designed their new flags.

The colours of the new flag were white, red, and blue, a clearly intended reference to the American and French revolutions, which had inspired the Norwegians' own revolution of 1814 to such a large extent. At the same time, the distribution of the colours, combined with the design of the flag, placed Norway squarely between her two neighbours and former or new Union partners: Denmark which the Norwegians had left politically in 1814, but were still closely attached to culturally, linguistically, and in terms of kinship, and Sweden, Norway's new Union partner. The ties to Denmark are obvious, already being referred to in the case of the 'Norwegian' badge in the Union flag. Take away the blue arms of the cross in the 1821 flag and you have the Danish flag. At the same time, those blue arms provided a necessary link, the bridge over to the Swedes, the blue being one of Sweden's national colours.

Yes, the Norwegian civil ensign of 1821 was new and original, no flag being exactly like it. At the same time, it displayed all kinds of similarities with the flags of its Scandinavian neighbours. Thus, there is an ineradicable Scandinavianism in the Norwegian flag, rarely recognized by the Norwegians themselves, a genuine reflection of that loose Scandinavian – or, better, Nordic – identity that has always been there, however impalpable. However, the heavy Scandinavian characteristics of the flag might also have implied Norway's dependence, rather than independence, in relation to her neighbours. This was avoided by the adoption of the French tricolours whose universal symbolism softened the strong Scandinavianism of the flag. The tricolours linked the flag to the noblest notions of the age, providing the flag with a strong idealistic connotation, that of liberty (more than equality and fraternity, I think). It still retains this in many contexts, however much it finds itself in less than lofty settings these days.

So did the Norwegian nation, the Norwegian state and the Swedish-Norwegian Union each get its own flag? The nation undoubtedly did, in the shape of the 1821 civil ensign. The Union also did, Carl Johan saw to that. The Norwegian state, however, was only partially provided for. The civil ensign did not serve as a state flag, since it was only used by private merchant ships. The military ensign, flown by the Norwegian navy on its ships and the Norwegian army on its fortresses (Norway possessed its own navy and army in the Union), could be seen as a state flag but reflecting only the military aspect of the state, not the civilian, and being more of a Swedish and Union flag than a specifically Norwegian one. Now, the European state at the beginning of the nineteenth century was still very much a military entity, so the fact that the state flag was exclusively military was not as anomalous as it would seem today. It was chiefly the fusion of the military and the Union flag, and the heavy Swedish imprint on that flag, which prevented the fledgling Norwegian state from having a satisfactory flag of its own.

To sum up, after 1821 Sweden and Norway each had their own civil ensign, which was a national flag in the Swedish case and one in embryo in Norway. They shared a common Union flag, which was identical with the Swedish military ensign, but with a supposedly Norwegian mark in it. Thus national and Union symbols, the relationship and tension between which are the main theme of Norwegian flag history in the nineteenth century, were distributed in such a way that national symbolism was embodied in two separate national flags, while Union symbolism was located in one common, mainly Swedish, flag.

The second formative period of Norwegian and Union flag history was the 1830s and beginning of the 1840s. It concluded in a major flag reform in 1844, a reform which marks a watershed in nineteenth-century flag history. A Norwegian national offensive in the 1830s triggered off the reform, which partly contributed to, and partly reflected, an important change in public opinion concerning the Union. After considerable tension and conflict between the Union partners during the 1820s and most of the 1830s a new harmony gradually developed from the late 1830s, inaugurating the heyday of the Union during the years 1840 to 1870. In this period, many in the Norwegian elite sincerely believed in the Union, even though all efforts to have it extended, reflecting that belief, were in the end thwarted. This was also the climax of political and ideological Scandinavianism, and of the so-called 'civil servants' state' (*embetsmannsstaten*) both of which served to strengthen the new Unionist sympathies.

During their national offensive the Norwegians picked on the military/Union ensign, voiced their dissatisfaction with the Swedish superiority in it, and were no longer content with its Danish-looking badge that was supposed to be a Norwegian symbol. The Norwegians asserted the principle of equality in flags, acknowledging, however, that there was also a need for symbols representing the Union. The Swedes now accepted the principle of equality, but their main concern was Union symbolism. Thus there was room for negotiations and compromise between the parties.

How do you go about creating a Union flag with the aim of having it reflect a complete and immaculate equality between the two members of the Union? Well, in this case you don't; it proved impossible. Devising such a flag would mean diminishing and altering the Swedish element in it, whereby the Swedes would lose their cherished military ensign that was so closely associated with Sweden's former great power status and victories on the battle field. If the Union flag and the military ensign had been two separate emblems it would have been easy to solve the problem, but such separation was constitutionally impossible. The Union flag was, according to the Constitution, tied to the military ensign and vice versa, the two had to be identical. The Swedes were adamant that their war ensign be retained, for once being just as nationalistic as the Norwegians. Thus there could be no common Union flag symbolizing equality.

Figure 10.1 Four Union flags from 1844: Swedish (top) and Norwegian (bottom).

Equality and harmonization of Union and national symbolism would have to be achieved in some other way, then. The point of departure was that Sweden must preserve its military ensign, the logical conclusion that Norway must have its own military ensign, too. There was no problem as to what that ensign would be: the 1821 national flag, to be marked as a military ensign by making it swallow-tailed, with a tongue. There was complete equality then: Swedish and Norwegian military ensigns side by side, both being their countries' national flag, respectively. But how then was the demand for Union symbolism to be met, once the idea of a common Union flag was scrapped? The solution was a Union mark, a major innovation of the 1844 flag reform. The mark was to be placed in the upper left corner of every Swedish and Norwegian flag, every military and civil ensign. Thus what the reform separated, by having all flags be national flags, Swedish or Norwegian, it tied together again by providing all those flags with a common mark symbolizing the Union.

In the Union mark the rule of equality was again observed. The mark was put together as a mixture of Swedish and Norwegian flag colours and design, in such a way that neither country would appear superior to the other. On the other hand, the Union mark did come to look rather motley, in its reflection of minute equality, a bit like a salad bowl or a 'dog's dinner'. The detractors of the flag pounced on this, and were to nickname the Union mark *'sildesalaten'* (Norwegian) or *'sillsaladen'* (Swedish), that is 'the herring salad'.

The symbolic and the real

There was an alternative to basing the Union mark on the colours and design of flags. Both countries had their own time-honoured and emotionally charged coats of arms (*riksvåpen*). Why not place a combination of those in the Union mark to symbolize the Union? The alternative was discussed but dismissed, possibly because the figures in the arms were considered difficult to discern at a distance, an argument that was often used against placing heraldic figures in flags.

Suspicious historians, with the benefit of hindsight, might point out that the 1844 reform was really a triumph for national symbolism. There was no longer one common Union flag, only national flags, whether represented by the military or civil ensign. Furthermore, the space which the Swedish and Norwegian national flag occupied was much larger than the space allotted to Union symbolism, in the shape of the new Union mark. However, mainstream elite opinion at the time, at least in Norway, hardly saw the reform as a victory for nationalism only. It was, rather, viewed as a successful harmonization of national and Union demands. It was noted with satisfaction that the principle of equality between the two nations was now wholly observed and that Norway had been granted its own military ensign, the Union mark even being accepted as a cherished symbol, and at least as a necessity, by a good many people. What counted was that everywhere there were now national flags and everywhere those flags bore a Union mark.

The military/Union flag of 1815 had represented the reality of the Union, i.e. Swedish superiority in it. The 1844 flag system represented the opposite, an ideal of equality; an ideal which was never fully implemented, since Sweden until the end of the Union always prevailed in some way or another. This raises the old and tricky question of the relationship between the symbolic and the real world. Did the symbolic world of the 1844 flag system, encapsulating equality, somehow alter the real world in the direction of that equality. Possibly it did, but how are we to trace such an influence of the symbolic on the real?

The 1844 reform had an unintended (as far as we know) effect during the subsequent decades in Norway. The military ensign ranked higher than the civil one, there was no doubt about that. The former was associated with state power, the latter with private shipping only. The eighteenth-century state had, to a large extent, been a military one, whereas the nineteenth-century state increasingly took on a civilian character, something which generated a demand for a flag which could be flown on a growing number of civilian state buildings and utilized at official festive occasions which the authorities wanted to have a civilian character. This demand was gradually met, not by the civil ensign, which was not sufficiently prestigious for that, but by extending the use of the military ensign to the civilian buildings of the state. In other words, in this second period the Norwegian state was, formally or informally, provided with a proper state flag, which was the national flag introduced in 1821, but swallow-tailed with a tongue, and bearing a Union mark, military in origin and essence but now also civilian through actual use.

The third phase of Norwegian flag history was the fifteen years prior to the dissolution of the Union, in 1905, particularly the 1890s. As far as the flag was concerned the two salient features of the 1890s were: (1) it became a hot political issue, being intimately associated with other major issues of the decade and contributing heavily to the deep political and national cleavage which was so characteristic of Norwegian society at the time; and (2) there was a breakthrough in the use of the flag, which now, for the first time, became a mass symbol.

The backdrop to this development was a complete change of scene compared to the earlier periods. After the foundation of a modern party system and the breakthrough of parliamentarism in 1884, the age of mass politics had come to Norway. Mass politics, mass nationalism and the use of the flag as a mass symbol became closely interconnected. Nationalism assumed a decidedly aggressive and, unlike most other countries, clearly leftist form. It also took on a military aspect, rearmament being introduced from 1895 onwards. Both cultural and political nationalism received a strong impetus, but political nationalism held sway. There was a deep rift in society between the radicals represented by the party of Venstre, which was the hegemonic party of the time, and the conservatives who also took a large share of the vote at the elections. The radicals were able to whip up and exploit nationalism more effectively than the conservatives, one of the principal issues between the two parties being that of the flag.

The flag in the 1890s should be studied at three levels, two of which are clearly political, the third being a popular level, which is also political in a sense but is primarily characterized by the actual use of the flag. First, there is the political level on which the nationwide parties and the Storting operated. Venstre was no longer satisfied with the 1844 flag system. In the grip of the new nationalist vogue, which was so typical of the 1890s Venstre no longer saw the Union mark as a token of equality, but, rather, as an intruder in the national flag, the Swedish colours in the mark defiling it. According to Venstre the Union mark gave a wrong impression of the Union, which, thanks to the mark, was too easily interpreted not as a Union between two independent states but as the equivalent of what the American flag and the Union Jack represented, that is a federal state. The radicals started campaigning against the Union mark as an emblem of inferiority, wishing to have it removed from the flag, preferably from both the military and civil ensign, but at least from the latter. The flag was to be 'cleansed', making way for a 'pure' unblemished Norwegian flag.

The conservatives, the King, and the Swedes were dead against this step, whereby Norway would unilaterally discard a Union symbol. They viewed the Union-marked flag as a national emblem, which laudably embodied Norway's ties to a Union that guaranteed the country's safety, constitution, and self-government. But Venstre was not to be stopped. At three consecutive sessions of the Storting, in 1893, 1896 and 1898, a radical majority passed a flag law that adopted a civil ensign without the Union mark, Venstre ultimately neutralizing the King's suspensive veto. On 15 December 1899, the new law came into effect. The law-abiding conservatives observed it loyally and only a few diehards continued to hoist the Union-marked flag in subsequent years.

Second, the political struggle was also carried out at a municipal level. In the course of the 1890s, a good many municipalities with a Venstre majority adopted the 'pure' flag for their municipal buildings. At this level, no national law was considered necessary, and no suspensive veto by the King applied. The conservatives argued that the municipalities were official agencies that ought not to use unauthorized flags but the radicals retorted that a municipality could hoist whatever flag it wanted, the more so since the flag was the 'pure' 1821 ensign which everybody, the conservatives included, considered to be the country's national flag. In the capital the flag issue produced an amusing incident. The local council of Kristiania (today Oslo) adopted the flag without a Union mark on May 6 1897, just in time to display it on the buildings of the municipality on the National Day of 17 May. The only exception was Police Headquarters, where the Commissioner of Police refused to fly the 'pure' flag, saying that as a state civil servant he could hoist no other flag than the official flag of the state. In order to prevent the flying of the Union-marked flag over the police station, the building of which belonged to the municipality, the local council promptly had the flagpole dismantled.

In 1892 the Kristiania Flag Association (Kristiania Flagsamlag) was founded to work for the unmarked flag. It acted as a pressure group, lobbying for the flag, in particular making an effort to persuade the municipalities to make use of the 'pure' flag. The Association collected data on the municipalities' adoption of the unmarked flag and wrote to different newspapers to have them publish this information, in order to influence municipalities which had not yet decided in favour of the 'pure' flag. The Association also adopted a method which was rather common among the radicals: it bought a number of flags, to offer them free of charge to a municipality which might thus be persuaded to convert to the 'pure' flag, or it distributed the flags to participants in the 17 May parades. Flag distribution of this kind was also something that the conservatives did. There was still an economic side to flags, which seemed expensive to retrenchment-oriented municipalities and common people.

Third, the struggle over the flag went on at a popular level. But first a note of caution: there has been very little in the way of scholarly study of flag history in Norway (and for that matter of other national symbols). Furthermore, what scholarly work there is, and what else that has been produced on the history of flags, has always focused on the struggle at the level of formal political organs for the introduction and maintenance of flags. The basis has chiefly been political source material which is easily accessible, as much of it is printed. What is neglected in these writings is the actual *use* of the flag. This is probably to be explained both by the attention that the political struggle for the flag attracted in its time, and by the problematic nature of the source material. Sources on actual usage are scattered, where they may be obtained is often a matter of conjecture, and it takes time and effort to trace and glean the heterogeneous material that there is. So far, little work has been done on this. What follows is an impressionistic sketch based on some preliminary dips into the source material.[1]

At the popular level, people showed their leanings and preferences by choosing between the 'pure' and the Union-marked flag. Those who displayed the flag without a Union mark were sympathetic to the radicals. It might mean that they went for the whole Venstre package: its national items (a flag without reference to the Union, a separate Norwegian foreign minister and a separate consular service), its democratic item (universal suffrage), its economic item (direct and progressive state tax), and its social item (the beginnings of national insurance). Or it might mean that they were first and foremost nationalists, advocating radicalism in Union matters, but being more reticent on democratic and socio-economic reforms. Those who displayed the Union-marked flag might be convinced conservatives, manifesting their sympathy for the Union, disassociating themselves from the scepticism towards the Union evinced by Venstre, and keeping their distance from the economic and social radicalism of the leftists. Or, they might out of inertia fly the Union-marked flag, which was the flag that everybody had been accustomed to, the authorized flag, the flag one used when not being politically committed. The 'pure' flag was the newcomer, a usurper, the flag on the offensive, whereas the Union-marked flag found itself in more of a defensive position, with the advantage, however, of being the established flag, its defenders ranging from zealots to the uncommitted.

The National Day was the principal arena for the flag dispute at the popular level. Even the socialists, staging their 1 May demonstrations and initiating the use of their own emblem, the red flag, participated in the 17 May celebrations, using the unmarked flag to show their stand on the flag controversy. The collectively recognized arena of 17 May was, in the 1890s, not a platform manifesting national harmony and commonly felt patriotic sentiments, as it is today, but a stage for political struggle. Throughout the 1890s, different factions organized their own processions, although to what extent, and in what form, varied considerably from time to time and place to place. The workers set up their own parades, in which the unmarked flag was mandatory. Venstre organized processions in which there were seldom anything but 'pure' flags. Sometimes there were special suffrage parades staged by the socialists or the radicals, or a combination of the two. In such processions a Union-marked flag was hardly possible.

On the other hand, there were 'joint' or 'ordinary' processions, more or less conservatively tinged, sticking to the ideal of a common non-factional celebration of the National Day, but unable to suppress the flag dispute, as both types of flags would invariably appear in the processions. The school or 'children's parade' was a cherished part of the 17 May tradition. On one hand, there was a consensus that it ought to be kept out of politics; on the other, it proved impossible to do just that. If the children were to carry flags at all, and there was a strong tradition for that since 1870, there was no way that their teachers or parents could escape a choice between Union-marked or 'pure' flags. So the flag dispute crept up on the younger generation, too.

The use of flags in the processions, on buildings and in front of houses was a particular kind of vote, parallel to the institutionalized vote on the flag issue in the national assembly and the local councils, but unfolding at a mass level, not formalized, haphazardly, more or less in a chaotic and spontaneous way, even though it was the object of incessant campaigning from the political parties and lobby groups. The highly politicized press participated in the contest, referring to the display of flags and attempting to judge which type of flag was most frequent. But a hasty count of flags used on a mass scale cannot procure exact and reliable information, and the newspapers felt free to reckon according to their political tastes. My suspicion is that when, or if, scholarly research really digs into the source material, to find out how marked and unmarked flags were distributed in the 1890s, it will find it hard to come up with a reliable answer to the question of which flag won the day. My own hypothesis would be that the Union-marked flag was preponderant during most or possibly the whole of the decade, but that the non-marked flag certainly was an aggressive and strong runner-up.

The flag contest took place on other occasions, and in other arenas, than the National Day. The flag was flown at exhibitions. There was a controversy over the Union-marked flag that was used on the replica of a Viking ship which sailed across the Atlantic to the World Exhibition in Chicago in 1893. When the King or members of the royal house visited Norway there were flags in abundance, a large majority of them undoubtedly Union-marked, although the King was also confronted with 'pure' flags at times. The 1890s were a decade of polar expeditions and of a polar nationalist fever, which reached a peak during the homecoming ceremonies of the polar explorer and hero Fridtjof Nansen, in 1896. Nansen was an adherent of Venstre and personally, no doubt, would have preferred to use only the unmarked flag on his expeditions and at his homecoming. But he depended on an all-party consensus for the financing of his ventures and, besides, it was probably felt that the polar undertakings ought to be truly national, that is kept above politics. Consequently, both marked and unmarked flags were flown at the numerous homecoming arrangements in 1896.

The usage of flags was no doubt more of an urban than a rural pheno-menon, but flags spread to the countryside, too. Venstre was typically a party for peasant mobilization, something which had its effect on the use of flags in rural areas. Eager followers of Venstre on the farms, and the many radical primary school teachers leading the way among the country people, showed their disposition by flying the 'pure' flag. In the county of Valdres there are still some 'rock flags' ('*bergflagg*') dating from this time: flags without a Union mark painted on the crest of a mountain. The new villas sprouting up in the suburban areas seem to have had a flagpole in front of the house as a regular part of their equipment. As far as I know, there is little information on the use of flags at sports meetings, but at ski-jumping competitions at least the front of the take-off may be draped with a flag. A true sign of the new mass character of the flag was the commercialism that cropped up in its wake. There was now a market for flags and flagpoles and advertisements for both appeared in the press. My hypothesis is that this was the time when flags also crept into private homes, being used in miniature form on Christmas trees or on the table at festive occasions, but the information on this is scanty, indeed, in the sources that I have had at my disposal.

There is an epilogue to all this: the year of the dissolution of the Union in 1905, when flags were used on a hitherto unprecedented scale, being part of an ostentatious panoply of all kinds of glittering and colourful national symbols. In that year, the Union mark was finally removed from the Swedish flag, where it had been preserved in both the military and civil ensign, and from the Norwegian military ensign, where the Union mark had been maintained even after 1898, when the Storting removed it from the civil ensign. Since 1905 there has been only one official flag in Norway, the national flag of 1821, although it is still kept in two versions: the official ensign, swallow-tailed with a tongue, for state use, and the civil ensign for ordinary use.

Note

1   This chapter is based on a broad reading of archival material and printed sources: records from official committees dealing with the flag issue, debates and motions in the Storting, newspaper articles, photographs from the 1880s onwards, and scattered information in the literature and primary sources. Two elderly overviews in the nationalist tradition are Amundsen and Strøm-Ølsen (1936) and Bull (1927). Scholarly studies are few. I have profited from two postgraduate theses: Bjørnson Hofstad (2006) and Imsen (2005)

11 The domestication of a national symbol

The private use of flags in Norway

Anne Eriksen

One day – so the story goes – my great-grandmother went into the garden with a gun, aimed it at the shiny glass ball on the top of the flagpole and hit it in one shot, splintering it completely. More information as to *why* she did this, *who* was present or *what* actually happened is never forthcoming. But the story is always told with smiling admiration for a rather unconventional lady.

This story is a typical example of the kinds of anecdote about living or past members found in most families. They are short, often humorous and – as normally they are well known within the family – are most often not told in their entirety, just referred to by a short phrase or quote. This makes them part of a kind of coded language representing a shorthand version of family history and family ethos. Through them, the family communicates something about itself and its members.

My great-grandmother's attack on the flagpole must have taken place around 1900, and the narrative has been passed down through three generations of the family. This implies that what has made the story attractive and 'tellable' resides not so much in the somewhat abrupt original event as in the meanings created in and by the narrative tradition. The story's message is created through an interweaving of elements from two different fields. One is the prevalent Norwegian understanding of flag symbolism and private use of the flag. The other is family history and, even more specifically, the protagonist's own biography. In a cultural context where the national flag has been thoroughly appropriated for private use, this domesticated symbol has also lent itself to messages playing on the oppositions between private and national, individual and collective, feminine and masculine – not saying as much about the national aspect as characterizing an individual.

The flag in its early years

Norway created its own flag in 1821. The badge marking the Union with Sweden, from 1814, was added in 1844 (see also Grimnes' chapter). During the last decades of the nineteenth century criticism of the Union intensified. Leftists succeeded in making the flag one of the central cultural codifications of this critique. Even though the design of the badge signalled the equality of the two countries, it became the very symbol of Norway's allegedly inferior position within the Union. The demand for a 'pure' flag, without the badge, accompanied the leftists' demand for greater equality or even dissolution of the Union.

Not much is known about the private use of flags in nineteenth-century Norway, but there are clear indications that the left succeeded in making the flag a popular symbol, representing not just the state, but also denoting the country, its landscape and the people itself. Through this process the flag gradually changed from being a political symbol of the left to becoming a sign with ever more generalized cultural meanings.

Originally, the use of the flag within Norway seems to have been quite restricted. While hoisted for royal visits and other state occasions, there was very little private use. In 1838 a royal resolution on the use of the Norwegian merchant flag in foreign trade was eagerly celebrated in the capital, but the festive decorations reported, even on this occasion, included hardly any flags. They were only seen in the harbour, at the Stock Exchange and at the students' union (*Morgenbladet*, 25 April 1838). The state, its foreign affairs and the navy were the main domains of the flag.

An important factor promoting civil, and gradually more private, use of the flag was the celebration of Constitution Day, 17 May. The first more elaborate public celebration took place in Trondheim, in 1826. A detailed report from the celebrations in 1827 shows that a civil parade was the central element. All the city's guilds and corporations took part, carrying their own banners and standards. In addition, banners with national symbols and allegories were used, e.g. one displaying the ancient Norse god Thor 'driving the chariot of the sun of freedom through the clouds', others with the Norwegian heraldic lion or a spruce, interpreted as the Norwegian tree of liberty. The national female allegory Nora was depicted holding the constitution (Aarnes 1994: 12). Inspiration for the symbols and rituals of this and other early 17 May celebrations very obviously comes from revolutionary France, as copies of the feasts and festival marking the revolutionary year during the period from 1789 to the first empire (Simonetti 1989). Hardly any of these symbols have entered the repertoire of Norwegian national iconography on a more permanent basis. While banners and standards seem to have been an important part of the festivities in Trondheim, national flags are not mentioned, nor the use of the Norwegian flag's colours – red, white and blue. One important reason for this is probably that the celebrations during the early years were partly illegal (Aarnes 1994: 17), while the national flag, on the other hand, was very much a state symbol. They conveyed different messages and belonged to different spheres.

The death of the Union's first king in 1844 also led to a change in the authorities' attitude to the Norwegians' wish to celebrate their constitution. The new king, Oscar I, very explicitly stressed formal equality within the Union. This may also have been the direct reason for the first large and more official celebration of Constitution Day in Christiania, also in 1844 (Aarnes 1994). The civil parade still was an important element, and the banners of the guilds and corporations dominated. But the revolutionary iconography was absent and the parade was led by national flags. Draped in black crepe to mourn the recently deceased king, two Norwegian flags and one Swedish flag were carried in front of the parade, which wound through the city centre and up to the royal castle, where all flags and standards were planted.

Political symbols and cultural competence

The next important step in the development of the celebrations was the establishment of a children's parade. Debuting in Christiania (which later became Oslo) in 1870, the idea is usually attributed to the poet and national ideologue Bjørnstjerne Bjørnson, a leading figure of the left wing. The idea was propagated as 'the boys' flag parade' and led to heated debates about which flag the boys were to carry: the 'tricolour' – using this word to refer to the red, white and blue Scandinavian cross – or the one with the Union badge. By now the Union badge had become a symbol of the conservative right, while the 'pure' flag was a symbol of the left and their critical stance. The dispute about the boys' parade thus had important political implications. Nevertheless, the solution to the problem came out of purely practical circumstances. To hold the parade as planned, a large number of small and preferably cheap flags had to be made available. This excluded the Union badge; these flags were too expensive for boys from the lower classes (Aarnes 1994: 18ff.). It is worth noting that the idea of using the national flag in this way was *not* disputed. It was the political significance of the *kind* of flags that was at issue, not the civil use of them. Something had happened during the 26 years that Bjørnson's idea was meant to celebrate: in the parade of 1844, the flag was still a state symbol, carried in front of the civil parade, in part detached from it and strongly related to the king. By1870 it had become a civil symbol to be carried by young boys.

The flag parade quickly became popular, and the practice spread to other cities. But it was not until 1889 that girls took part, without flags, but wearing flowers in their hair. The flag had become a civil symbol, but its use was still reserved for the masculine sphere. The flags they carried marked the boys as the responsible citizens they would become, the future men of the nation. Even though they were taking part in a public parade, the girls were not originally assigned a corresponding role. Their symbolism resigned them to a private/aesthetic sphere of beauty and reproduction. However, after a very period short time, the girls took part on equal footing and the parade acquired its present name: 'the children's parade' (Rolfsen 1892: 223ff.).

In February 1879 a proposal was tabled in the Norwegian Parliament (Odelstinget, the parliament's larger division), to abolish the Union badge, The proposal was not passed, but the issue polarized the political parties and led to a marked growth in the private use of flags and a corresponding increase in the demand for them. A growing number of people bought or made flags, with or without the badge, according to their political stance. The tradition of erecting large, private flagpoles seems to have started in the countryside in this period (Koht 1896: xv). In the cities the polarization found clear expressions during the Constitution Day celebrations. An increase in the use of flags with the badge was reported from the children's parade, while adult citizens added the colours of the badge to the decorations normally worn on this day (*ibid.*).

The urban practice of hoisting flags on buildings – private and public – seems to have become gradually more common from 1844 onwards and was related to the Constitution Day celebrations. Photographs of Norwegian cityscapes show that flagpoles were used on representative buildings in city centres, from Kristiansand in the south to Tromsø in the north, from the 1870s onwards (Digranes *et al.* 1988). These poles normally were fixed on the roofs of the buildings so that the flag could be seen at a distance, even if the pole itself was not very high. On the other hand, hoisting a flag on the top of a steep roof would mean using a ladder or climbing the roof, which suggests that these poles were not used very often. They also presented another problem: the poles might break and fall in stormy weather, causing severe damage. In 1884 a journal in the capital reported that 'some time ago during a strong wind, two flagpoles fell from a roof here in Christiania'. The article referred to Berlin, where such dangers were taken seriously: here it was the responsibility of all property owners to have their flagpoles inspected and certified by the authorities once a year. The journal recommended a similar system for Christiania, but also stressed that iron poles were more solid than wooden ones (if properly fastened!) and had the additional quality of functioning as lightning rods (*Teknisk Ugeblad*, 12 December 1884: 214).

The period from the late 1870s was one of flourishing architectural development, marked by a strong wish to create a specific national architecture. 'The new wooden style', later named 'the Swiss style', came from abroad, but was quickly nationalized and became highly fashionable. Numerous villas and farm dwellings were erected according to these trends, and even today the Norwegian countryside, at least in the southern part of the country, is characterized by the farms' large white 'Swiss style' buildings. The national qualities already attributed to these architectural styles were further enhanced by the close-to-obligatory flagpole, which became a staple element in vernacular garden design in this period. The pole was normally placed in the garden, not in the courtyard, thus belonging to the more private and closed side of the villa or farm. Nonetheless, due to their height (2–3 metres above the roof), the poles – with or without their flags – were visible at a considerable distance. In this way they made up a national signal system. Their message was not just that each farm or villa was a part of the nation, but also that the nation was firmly planted in each garden. The macrocosm of the nation and the microcosm of the family or household mirrored each other.

After the debates of 1879, the left wing continued to diligently work on promoting popular use of the ('pure') flag, and communicating the correct understanding of its symbolism. In the capital, a flag society was established in 1892 to support this cause. A week before Constitution Day, 1893, a considerably successful nationwide appeal was made, calling on the people to hoist the flag. One year later it was proudly reported that on Constitution Day no less than 2,000 flags had been seen on buildings in the capital, approximately 700–800 of them 'pure' tricolours (Koht 1896: xvi). Furthermore, the windows of many shops had been decorated with flags, and even the merchants were now beginning to use the flag without the badge.

In 1896, the Kristiania Flag Association (Kristiania Flagsamband) published a small book of flag songs. The oldest song in this collection is from 1823, the number increasing steadily over the years. Two elements are worth noting. The majority of songs seem to have been written for Constitution Day festivities. Nonetheless, the Norwegian citizen described in the songs – who loves his flag and is proud of it – very frequently is a young sailor in foreign waters. This indicates that the maritime tradition still was strong in the use of the flag: despite its growing popular use, and its meaning as a political symbol within the Union, the primary model for civil use of national flags was still the merchant navy. The other element is a tendency to portray the flag as the nature and landscape of Norway, or to see its nature in the flag: the red, white and blue of the flag are also found in the sky, flowers, snow, and so on, or even in the (feminine) inhabitants' eyes, hair and cheeks. This – very literal – naturalization of the flag has continued to this day, and lyrics equating flag and country with nature still hold a position in the repertoire of songs for the children's parade.

By the end of the nineteenth century, the Norwegian population seems to have developed a considerable cultural competence in the use of the flag. It still was a political symbol, relating to the Union dispute, but as the tricolour gained the (garden) ground, the flag was gradually endowed with broader cultural meanings of undisputed nationality relating to an ordered, civil society as well as to landscape and nature.

Dissolving the Union

In 1898 the Union badge was removed from the merchant flag, an event that cannot have gone unnoticed. But in collective memory, the victory of the tricolour is above all else related to 1905, when the Union with Sweden was dissolved. The 'pure flag' had been the symbol of opposition against the Union (or Norway's position in it) for decades, and the victory of the flag correspondingly is associated with the victory of this opposition. In her memoirs, a woman from northern Norway offered this description of the end of the Union:

> I remember mother's smiling face as she cut the Union badge from our flag. She said, ' – at last we're getting rid of the Swedes – I wonder who

is going to be our new king. There are no Norwegian princes. But a
Swede can't be elected, I would never believe that – that would bring the
old ways back.' Father himself hoisted the pure flag and we all thought
it looked so beautiful, now all those stripes and crosses were gone.

(MO64, no. 59: 16)

The narrative very explicitly equates the removal of the badge with the
dissolution of the Union. Even if it is historically incorrect, the narrative
works well as an allegory for the political events, or rather for the popular
understanding of them. The political drama is condensed in the description
of the mother's treatment of the flag, which in a very concrete way
transforms the issues of Norway's independence and sovereignty into
something domestic and homely. The story creates an impression that what
brought the Union to an end was the resolute activity of ordinary citizens.
The dissolution was executed with a pair of scissors at the kitchen table, at
last cutting the nation free from its long and humiliating bondage. This
vigorous feminine act is then completed by the father's task, and after he has
hoisted the pure flag, the entire family/nation can admire the result of their
common efforts.

1905 also brought two referendums on whether Norway should be a
republic or a monarchy, and (later) on who should be the new king. On these
occasions, flags were mandatory on all public buildings, and a number of
private citizens also chose to hoist their flags. A man from northern Norway
tells that his father, who was Chairman of the county council, wanted to
hoist a flag at their home to mark the political leanings of the family. They
had no pole, but the problem was solved with the aid of a telephone pole
in the street running past their house. The neighbouring vicar, on the other
hand, had two poles in his garden, but as a conservative who did not support the Union's dissolution, he left them demonstratively bare. However,
when the vicar returned from church, where the referendum was being
held, his home had dramatically taken on a new appearance. His energetic,
and somewhat malicious, neighbour had used his authority as Chairman
of the municipality (*rådmann*) to order two flags from the local shop, and
had hoisted them at the vicarage. On coming home the vicar saw the flags
happily billowing in the wind (MO81, No. 94: 21).

The story does not just bear witness to the diffusion and distribution of
flags and poles, even in rather remote parts of the country, but also to the
flag competence of the population. It becomes quite obvious that if the flag
is a sign of its owner's political affiliation, the pole is no less so. Having a
pole and not using it, in this context, is just as clear a statement as flying the
flag. The Chairman's hoisting of flags on the vicar's poles thus is not just a
violation of his private property, but also of his political opinions.

The only way to avoid taking direct part in the national and political
discourse developing around the use of flags was to not have a pole in the
garden. A Norwegian woman who grew up in Sweden, due to her family's

business, relates that during the summer of 1905, when there was a very strong possibility that Norway's break from the Union could lead to war between the two countries, her family encountered severe problems concerning the two flagpoles in their garden: should they fly the Norwegian or the Swedish flag? What about the Union badge? What would bare poles communicate? For this family, living close to the border where soldiers passed daily and the tension was mounting, the only solution was to cut down both poles (MO.81, Os.89: 2).

War and resistance

After the winning of national independence in 1905, Constitution Day continued to be an occasion for political manifestations, now mainly related to the struggles of the Labour movement. Their 'pure' flag was the red one, and it was flown in the parades on Constitution Day as well as on 1 May (May Day). But despite these new political connotations, equating the national with the bourgeois, and the international with the radical working class, the tricolour by now also seems to have acquired indisputable national meanings, placing it above political strife. Growing up in a fishing village in northern Norway, a man born in 1922 claims that Constitution Day normally was not celebrated in his community: in May all the men were working in the great fisheries, while the women and children were busy tending the small farms. He remembers the teacher one year, in his best clothes and with a flag, passing his mother who was planting potatoes. He reprimanded her for working on Constitution Day, but was told that she had more important things do to than strutting along the road. Still, this man also underlines the importance of the flag: the fishing boats always had it with them, hoisting it on return to signal that all was well, the catch good and no lives lost. Ashore it was used to signal births and deaths (at half mast) in the community. For this man, the meaning of the flag was primarily local, not related to politics, the Constitution or the king, but to the life and death of people in the village (NEG 161, no. 30360).

One factor serving both to strengthen the flag competence developed during the last part of nineteenth century, and to pass this on to new generations, was the Scout movement. Founded in Great Britain in 1907, it was established in Norway in 1911 (for boys) and 1921 (for girls). Primarily an educational organization for children and youth, the organization also has its own symbols and rituals. Greeting and honouring the flag (the national flag and the organization's own flag) are important rituals in the Scouting movement. Even today, many Norwegians refer to the Scouts when asked where they have learned how to treat the flag (NEG 161).

On 9 April 1940, Norway was invaded by German forces. Two months of fighting ended with capitulation in June. The country was governed by the Germans until liberation in May 1945, part of the time with the aid of a Norwegian puppet government. From 1942 onwards a resistance movement developed, and, in addition to this, popular resistance to the occupation was expressed through a variety of symbols and symbolic actions. Symbolic resistance is communication: to be effective, somebody must read it as resistance. 'Luckily', for the Norwegian population, restrictions on the use of the national flag were introduced from 1941, prohibiting, for example, the carrying of flags, use of the flag (or the colours referring to it) on clothing and so on. Regulations 'for the protection of the flag' implied that it could only be legally used by the authorities. Even if no restriction ever directly forbade the celebration of Constitution Day, the various regulations left no doubt in mind that it was not allowed, thus creating a unique opportunity for symbolic resistance. Secret celebrations of Constitution Day are a very important motif in the collective memory about the war. Such celebrations were private and hidden, disguised as picnics or family gatherings. The flag was present as red, white and blue flowers, or other non-conspicuous decorations (Esborg 1995: 76ff.). During the rest of the year the flag was also an important element of the symbolic resistance. In some parts of the country anonymous dare-devils painted large flags on rocks and cliffs, in places that were very difficult to reach, but where the flags could be clearly seen from the sea or the air (cf. for example, NEG 161, no. 30404). Postcards and other images that 'happened' to contain something that might be read as a flag were popular. As the flag could not be carried openly, hidden ones, or objects with its colours, served the same function. A woman from Oslo says:

> The colours of the flag were our first symbols. Shops which still sold something with the flag in it were extremely popular. It could be postcards, pencils, corkscrews or ribbons. Myself, I owned a hexagonal pencil with our colours, which I used to carry in my pocket.
>
> (NEG 161, no. 30443; Esborg 1995)

Such use of pencils or corkscrews probably did not have great impact on the outcome of Word War II, but it was very much a part of developing a national ethos in Norway, and reinforced the understanding of the flag as a common symbol, uncontestedly denoting the people, the national landscape and the national community. The woman above refers to the flag as *our* symbol and *our* colours, and describes how this national symbol also is the expression of a personal identity – the nation is firmly kept in her own pocket.

Liberation, in May 1945, also meant liberation of the flag. As was the case with the collective memory of 1905, the flag again works as an image of the political events. As the news about the German defeat spread, flags were hoisted on flagpoles, and were hung on buildings, fences, and from verandas. Suddenly the country was covered with flags that had been hidden away for five years waiting patiently for the Day (cf. Eriksen 1995).

The flag today

In 1992 a questionnaire on national symbols was sent by Norsk etnologisk gransking (Norwegian Ethnological Research) to its habitual network of informants who supplied information on a wide range of cultural-history topics (NEG 161). One of the queries was about the flag, and the, approximately 125, answers are remarkably unanimous, regardless of gender or age. The only geographical variation concerning the use of the flag seems to be that in the northern and western parts of the country the poles tend to break in stormy weather. Modern steel poles are reported to have increased the use of flags in these regions.

Flags fixed to the house by means of a short diagonal pole are becoming increasingly popular all over the country for a number of reasons. For people living in flats, it is a practical solution; the flag can be fixed to the balcony. Modern single-family houses frequently do not have large gardens, and thus do not have the space needed to lower the pole for repair and inspection. But the main reason for the popularity of these smaller flags appears to be that the flag does not need to be lowered, both the pole and flag are easily removed from the fitting on the wall. The main advantage of this is to avoid showing a bare pole on the days where the flag ought to be hoisted. A man from Oslo explains:

> The grounds around my house are spacious enough for a flagpole, but [this necessitates] hoisting and lowering the flag according to the prescribed laws and times of the day. I used to be away in the weekends, at least in my younger years. I think this is the reason why a tall pole has never been erected, even if I think that a tall white pole with a large pure Norwegian flag flying in the wind speaks directly to the heart.
>
> (NEG 161, no. 30527)

A flag hanging in the dark is a major *faux pas*, to be avoided at all costs. His comment about the 'prescribed laws and times of the day' thus does not criticize these regulations, but rather reveals his respect for them: it is better not to have a flagpole than not to be able to comply with the rules. Several answers comment on this in the same way. The flag must be hoisted at dawn and lowered at sunset, and it must be flown on all flag days – if one has a pole. A removable pole gives greater freedom. Then the flag is 'hoisted' for Constitution Day, Christmas and some other flag days, but not, it is underlined, on royal birthdays. The flag is also used on a number of private occasions, family and neighbourhood birthdays being the most frequent. A closer reading of the answers shows that those who actually have a large fixed pole also use it according to this pattern: they also skip a number of official flag days and add a number of their own. This would not be so remarkable if the same answers did not also heavily stress the importance of complying with the regulations, and the social disgrace that bare poles on flag days represented.

Flag regulations in Norway, for example printed in all calendars, are in accordance with what the answers report: the flag is to be hoisted at 9 am during winter, at 8 am in summer. It is to be lowered at sunset, but no later than 9 pm. Special rules apply in northern Norway and Svalbard for the winter season.[1] But in vernacular culture other rules are added. They are not found in any public regulations, but are quoted and treated as if they have such a position. The flag must be honoured. It must never touch the ground. It must be properly folded (some even stress that a correctly folded flag should only show the red colour). It may drape a coffin, but nothing else. When worn out the flag must be burnt or destroyed in such a way that it is unrecognizable. Such rules are also to be found on the websites of Norwegian producers and vendors of flags and poles. The probable origin of these rules is the Scout movement. Some of the answers explicitly mention the Scouts, but a far greater number refer to the rules in a self-evident way, on a par with the other flag regulations. In this way the answers create the impression that the use of the Norwegian flag is governed by a large number of very strict regulations, which the citizens strive to comply with, even if this is demanding. This severe image is accompanied by utterances which further underline that the flag is no joking matter. Flags as decoration on clothes are ugly, incorrect and unworthy. Flags do not belong to fashion. Painting one's face with the flag colours for sports events, or draping oneself in the flag, is disrespectful.

But on the other hand, the flag and the flag colours are used for home decorations on Constitution Day. Candles and napkins may be in red, white and blue. Flags are used on Christmas tree and on cakes. Flags on clothes may be excusable if the clothes are for outdoor activities like skiing, and even painting the face for a sports event may be acceptable if a Norwegian wins! And the ceremoniously hoisted flag may also be flying to celebrate the acquisition of a new diving board at the summer house (NEG 161, no. 30443). This somewhat inconsistent attitude probably gives a good picture of the position of the flag in Norwegian culture. On the one hand it is loved and respected as a very solemn national symbol, and, on the other, it is domesticated and appropriated as the property of every individual Norwegian, fit for his or her private use. To quote one of the flag producers on its website: 'If you have a pole, you can use the flag whenever you want. Private individuals may choose whether or not to hoist their flag on flag days'.[2]

A return to the anecdote

This cultural history of the flag is the background for the anecdote about my great-grandmother, and the context for the meanings that have been read into it during a century of tradition. The event took place on a farm just outside Oslo. Today, its grounds have been incorporated into one of the capital's new suburbs, but the large, white dwelling is heritage protected and has been preserved. The flagpole no longer stands in the slightly sloping garden, but, apart from this, the building still looks just as it did in the large photograph in my grandmother's sitting-room. This photograph is not just a part of family history, it also relates to a larger frame of national iconography, which is alive and well, even today. It still represents an image of how farms in Norway are supposed to look, at least in the southern part of the country and at least in the period from the late 1800s to the present: the red barn, white house, and white flagpole in the garden are the standard elements of this rural landscape. When a flag is hoisted on each pole – as it is for Christmas, Constitution Day, and so on – the result is an effective and impressive nationalization of the landscape, with the flag at the same time incorporated as one of its natural elements. The farms, with their red and white buildings, preferably under a blue sky, denote 'the past', 'the rural' and 'the national roots'.

The pole is part of the symbolic language of these farms and the national landscape they create. During the latter part of the nineteenth century, when such poles were first erected, they above all supplied the means to mark political standpoints. But in a local context the white pole crowned by its shining ball also signifies a degree of affluence, revealing resources above what had been strictly necessary for the daily life of the family and the running of the farm. And, as the answers to the questionnaire clearly demonstrate, the pole signals a well-ordered life. Respectable citizens honour their fatherland by hoisting its flag, but this has to be done according to the rules: one has to remember the flag days, and to be at home at dawn and dusk to hoist and lower the flag, one's life has to be governed by a degree of discipline. A bare pole on flag days, or a flag still flying when it should have been taken down, become very explicit – and highly visible – signs of disorder and chaos.

The pole signifies that the self-sufficient and harmonious microcosm of the farm with its family and servants is part of the nation's larger macrocosm. Through the pole and its flag, the nation is literally rooted in the private garden, in the centre of family life and happy family reunions. Seen from a distance the pole and its flag signal that 'this farm is part of the nation'. In the closer perspective of flower arrangements and playing children, the same pole says: 'the nation is here, in our garden'. Through the pole the nation is domesticated.

The anecdote about my great-grandmother plays on the contrast between this harmonious scene of respectable family life and the sudden shot splintering the peace and tranquillity as well as the glass ball. The effect is amplified by the fact that a woman pulls the trigger. On the one hand the place where the event takes place belongs to the feminine sphere of the farm. The garden and flagpole are situated on the private side of the building, as opposed to the more public farmyard. This is the place for family life and peacefully playing children. The tending of the garden is also a feminine task, as opposed to the men's farm work with the soil. On the other hand, the woman who in this case enters her garden is not there to prepare the table for a peaceful summer meal, to cut her roses, or to admonish her children. She is carrying a gun and very resolutely fires it. The story says only one thing about her motivation for doing this: she wants to prove that she is a good shot. The shot is a demonstrative act of loud bragging, a very unfeminine thing to do.

The story is told with smiling admiration. This is probably not due so much to the fact that the shot hit quite a small object at rather a long distance, but more to the paradox that it was fired in the thoroughly domestic, even feminine, sphere of the garden. The anecdote would not have had the same effect if it told that a flowerpot on the fence was the target. It is an important narrative point that the shot was fired at the one element in the garden that does not purely relate to the domestic and feminine context, but, on the contrary, represents the link between the familial and private on the one hand and the official or national on the other: the pole. The shot goes far beyond the garden, not just above it. It reaches out of the private and into the public sphere.

Hitting the glass ball means showing off shooting skills, but it also represents a rather arrogant domination of the national. The flagpoles in the gardens communicate a message about national identity successfully constructed: the private sphere has become part of the national sphere. But my great-grandmother's shot shows that there are other sides to the relationship. The nation is not just domesticated, but tamed and commodified, becoming subject to the will of private persons. In this case, the shot shows that the domestic sphere of family and femininity is not without its own dangers, or without force and a will to commit subversive acts. Still, the shot could not have been fired when the flag was hoisted; at least, that would have made quite another story. Shooting at the flag, even in one's own garden, would have been an act of national sacrilege far beyond friendly admiration and humorous family anecdotes. Hitting the pole is sufficiently arrogant to be amusing, so much of a paradox to give the story a point – but it is not outrageous.

So far the meanings of the story have been of a general kind, concerning the relationship between public and private, national and feminine, peaceful family life and unexpected skill, will and force. In addition to this, the narrative carries a message that more directly concerns the protagonist herself, and which probably is the reason why it has been a family tradition for so long. It is also close to the only narrative I have heard about my great-grandmother. My grandmother – her daughter – in general spoke very little about her parents, and my knowledge about them comes from other sources. My great-grandmother was married to the son of a wealthy neighbourhood farmer. The marriage was probably arranged by the parents, as her brother married her husband's sister at about the same time. This made it possible to keep the property of the two families undivided. The marriage was not a happy one, and after giving birth to three children my great-grandmother obtained a divorce. She acquired one of her fathers' farms and ran it herself, also taking her name from this farm. Later, she married a man of her own choice, 20 years her junior and socially somewhat below her, and moved with him to another part of the country. The episode with the pole took place during the time she lived with her children as a divorced woman.

Her biography may be read as presenting a strong and resourceful woman, but there was probably little admiration for her choices at the time when the events took place. Divorce was a scandal in the 1890s, a social disgrace. That the husband was a hopeless drunkard did not improve matters, nor did the fact that the divorcee later married her children's young teacher. My grandmother refused to speak about these events, and she and her siblings also refused to bear their father's name. They removed his picture from all the family albums and his name from family documents. I will not attempt to provide any deep psychological interpretation of my grandmother's feelings towards her family, but find it obvious that the short anecdote has worked as a means to communicate a message that was otherwise difficult to articulate, giving a kind of condensed portrait of her mother. The family of the woman who broke the domestic peace of her garden by shooting at the pole and hitting the glass ball had already been splintered. The happy family in the national microcosm of the garden did not really exist in this case. This was in part her own doing: to save herself and her children she had broken her marriage and left her husband. The financial position of her own family made such an act possible, but not acceptable. At the time of the shot she had her own property and ran her farm like a man. Later, she secured her happiness with a husband of her own choice. She proved herself a resourceful person, but hardly one following the conventions of the period, or her age, gender and social class. She had splintered her social role and lost much of her social position long before she shot the flagpole.

This is not intended as an interpretation of what the shot meant when it was fired, but one that has been generated and passed on by the narrative tradition. It has been possible to make the short narrative convey such a message of contrasts, paradoxes and difficult emotions just because the flag and the pole work as cultural ready-mades, with vague, generally accepted and not too complicated meanings. As any other convenient household articles, they were useful tools, coming in handy when needed.

Abbreviations

NEG 161: Answers to Questionnaire no. 161, distributed in 1992 by Norsk etnologisk granskning (Norwegian Ethnological Research, at Norsk Folkemuseum, Oslo).

MO64, MO81: *Minneoppgave for eldre*, 1964 and 1981, respectively. Collections of memoirs of older people in Norsk folkeminnesamling (Norwegian Folklore Archives) at the University of Oslo.

Notes

1   http://www.lovdata.no/for/sf/ud/xd-19271021-9733.html
2   http://www.hytte.no/flaggstang.html

12 Afterword

Iver B. Neumann

According to C. S. Pierce (1977), there are three basic kinds of signs. 'Icons' have a physical resemblance to what they signify. 'Indices' have a causal relationship to what they signify. 'Symbols' have an arbitrary relationship to what they signify. The symbol, which to Pierce is the proper sign, is distinct from an icon or an index in having no intrinsic meaning. Without explanation, the uninitiated will know nothing of what it signifies.

At first glance, a flag is a symbol. Indeed, the class of flags called 'semaphores' may be the closest thing we have to a pure symbol. But let's glance again. First, flags may include icons and indices. The red circle on Japan's flag bears a physical resemblance to the sun, perhaps even to the rising sun. It is an icon. So are the different-shaped crosses that appear in a number of flags of Christian origins. The sword on the flag of Saudi Arabia bears witness to the military strength and prowess of the state (and, since this is a state that bears the name of a family, presumably of the Sauds as well). It is an index.

Secondly, the national flag is a symbol of the second order. It symbolises something that in turn symbolises something else. What this something is, has changed historically. At first, the flag signified the King and the dynasty, or more precisely, the ruler. The flag of the Sovereign Military and Hospitaller Order of St John of Jerusalem, Rhodes and Malta, recognised as a sovereign entity by 89 others of that class, remains the flag of its Grand Master (a good idea, inasmuch as the order of St John presently has no territory).[1] The King's colours had everything to do with the territory ruled by the king, and little or nothing to do with a specific territory as such. During the sixteenth and seventeenth centuries, the concept of Kingly power as such transmuted into the concept of Kingly power over a specific (and increasingly contiguous) territory. The meaning of extant national flags changed. They still symbolised dynasty (cf. the expression 'the King's colours') but, increasingly, also began to signify the territory as such. But all the way up to the Napoleonic Wars, in times of peace flags were only used at sea and on fortresses. It was the military aspect of the King that was symbolised by the flag, and not the other aspects.

With the change in the principle of sovereignty that began in the late-eighteenth century, as the people took the place of God as the legitimating force, the flag developed yet another referent, namely the people. With reference to the US, Marvin and Ingle (1996) suggested that the root meaning of the flag is bodily sacrifice, and that this speaks first and foremost to the working classes, who have nothing to offer but their bodies. Be that as it may, if the King flies a flag these days, it is not necessarily the same flag as the national one. In those cases where he does not, the symbolic separation has manifested itself in a separation of flags as well.

At issue here is the awareness of the subjects, as to whether a flag symbolises the King, his territory, the people or perhaps some other state entity. Before the Boston tea party, for example, certain US rebels used the Union Jack in order to signal that their quarrel was with the government, and not with the King. The paradigmatic event for the change of symbolism that is at issue here hails from the same period. It is the change of national standard in revolutionary France, away from the lily flag of the Bourbons and the *ancien régime*, to the revolutionary *tricolore*. A similar move may be observed where other national standards are concerned, however. As pointed out by Richard Jenkins, Dannebrog, which fell down from the sky in 1219 and is the oldest flag now used as a national one, found its way from a nobility that was unwilling to share it to a people that was increasingly keen on having it. But as Orvar Löfgren reminds us, in the old military state of Sweden, as recently as in the late nineteenth century the people were at first unwilling to accept non-military uses of the flag.

Negotiations about the flag seem, in this regard, to be an ongoing business, which make for all kinds of interesting comparative usages. In the US, flags are routinely flown in front of state (or, to underline the rather timid nature of this aspect of statehood, 'official') buildings such as post offices. That is not the case in most other countries. In Denmark, the flag insinuates itself into many, if not most, private festivities. That would never happen in Chechnia. One way of thinking about this is in terms of Walter Benjamin's concept of aura, which he defined as 'the unique manifestation of a distance, however close at hand' (Shiff 2003). The flag manifests the nation at a distance. Historically, as national sovereignty spreads, the distance between what is represented and the citizen becomes shorter and shorter; from the battlefield and the fortress to the King's castle to state buildings to homes. This seems to hold for all cases, regardless of variations in contexts such as regime type and state/society configuration.

The flag symbolises the sovereign state, and the state may be understood as one of, or as any one constellation of, the following three entities: the central administration (e.g. King), the territory and the people. The quarrels about the Norwegian flag in the late nineteenth century, discussed above by Anne Eriksen and Ole Kristian Grimnes, may be seen as one instance of a debate about what this constellation should be. Should the Swedish King's colours be included in the upper left-hand corner, which is the most prestigious quadrant of the flag, or should the King be left out? Similar problems mark the history of the Australian, New Zealand and Canadian flags.

Thirdly, as demonstrated by the previous point, the national standard is a European symbol, which is much older than the nation. It has spread from Europe to the states system, and beyond that to the global system of both state and non-state entities. This is not to say that flag symbolism is exclusively European; far from it. Most states associated with Islam will fly green, the colour of the prophet, as one of their colours. It does, however, mean that flags are embedded in a heraldic tradition with rules of its own. One consequence of this is that one may often use the colours involved, and not least the shades of colour, to spot which flags have a long history as national ones, and which do not. Like nationalisms themselves, national standards have a modular quality about them. They tend to depend on a colour scheme of horizontals or verticals. Like sovereignty itself, the national flag has a dual quality. It is part of a series of flags, and as such it is ordinary. On the other hand, given the subtle differences, it stands out from the series as unique.

From Nietzsche to Foucault and beyond, one approach to the history of a certain phenomenon has been genealogical, in which the point of departure is how things are today. The researcher will then fast-rewind to a time when things were different, and identify the historical breaking point that ushered in today's state of affairs. This work is often facilitated by the presence of remnants of previous orders in our world, here and now. An example would be the plural of nouns in English; they usually end in -s, but there was a time when they usually ended in -en. Certain nouns, such as oxen, still serve as living reminders of that. Where national flags are concerned, they are all, bar one, square or rectangular. The exception is the Nepali flag, which, on closer inspection, turns out to be a remnant of a whole class of sub-continental flags that were often pennant-shaped, and certainly not rectangular.[2] It has been said that a language is a dialect with an army and a navy behind it; the European rectangular-shaped flag certainly became dominant as a consequence of colonialism. For additional empirical evidence, witness the fact that the Ethiopian flag derives from a three-pennant flag. The pennants were red, yellow and green. These colours were later used in a number of other African flags, but the Ethiopian as well as the other national flags stuck to the rectangular shape that had been introduced by the Europeans.

The logic of the sovereign state having a flag is so strong that any other political entity with aspirations not only to sovereignty, but to some kind of agency, in global politics will acquire a flag under which to fight their campaign for recognition. From the Palestine Authority to Assam, aspiring nation states have flags. Trans-national firms like Shell and Nissan have flags. NGOs traditionally have flags, from the Red Cross to Amnesty International. Multinational organisations – the UN, NATO, ASEAN – they all have flags. The EU even took over the old flag of the Council of Europe. The Jolly Roger is no historical anomaly. Pirates were the enemies of the state par excellence, excommunicated by international law as *hostes generi humanis*, enemies of mankind. Pirates were no collective actor, but they were treated as a category by the powers that be, and they recognised that by flying their own flag. Conventionally, so has that other enemy of mankind recognised by international law, the terrorist. The Red Brigades, for example, had a flag. We will get to know if things have changed in this respect when we see whether Al Quaida will adopt a flag (green banners already being in evidence). We have here also a reminder of the limits of a flag's multivocality; it may mean different things to different people in different contexts, but it still carries with it the basic function it had on the battlefield, namely separating 'us' from 'them'. When different flags are flown side by side, it is a way of signalling solidarity or 'brotherhood', not integration. On state territory, that state's flag bows to no other, except the invisible flag of death that is supposed to outrank it, when it is flown at half mast (that is, two-thirds up the pole).

As a European symbol of a symbol, the flag's arbitrariness is somewhat circumscribed. For example, given that the colour schemes of flags seem to be tied up either with natural features or with heraldry, it is possible to guess that the Ukrainian flag – top blue half above bottom yellow half – symbolises the sky above a cornfield. Again, given that orange is not rampant in natural environments, and definitely not on the parallel where the Netherlands and Ireland are to be found, it is clear that the colour's symbolism in the Dutch and Irish flags derives from the heraldic colour of the House of Orange.

This book is rich in accounts of the flag featured in symbolic interaction. It sutures in-groups and excludes out-groups by demarcating geographical and social boundaries.[3] It seems to be able to do so in the most quotidian as well as in the most sublime settings. It hangs at, or from, the top of the most elevated buildings. In Britain, at least, it adorns the torsos of royalty and the backsides of commoners. American politicians wrap themselves in it, sometimes even literally. Sports spectators go one better, by painting it onto their faces or their entire bodies. Some even better that by having it tattooed or branded on their skins. In pre-modern societies, flags belonged to royalty and nobility. In modern societies, they were extended to the people, understood as an entity. In post-modern societies they emerged on the bodies of individuals, finally to creep onto, or perhaps even under, their skin. A good symbol should be all things to all people, anytime, anywhere. That is, of course, impossible, but the flag may be the closest thing the world has seen so far.

Notes

1 As if to underline the point, upon taking office, each Grand Master may make small modifications to the Grand Master's flag, and fly it as his very own.
2 See: http://fotw.vexillum.com/flags/in-princ.html#alpha
3 See, particularly, Dominic Bryan's chapter in this collection.

Bibliography

Aarnes, S. A. (1994) 'Oppfinnelsen av 17. mai', *Nytt norsk tidsskrift*, vol. 1: 10–23.

Adriansen, I. (1999) 'Dannebrog – statens symbol eller folkets? Danske flagstikke gennem 150 år', in B. Stoklund (ed.) *Kulturens Nationalisering: Et etnologisk perspektiv på det nationale*, Copenhagen: Museum Tusculanums Forlag.

Alderman, D. H., Mitchell, P. W., Webb, J. T. and Hanak, D. (2003) 'Carolina Thunder Revisited: Toward a Transcultural View of Winston Cup Racing', *Professional Geographer*, vol. 55: 238–49.

Allen, T. (1994) *The Invention of the White Race*, New York: Verso.

Amundsen, S. S. and Strøm-Olsen, A. (1927) *Norges Flagg*, Oslo: J. W. Cappelens forlag.

—— (1936) *Norges Flagg*, 2nd edn, Fagbiblioteket fri lesning, Oslo: J. W. Cappelens forlag.

Anderson, B. (1991) *Imagined Communities. An Inquiry into the Origins and Spread of Nationalism*, 2nd edn, London: Verso.

Andio, A. T. (2001) 'Lake City Clash over Flag Coincides with Olustee Fest', *Jacksonville Time-Union*, February 15, 2001.

Associated Press (2006) 'At L.S.U., Tailgating Instead of Marching', *New York Times*, September 3, 2006.

Atlanta Journal-Constitution (2004) 'Flags Have Inclusion in Common' (editorial), February 27, 2004.

Ayers, E. L. (1996) 'What We Talk About When We Talk About the South', in E. L. Ayers, P. N. Limerick, S. Nissenbaum and P. S. Onuf, *All Over the Map: Rethinking American Regions*, Baltimore, MD: Johns Hopkins University Press.

Balle-Petersen, M. (1979) 'Commentary', *Ethnologica Scandinavica* 1979: 29–33.

Barker, S., Balloch, J. and Alapo, L. (2005) 'Rebel Flag Fuss: School Board Decision to Ban Emblem at Games Divides City', *Knoxville News*, September 11, 2005, http://www.knoxnews.com/kns/local_news/article/0,1406,KNS_347_407——,00.html

Barth, F. (1969) *Ethnic Groups and Boundaries: The Social Organization of Culture Difference*, Boston, MA: Little Brown.

Beirich, H. and Moser, B. (2003) 'Outfitting Dixie', *Intelligence Report* no. 110, Southern Poverty Law Center.

Belfast City Council (2004) *Flying the Flag: An Equality Impact Assessment*, http://www.belfastcity.gov.uk/equality/docs/FlyingOfUnionFlagEQIA.pdf

Berger, P. L. and Luckmann, T. (1967) *The Social Construction of Reality*, London: Allen Lane.

Bergsten, M. (1997) 'Flagga för kung och fosterland', *Populär Historia*, no. 2: 38–9.
Bessinger, M. (2001) *Defending My Heritage: The Maurice Bessinger Story*, West Columbia, SC: Lmbone-Lehone Publishing Company.
Billig, M. (1995) *Banal Nationalism*, London: Sage.
Biörnstad, A. (1976) 'Svenska flaggans bruk', *Fataburen* 1976: 43–56.
Bjørnson Hofstad, M. (2006) 'Et splittelsens tegn': Flaggstriden i Norge på 1890 tallet, Ph.D thesis (*Hovedoppgave*), University of Oslo.
Blackmon, D. A. (2001) 'Foes of Confederate Flag Struggle in Mississippi Vote', *The Wall Street Journal*, April 17, 2001.
Boas, K. (1994) 'En ægte sællert', *Politiken Søndag*, 10 July 1994: 9.
Bodnar, J. (1992) *Remaking America: Public Memory, Commemoration, and Patriotism in the Twentieth Century*, Princeton, NJ: Princeton University Press.
—— (1994) 'Public Memory in an American City: Commemoration in Cleveland', in J. R. Gillis (ed.) *Commemoration: The Politics of National Identity*, Princeton, NJ: Princeton University Press.
—— (ed.) (1996) *Bonds of Affection*, Princeton, NJ: Princeton University Press.
Boime, A. (1998) *The Unveiling of the National Icons*, Cambridge: Cambridge University Press.
Bonner, R. E. (2002) *Colors and Blood: Flag Passions of the Confederate South*, Princeton, NJ: Princeton University Press.
Bonnett, A. (2000) *White Identities: Historical and International Perspectives*, Harlow: Prentice Hall.
Borish, S. (1991) *The Land of the Living: The Danish Folk High Schools and Denmark's Non-violent Path to Modernization*, Nevada City, CA: Blue Dolphin.
Borneman, J. (1992) *Belonging in the Two Berlins: Kin, State, Nation*, Cambridge: Cambridge University Press.
Bourdieu, P. (1977) *Outline of a Theory of Practice*, Cambridge: Cambridge University Press.
—— (1990) *The Logic of Practice*, Cambridge: Polity.
Boutell, C. (1978) *Boutell's Heraldry*, rev. J. P. Brooke-Little, London: Warne.
Brack, A. (2004) 'Palmetto Bowl May Become Victim to Confederate Flag', *South Carolina State House Report*, http://www.statehousereport.com/columns/04.0627.bowl.htm
Brant, M. (2002) *Freebirds: The Lynyrd Skynyrd Story*, New York: Billboard Books.
Brown, K. and MacGinty, R. (2003) 'Public Attitudes towards Partisan and Neutral Symbols in Post-Agreement Northern Ireland', *Identities: Global Structures in Culture and Power*, vol. 10: 83–108.
Bryan, D. (2000) *Orange Parades: The Politics of Ritual Tradition and Control*, London: Pluto.
—— (2004) 'Parading Protestants and Consenting Catholics in Northern Ireland: Communal Conflict, Contested Public Space, and Group Rights', *Chicago Journal of International Law*, vol. 5, no. 1: 233–50.
Bryan, D. and Gillespie, G. (2005) *Transforming Conflict: Flags and Emblems*, Belfast: Institute of Irish Studies.
Bryan, D. and McIntosh, G. (2005) 'Symbols: Sites of Creation and Contest in Northern Ireland', *SAIS Review*, vol. 25, no. 2: 127–37.
Bryson, L. and McCartney, C. (1994) *Clashing Symbols: A Report on the Use of Flags, Anthems and Other National Symbols in Northern Ireland*, Belfast: Institute of Irish Studies, for the Community Relations Council.

Buckley, A. D. (1985–6) '"The Chosen Few": Biblical Texts in the Regalia of an Ulster Secret Society', *Folk Life*, vol 29.

—— (ed.) (1998) *Symbols in Northern Ireland*. Belfast: Institute of Irish Studies.

Buckley, A. D. and Kenny, M. (1995) *Negotiating Identity: Rhetoric, Metaphor and Social Drama in Northern Ireland*, Washington, DC: Smithsonian Institute Press.

Bull, E. (1927) 'Det norske flags historie', in J. S. Worm-Müller (ed.) *Den norske sjøfarts historie fra de ældste tider til vore dager, volume 3*, Oslo: Steenske Forlag.

Bulmer, M. (ed.) (1982) *Social Research Ethics: An Examination of the Merits of Covert Participation*, London: Macmillan.

Burgess, R. (1984) *In the Field: An Introduction to Field Research*, London: Allan and Unwin.

Cannon, D. D. (1998) *The Flags of the Confederacy: An Illustrated History*, Memphis, TN: St Luke's Press.

Carter, D. T. (1995) *The Politics of Rage*, New York: Simon and Schuster.

Cawthorne, N. (2004) *The Strange Laws of Old England*, London: Portrait.

CBS News (2005) 'The Real NASCAR Family', *60 Minutes*, October 6, 2005, http://www.cbsnews.com/stories/2005/10/06/60minutes/main919340.shtml

Chatterjee, P. (1999) *The Partha Chatterjee Omnibus*, Oxford: Oxford University Press

Clark, E. C. (1993) *The Schoolhouse Door: Segregation's Last Stand at the University of Alabama*, New York: Oxford University Press.

Cohen, A. P. (1982) 'Belonging: The Experience of Culture', in A. P. Cohen (ed.) *Belonging: Identity and Social Organisation in British Rural Cultures*, Manchester: Manchester University Press.

—— (1985) *The Symbolic Construction of Community*, London: Tavistock (subsequently Routledge).

Cohodas, N. (1997) *The Band Played Dixie: Race and the Liberal Conscience at Ole Miss*, New York: Free Press.

Coski, J. M. (2005) *The Confederate Battle Flag: America's Most Embattled Emblem*, Cambridge, MA: The Belknap Press of Harvard University Press.

Craige, B. J. (1996) *American Patriotism in a Global Society*, Albany, NY: State University of New York.

Crampton, W. (1992) *The World of Flags: A Pictorial History*, 2nd edn, London: Studio Editions.

—— (1989) *The Complete Guide to Flags: Identifying and Understanding the Flags of the World*, London: Kingfisher.

Cronin, M. and Adair, D. (2002) *The Wearing of the Green: The History of St Patrick's Day*, London: Routledge.

Curtis, M. K. (ed) (1993) *The Constitution and the Flag: The Flag Burning Cases*, New York: Garland.

Danmarks-Samfundet (1992), *Sådan bør man bruge Dannebrog*, 5th edn, Brøndby: Danmarks-Samfundet.

Davenport, J. (2006) 'Confederate Group to Challenge NCAA Ban', Associated Press, November 22, 2006.

Davey, K. (1999) *English Imaginaries: Six Studies in Anglo-British Modernity*, London: Lawrence and Wishart.

Davis, J. (1992) *Exchange*, Buckingham: Open University Press.

Davis, J. W. (1998) 'An Air of Defiance: Georgia's State Flag Change of 1956', *Georgia Historical Quarterly*, vol. 82: 305–30.

Delgado, R. and Stefancic, J. (2001) *Critical Race Theory: An Introduction*, New York: New York University Press.

Devereux, E. (1992) *The Book of World Flags*, London: New Burlington Books and Apple Press.

Digranes, Å., Greve, S. and Reiakvam, O. (ed.) (1988) *Det norske bildet: Knud Knudsens fotografier 1864–1900*, Oslo: Grøndahl.

Du Bois, W. E. B. (1989) [1903] *The Souls of Black Folks*, New York: Bantam Classic.

Duara, P. (1993) 'De-constructing the Chinese Nation', *Australian Journal of Chinese Affairs*, no. 30: 1–26.

Durkheim, E. (1976) *The Elementary Forms of Religious Life*, 2nd edn, London: George Allen and Unwin.

Durkheim, E. and Mauss, M. (1963) [1903] *Primitive Classification*, trans. Rodney Needham, London: Cohen and West.

Ehn, B. and Löfgren, O. (1982) *Kulturanalys*, Lund: Liber.

Ehn, B., Frykman, J. and Löfgren, O. (1993) *Försvenskningen av Sverige: Det nationellas förvandlingar*, Stockholm: Natur och Kultur.

Elgenius, G. (2005a) 'Expressing the Nation: National Symbols and Ceremonies in Contemporary Europe', Ph.D thesis, London School of Economics.

—— (2005b) 'National Days and Nation-building: A Contemporary Survey', in L. Eriksonas and L. Müller (eds), *Statehood Beyond Ethnicity*, Brussels: Peter Lang.

—— (2007) *Symbols of Nationalism: Expressing the Nation*, Basingstoke: Palgrave Macmillan.

Eliot, T. S. (1973) *Notes Towards the Definition of Culture*, London: Faber.

Engene, J. (1997a) *First Flag of Independence 1814*, http://www.crwflags.com/fotw/flags/no-hrank.html#1814

—— (1997b) *Norway Historic Flags: National War Ensign, Union Flags 1844–*, http://www.crwflags.com/fotw/flags/no-hrank.html

—— (1996) *Sweden: History of the Flag*, http://fotw.digibel.be/flags/se-3kron.html#his

English, R. (2003) *Armed Struggle: The History of the IRA*, Basingstoke: Macmillan.

Enloe, C. (2000) *Maneuvers: The International Politics of Militarizing Women's Lives*, Berkeley, CA: University of California Press.

Equality Commission For Northern Ireland (2006) *Final Report of Commission Investigation under Paragraph 10 of Schedule 9 of the Northern Ireland Act 1998: Paul Butler & Lisburn City Council*, www.equalityni.org/uploads/word/CommissionInvestigationReport040706.doc

Eriksen, A. (1995) *Det var noe annet under krigen: 2. verdenskrig i norsk kollektivtradisjon*, Oslo: Pax forlag.

—— (2005) 'Den nasjonale erindring – minner om 1905', in Ø. Sørensen and T. Nilsson (eds) *1905 – Nye perspektiver*, Oslo: Aschehoug.

Eriksen, T. H. (1993) 'Formal and Informal Nationalism', *Ethnic and Racial Studies*, vol. 16: 1–25.

Esborg, L. (1995) '. . . og så var vi alle gode nordmenn': Fortellinger on den symbolske motstanden under okkupasjonen av Norge 1940–45', Ph.D thesis (*Hovedoppgave*), Oslo University.

Eubanks, W. R. (2003) *Ever is a Long Time: a Journey into Mississippi's Dark Past, A Memoir*, New York: Basic Books.

Evans-Pritchard, E. E. (1965) *Theories of Primitive Religion*, Oxford: Oxford University Press.

Fanon, F. (1967) *Black Skins, White Masks*, New York: Grove.

Feldman, A. (1991) *Formations of Violence: The Narrative of the Body and Political Terror in Northern Ireland*, Chicago, IL: University of Chicago Press.

Fenton, S. (2003) *Ethnicity*, Cambridge: Polity.

Firth, R. (1973) *Symbols: Public and Private*, 2nd edn, London: George Allen and Unwin.

Flagmaster (1998) 'The 1998 Flag Change. Proposals from the Westerndorp Commission. Bosnia and Herzegovina: A New 'Neutral' flag', *Flagmaster*, no. 89: 9–12.

Ford, O. (2003) 'Locals Gather for Confederate Flag Rally at Waterfront Park', *Beaufort Gazette* (Beaufort SC), April 27, 2003.

Fortson, B. W. (1957) *Georgia Flags*, Atlanta, GA: Office of the Secretary of State.

Foster, R. J. (2002) *Materializing the Nation: Commodities, Consumption and Media in Papua New Guinea*, Bloomington, IN: Indiana University Press.

FOTW (1995) *Denmark: History of the Flag*: http://fotw.digibel.be/flags/dk.html#hist

—— (2003) *The Princevlag of the Netherlands*, http://www.crwflags.com/fotw/flags/nl_prvlg.html, 2003

—— (2004) *Denmark*, http://www.crwflags.com/fotw/flags/dk.html

Fox-Davies, A. C. (1949) *A Complete Guide to Heraldry*, London: Nelson.

Frankenberg, R. (1993) *The Social Construction of Whiteness: White Women, Race Matters*, Minneapolis, MN: University of Minnesota Press, and London: Routledge.

—— (1997a) 'Introduction: Local Whitenesses, Localising Whiteness', in R. Frankenberg (ed.) *Displacing Whiteness*, Durham, NC: Duke University Press.

—— (1997b) *Displacing Whiteness: Essays in Social and Cultural Criticism*, Durham, NC: Duke University Press.

Gallatin Anderson, B. (1990) *First Fieldwork: The Misadventures of an Anthropologist*, Prospect Heights, IL: Waveland.

Geertz, C. (1973) *The Interpretation of Cultures*, New York: Basic Books.

Gellner, E. (1983) *Nations and Nationalism*, Oxford: Blackwell.

Gilroy, P. (2002) *There Ain't No Black in the Union Jack*, London: Routledge.

Girardet, R. (1998) 'The Three Colors: Neither White nor Red', in P. Nora and L. D. Kritzman (eds), *Realms of Memory: The Construction of the French Past, vol. 3: Symbols*, New York: Columbia University Press.

Giuliano, G. (1996) *Behind Blue Eyes: The Life of Pete Townshend*, London: Dutton.

Goldstein, R. (1995) *Saving 'Old Glory': The History of the American Flag Desecration Controversy*, Boulder, CO: Westview Press.

—— (1996a) *Burning the Flag: The Great 1989–90 American Flag Desecration Controversy*, Ashland, OH: Kent State University Press.

—— (ed.) (1996b) *Desecrating the American Flag*, Syracuse, NY: Syracuse University Press.

—— (2000) *Flag Burning and Free Speech: The Case of Texas v. Johnson*, Lawrence, KS: University of Kansas Press.

Gottmann, J. (1952) 'The Political Partitioning of the World: An Attempt at Analysis', *World Affairs*, vol. 4: 512–19.

Green, J. (1998) *Days in the Life: Voices from the English Underground, 1961–71*, London: Pimlico.

Groom, N. (2006) *The Union Jack: The Biography*, London: Atlantic.

Hague, E., Giordano, B. and Sebasta, E. H. (2005) 'Whiteness, Multiculturalism and Nationalist Appropriation of Celtic Culture: The Case of the League of the South and the Lega Nord', *Cultural Geographies*, vol. 12: 151–73.

Hague, E., Beirich, H. and Sebesta, E. (eds) (2007) *The Neo-Confederate Movement in the United States*, Austin, TX: University of Texas Press.

Hale, G. E. (1998) *Making Whiteness: the Culture of Segregation in the South, 1890–1940*, New York: Pantheon Press.

Hall, S. (1996) 'New Ethnicities', in J. Hutchinson and A. D. Smith (eds) *Ethnicity*, Oxford: Oxford University Press.

Handelman, D. (1990) *Models and Mirrors: Towards an Anthropology of Public Events*, Cambridge: Cambridge University Press.

Harris, R. (1972) *Prejudice and Tolerance in Ulster: A Study of Neighbours and Strangers in a Border Community*, Manchester: Manchester University Press.

Harrison, S. (1995) 'Four Types of Symbolic Conflict', *Journal of the Royal Anthropological Institute* (n.s.), vol. 1: 255–72.

Hartsock, N. C. M. (1987) 'The Feminist Standpoint: Developing the Ground for a Specifically Feminist Historical Materialism', in S. Harding (ed.) *Feminism and Methodology*, Bloomington, IN: Indiana University Press.

Hattenauer, H. (1990) *Geschichte der deutschen Nationalsymbole: Zeichen und Bedeutung*, Munich: Orlag Verlag.

Hayes-McCoy, G. A. (1979) *A History of Irish Flags From Earliest Times*, Dublin: Academy Press.

Hebdige, D. (1979) *Subculture: The Meaning of Style*, London: Routledge.

Hennessey, T. (2005) *The Origins of the Troubles*, Dublin: Gill and Macmillan.

Henry, M. J. (2004) 'Student Display of the Confederate Flag in Public Schools', *Journal of Law and Education*, vol. 33: 573–9.

Hill, J. (1984) 'National Festivals, the State and Protestant Ascendancy in Ireland, 1790–1829', *Irish Historical Studies*, vol. 24: 93.

Hill, R. (2002) 'Understanding the Drive to Make the Confederate Flag Official in South Carolina', in A. Willingham (ed.) *Beyond the Color Line? Race, Representation, and Community in the New Century*, New York: Brennan Center for Justice at New York University School of Law.

Hjermind, J. (1995) 'Flagdage', in J. Hjermind and K. Melgaard (eds) *Om Dannebrog jeg ved . . .*, Viborg: Forlaget Viborg.

Hobsbawm, E. (1990) *Nations and Nationalism since the 1780s: Programme, Myth, Reality*, Cambridge: Cambridge University Press.

—— (1999) *Industry and Empire: From 1750 to the Present Day*, Harmondsworth: Penguin.

Holdaway, S. (1982) 'An Insider Job: A Case Study of Covert Research on the Police', in M. Bulmer (ed.) *Social Research Ethics: An Examination of the Merits of Covert Participation*, London: Macmillan.

hooks, b. (1990) *Killing Rage*, New York: Owl.

Hulme, E. (1915) *Flags of the World*, London: Frederick Warne.

Huntington, S. (1996) *The Clash of Civilizations and the Remaking of World Order*, New York: Simon and Schuster.

Hurt, D. A. (2005) 'Dialed In? Geographic Expansion and Regional Identity in NASCAR's Nextel Cup Series', *Southeastern Geographer*, vol. 45: 120–37.

Hutchinson, J. and Smith, A. D. (eds) (1994) *Nationalism*, Oxford: Oxford University Press.

Iacobelli, P. (2006) 'At Black Coaches' Request, NCAA May Expand Confederate Flag Ban', Associated Press, http://www.blackamericaweb.com/site/aspx/baw news/flagban803

Ignatieff, M. (1993) *Blood and Belonging: Journeys into the New Nationalisms*, London: Vintage.

Ignatiev, N. (1995) *How the Irish Became White*, New York: Routledge.

Imsen, Ø. (2005) 'Flaggsak og flaggbruk i 1890-åra – fra Stortinget til Ilevolden', Ph.D thesis (*Hovedoppgave*), University of Oslo.

Independent Commission on Policing for Northern Ireland (1999) *A New Beginning: Policing in Northern Ireland*, www.nio.gov.uk/a_new_beginning_in_policing_in_ northern_ireland.pdf

Jacobson, M. F. (1998) *Whiteness of a Different Color*, Cambridge, MA: Harvard University Press.

James, L. (2001) *Warrior Race: A History of the British at War*, New York: Little, Brown.

Jansson, D. R. (2003) 'Internal Orientalism in America: W. J. Cash's "The Mind of the South" and the Spatial Construction of America National Identity', *Political Geography*, vol. 22: 293–316.

Jarman, N. (1992) 'Troubled Images: The Iconography of Loyalism', *Critique of Anthropology*, vol. 12, no. 2.

—— (1993) 'Intersecting Belfast', in B. Bender (ed.) *Landscape: Politics and Perspectives*, Oxford: Berg.

—— (1997) *Material Conflicts: Parades and Visual Displays in Northern Ireland*, Oxford: Berg.

—— (1998) 'Material of Culture, Fabric of Identity', in D. Miller (ed.) *Material Cultures: Why Some Things Matter*, London: UCL Press.

—— (1999) *Displaying Faith: Orange, Green and Trade Union Banners in Northern Ireland*, Belfast: Institute of Irish Studies.

—— (2000) 'For God and Ulster: Blood and Thunder Bands and Loyalist Political Culture', in T. G. Fraser (ed.) *The Irish Parading Tradition: Following the Drum*, Basingstoke: Macmillan.

—— (2001) 'The Orange Arch: Creating Tradition in Ulster', *Folklore*, vol. 112, no. 1: 1–21.

Jarman, N. and Bryan, D. (1998) *From Riots to Rights: Nationalist Parades in the North of Ireland*, Coleraine: Centre for the Study of Conflict.

—— (2000) 'Green Parades in an Orange State: Nationalist and Republican Commemorations and Demonstrations from Partition to the Troubles, 1920– 1970', in T. G Fraser (ed.) *The Irish Parading Tradition: Following the Drum*, Basingstoke: Macmillan.

Jenkins, R. (1997) *Rethinking Ethnicity: Arguments and Explorations*, London: Sage.

—— (1998) *Fra Amalienborg til Kvickly: Dannebrog i dansk dagligliv*, Skive: Skive Museums Forlag.

—— (2002) 'Modern Monarchy: A Comparative View from Denmark', *Sociological Research Online*, vol. 7 no. 1: http://www.socresonline.org.uk/7/1/jenkins.html

—— (2004) *Social Identity*, 2nd edn, London: Routledge.

Jespersen, K. J. V. (2004) *A History of Denmark*, London: Palgrave Macmillan.

Jeter, B. (2006) 'Cotton, Slavery at Heart of War', letter to the editor, *Birmingham News*, October 29: 3D.

Johnson, N. C. (2004) 'Public Memory', in J. S. Duncan, N. C. Johnson, and R. H. Schein (eds) *A Companion to Cultural Geography*, Oxford: Blackwell.

Kapferer, B. (1984) 'The Ritual Process and the Problem of Reflexivity in Sinhalese Demon Exorcism', in J. MacAloon (ed.) *Rite, Drama, Festival, Spectacle*, Ithaca, NY: Cornell University Press.

Kertzer, D. I. and Arel, D. (eds) (2002) *Census and Identity: The Politics of Race, Ethnicity and Language in National Censuses*, Cambridge: Cambridge University Press.

Koht, H. (1896) *Norske Flagsange, Med indledning og anmærkninger af . . .*, Kristiania: Kristiania flagsamlag.

Kolstø, P. (2006) 'National symbols as signs of unity and division', *Ethnic and Racial Studies*, vol. 29: 676–701.

Kureishi, H. and Savage, J. (eds) (2002) *The Faber Book of Pop*, London: Faber.

Lamont, M. and Fournier, M. (eds) (1992) *Cultivating Differences: Symbolic Boundaries and the Making of Inequality*, Chicago, IL: University of Chicago Press.

Larsen, S. S. (1982) 'The Glorious Twelfth: A Ritual Expression of Collective Identity', in A. P. Cohen (ed.) *Belonging: Identity and Social Expression in British Rural Cultures*, Manchester: Manchester University Press.

Laurin, C. (1916) *Folklynnen*, Stockholm: Nordstedts.

Lee, A., Hammack, D. and Dodd, S. (2005) 'Mississippi Governor: Possible 80 Dead', *The Sun-Herald*, August 30, 2005.

Leepson, M. (2005) *Flag: An American Biography*, New York: St Martin's Press.

Leib, J. I. (1995) 'Heritage versus Hate: A Geographical Analysis of Georgia's Confederate Battle Flag Debate', *Southeastern Geographer*, vol. 35: 37–57.

—— (1998) 'Teaching Controversial Topics: Iconography and the Confederate Battle Flag Debate in the South', *Journal of Geography*, vol. 97: 229–40.

—— (2002) 'Separate Times, Shared Space: Arthur Ashe, Monument Avenue and the Politics of Richmond, Virginia's Symbolic Landscape', *Cultural Geographies*, vol. 9: 286–312.

—— (2004) 'Robert E. Lee, "Race", Representation, and Redevelopment along Richmond, Virginia's Canal Walk', *Southeastern Geographer*, vol. 44: 236–62.

Leib, J. I. and Dittmer, J. (2006) 'Not Just Wearing Dixie? Performativity, Dixie Outfitters and 'Southern' Identity', paper presented at the annual meeting of the Southeastern Division of the Association of American Geographers, Morgantown, West Virginia.

Leib, J. I. and Webster, G. R. (2002) 'The Confederate Flag Debate in the American South: Theoretical and Conceptual Perspectives', in A. Willingham (ed.) *Beyond the Color Line? Race, Representation, and Community in the New Century*, New York: Brennan Center for Justice at New York University School of Law.

—— (2003) 'A New "Stars and Bars"?: The Confederate Battle Emblem and Mississippi's 2001 State Flag Referendum', paper presented at the annual meeting of the Association of American Geographers Annual Conference, New Orleans, Louisiana.

—— (2004a) 'Banner Headlines: The Fight Over Confederate Flags in the American South', in D. Janelle, B. Warf and K. Hansen (eds) *WorldMinds: Geographical Perspectives on 100 Problems*, Dordrecht: Kluwer.

—— (2004b) 'Stars and Bars, Rebel Cross, or "Denny's Placemat"?: Race, Party, Iconography, and the Battle over Georgia's State Flags, 2001–2004', paper presented at the Association of American Geographers Political Geography Specialty Group Conference, Atlantic City, New Jersey.

—— (2006) 'District Composition and State Legislative Votes on the Confederate Battle Emblem', *Journal of Race and Policy*, vol. 2: 53–75.

Leib, J. I. , Webster, G. R. and Webster, R. H. (2000) 'Rebel with a Cause?: Iconography and Public Memory in the Southern United States', *Geojournal*, vol. 52: 303–10.

Lévi-Strauss, C. (1962) *La pensée sauvage*, Paris: Plon.

Levine, B. (2006) 'In Search of a Useable Past: Neo-Confederates and Black Confederates', in J. O. Horton and L. E. Horton (eds) *Slavery and Public History: The Tough Stuff of American Memory*, New York: The New Press.

Lingren, C. (2000) *Den høje flagbog*, Copenhagen: Borgen.

Löfgren, O. (1993) 'Materializing the Nation in Sweden and America', *Ethnos*, vol. 38, nos. 3–4: 161–96.

—— (1999) *On Holiday: A History of Vacationing*, Berkeley, CA: University of California Press.

—— (2000) 'The Disappearance and Return of the National: The Swedish Experience 1950–2000', in P. J. Anttonen (ed.) *Folklore, Heritage Politics, and Ethnic Diversity: A Festschrift for Barbro Klein*, Botkyrka: Botkyrka Multicultural Centre.

Loftus B. (1990) *Mirrors: William III and Mother Ireland*, Dundrum: Picture Press.

—— (1994) *Mirrors: Orange and Green*, Dundrum: Picture Press.

McCormick, J. and Jarman, N. (2005) 'Death of a Mural', *Journal of Material Culture*, vol. 10: 49–71.

—— (forthcoming) 'Culture in a Corner: Survival and Adaptation of Material Culture in Northern Ireland', *Journal of Design History*.

McCrone, D. (1998) *The Sociology of Nationalism*, London: Routledge.

Macdonald, S. (1987) 'Drawing the Lines: Gender, Peace, and War: An Introduction', in S. Macdonald, P. Holden, and S. Ardener (eds) *Images of Women in Peace and War*, Basingstoke: Macmillan.

McElroy, O. M. (1995) 'The Confederate Battle Flag: Social History and Cultural Contestation', Master's Thesis, University of Alabama.

McFarlane, G. (1986) '"Its not as simple as that": The Expression of the Catholic and Protestant Boundary in Northern Irish Rural Communities', in A. P. Cohen (ed.) *Symbolising Boundaries: Identity and Diversity in British Culture*, Manchester: Manchester University Press.

MacGinty, R. and Darby, J. (2002) *Guns and Government: The Management of the Northern Ireland Peace Process*, Basingstoke: Palgrave.

Mackay, H. (ed.) (1997) *Consumption and Everyday Life*, London: Sage.

McMurray, J. (2000) 'Georgia State Flag Prompts Quiet Protest', *Tallahassee Democrat* (Tallahassee FL), August 28, 2000.

Madriaga, M. (2005) 'Understanding the Symbolic Idea of the American Dream and its Relationship with the Category of "Whiteness"', *Sociological Research Online*, vol. 10, no. 3, http://www.socresonline.org.uk/10/3/madriaga.html

Manis, A. M. (2005) 'The Civil Religions of the South', in C. R. Wilson and M. Silk (eds) *Religion and Public Life in the South: In the Evangelical Mode*, Walnut Creek, CA: AltaMira Press.

Marcoplos, L. (2006) 'Drafting Away From it All', *Southern Cultures*, vol. 12: 33–41.

Marvin, C. (1991) 'Trooping the Colors on TV', *Public Culture*, vol. 3: 155–8.

—— (2005) 'Iconoclastic Strains of American Patriotism', paper presented at Culcom conference 'Flying the Flag', University of Oslo, November 2005.

Marvin, C. and Ingle, D. W. (1996) 'Blood Sacrifice and the Nation: Revisiting Civil Religion', *Journal of the American Academy of Religion*, vol. 64: 767–80.

—— (1999) *Blood Sacrifice and the Nation: Totem Rituals and the American Flag*, Cambridge: Cambridge University Press.

Melly, G. (1989) *Revolt into Style: The Pop Arts in the 50s and 60s*, Oxford: Oxford University Press.

Memmi, A. (1990) [1957] *The Colonizer and the Colonized*, London: Earthscan.

Meyer, J. A., Kamens, D. and Benavot, A. (1992) *School Knowledge for the Masses: World Models and National Primary Curricular Categories in the Twentieth Century*. Washington, DC: Falmer.

Miles, D. (2005) *The Tribes of Britain*, London: Weidenfeld and Nicolson.

Miles, R. (1993) *Racism after 'Race Relations'*, London: Routledge.

Miller, D. (1998) *A Theory of Shopping*, Cambridge: Polity.

—— (2001) *The Dialectics of Shopping*, Chicago, IL: University of Chicago Press.

Mitchell, D. (2000) *Cultural Geography: A Critical Introduction*, Oxford: Blackwell.

Morely, V. (1998) *The Tricolour*, http://www.connect.ie/users/morley/tric.htm

Morrello, C. (1997) 'Rebel Banner Roils Ole Miss Anew', *USA Today*, October 23, 1997.

Morrison, T. (1998) 'From Playing in the Dark', in D. R. Roediger (ed.) *Black on White: Black Writers on What It Means to be White*, New York: Schocken.

Multi-Party Agreement (1998) The Agreement: Agreement Reached in the Multi-Party Negotiations, see http://www.nio.gov.uk/agreement.pdf

Nairn, T. (2001) *After Britain: New Labour and the Return of Scotland*, London: Granta Books.

NCAA (2001a) 'Moratorium Set for Championships in South Carolina', news release, August 10, 2001, http://www.ncaa.org

—— (2001b) 'NCAA Executive Committee Acts on Confederate Flag Issue', news release, April 27, 2001, 2001, http://www.ncaa.org

—— (2003) 'NCAA Executive Committee Passes Recommendations Regarding American Indian Mascots, Confederate Flag and NCAA Budget', August 12, 2003, news release, http://www.ncaa.org

Netherlands Ministry of Foreign Affairs (1999) *Holland: Information*, The Hague: Foreign Information Service.

Nevéus, C. (1992) *Ny Svensk Vapenbok*, Stockholm: Streiffert.

—— (1993) 'Svenska flaggan: Historik och utveckling i praxis och lagstiftning', in Nordic Association, *From Campaigns to National Festivals*, Stockholm: Nordic Association.

Nic Craith, Máiréad (2002) *Plural Identities, Singular Narratives: The Case of Northern Ireland*, Oxford: Berghahn Books.

Northern Ireland Life and Times Survey (various years), http://www.ark.ac.uk/nilt/

Notholt, S. (1995) *Denmark: History of the Flag*, http://fotw.digibel.be/flags/dk. html#hist

—— (1996) *United Kingdom: History of the Flag*, http://fotw.digibel.be/flags/gb. html#hist

Nuttall, J. (1970) *Bomb Culture*, London: Paladin.

O'Dell, T. (1997) *Culture Unbound: Americanization and the Swedish Experience*, Lund: Nordic Academic Press.

OFMDFM (2005) *A Shared Future*, Belfast: Community Relations Unit of the Office of the First Minister and Deputy First Minister.

Ohta, Russell J. (1998) 'My Eyes Have Seen the Glory: Visitor Experience at a Controversial Flag Exhibition', *Current Trends in Audience Research and Evaluation*, vol. 11: 48–58.

O'Leary, C. (1999) *To Die For: The Paradox of American Patriotism*, Princeton, NJ: Princeton University Press.

Omi, M. and Winant, H. (1994) *Racial Formation in the United States*, 2nd edn, London: Routledge.

Ortner, S. (1973) 'On Key Symbols', *American Anthropologist*, vol. 75: 1338–46.

Paris, M. (2000) *Warrior Nation: Images of War in British Popular Culture, 1850–2000*, London: Reaktion.

Paxman, J. (1999) *The English: A Portrait of a People*, Harmondsworth: Penguin.

Percy, W. (1997) [1965] 'Mississippi: The Fallen Paradise', in M. Barnwell (ed.) *A Place Called Mississippi: Collected Narratives*, Jackson, MS: University Press of Mississippi.

Perryman, M. (2005) 'Keep the Flags Flying: World Cup 2002, Football and the Remaking of Englishness', in J. Littler and R. Naidoo (eds) *The Politics of Heritage: Legacies of 'Race'*, London: Routledge.

Person, J. (2006) 'Clemson's Role as Baseball Host Unfurls Flag Flap', *The State* (Columbia, SC), July 23, 2006.

Pierce, C. S. (ed. C. Hardwick) (1977) *Semiotics and Significs*, Bloomington, IN: Indiana University Press.

Pierce, D. (2001) 'The Most Southern Sport on Earth: NASCAR and the Unions', *Southern Cultures*, vol. 7 : 8–33.

Pillsbury, R. (1995) 'Stock Car Racing', in K. Raitz (ed.) *The Theater of Sport*, Baltimore, MD: Johns Hopkins University Press.

Potok, M. (ed.) (2000) *Rebel with a Cause, Intelligence Report* no. 99, Southern Poverty Law Center.

Preble, G. H. (1980) *The Symbols, Standards, Flags, and Banners of Ancient and Modern Nations*, Winchester, MA: The Flag Research Centre.

Prince, K. M. (2004) *Rally 'Round the Flag, Boys!: South Carolina and the Confederate Flag*, Columbia, SC: University of South Carolina Press.

Ringer, B. (1983) *'We the People' and Others: Duality and America's Treatment of its Racial Minorities*, New York: Tavistock.

Ringgaard Lauridsen, H. (1995) 'Dannebrog og danskerne', in J. Hjermind and K. Melgaard (eds) *Om Dannebrog jeg ved . . .*, Viborg: Forlaget Viborg.

Roediger, D. R. (1991) *Wages of Whiteness: Race and the Making of the American Working Class*, New York: Verso.

—— (1998) *Black on White: Black Writers on What it Means to Be White*, New York: Schocken.

Rolfsen, N. (1892) *Læsebog for folkeskolen, første del*, Christiania: Jacob Dybwads forlag.

Rolston, B. (1991) *Politics and Painting: Murals and Conflict in Northern Ireland*, Toronto: Associated Universities Press.

—— (1992) *Drawing Support 1: Murals in the North Ireland*, Belfast: Beyond the Pale.

—— (1995) *Drawing Support 2: Murals of War and Peace*, Belfast: Beyond the Pale.

—— (1999) *Drawing Support 3: Murals and Transition in the North of Ireland*, Belfast: Beyond the Pale.

Rothenberg, P. S. (ed.) (2005) *White Privilege: Essential Readings on the Other Side of Racism*, New York: Worth.

Sabin, R. (ed.) (1999) *Punk Rock: So What? The Cultural Legacy of Punk*, London: Routledge.

Sahlins, M. (1974) *Stone Age Economics*, London: Tavistock.

Said, E. W. (1978) [1995] *Orientalism*, Harmondsworth: Penguin.

—— (1993) *Culture and Imperialism*, London: Chatto and Windus.

Samuel, R. (1998) *Island Stories: Unravelling Britain*, London: Verso.

Santino, J. (2001) *Signs of War and Peace: Social Conflict and the Use of Public Symbols in Northern Ireland*, Basingstoke: Palgrave.

Savage, J. (1991) *England's Dreaming: Sex Pistols and Punk Rock*, London: Faber.

Schein, R. H. (ed.) (2006) *Landscape and Race in the United States*, New York: Routledge.

Scruggs, M. (2006) 'My Turn: Defining the Confederate Flag', *Birmingham News*, October 22, 2006: 2D.

Sebasta, E. (2004) 'The White Supremacist Design Ideas in the 2nd and 3rd National Confederate Flags', http://www.temple of democracy.com/2ndnat.htm

Sebasta, E. and Hague, E. (2002) 'The U.S. Civil War as a Theological Struggle: Confederate Christian Nationalism and the League of the South', *Canadian Review of American Studies*, vol. 32: 253–83.

Shiff, R. (2003) 'Digitized Analogies', in H. U. Gumbrecht and M. Marrinan (eds) *Mapping Benjamin: The Work of Art in the Digital Age*, Stanford, CA: Stanford University Press.

Shirlow, P. and Murtagh, B. (2006) *Belfast: Segregation, Violence and the City*, London: Pluto.

Simonetti, P. (1989) '"Vivants piliers": Les arbres de la liberté', in: B. de Andia *et al.*, *Fêtes et révolution*, Paris: Hachette.

Smith, A. D. (1991) *National Identity*, Harmondsworth: Penguin.

Smith, W. (1969) 'Prolegomena to the Study of Political Symbols', Ph.D. thesis, Boston University.

—— (1975) *Flags throughout the World and across the Ages*, London: McGraw-Hill.

—— (2004a) 'Flag of France', *Encyclopædia Britannica*.

—— (2004b) 'Flag of Norway', *Encyclopædia Britannica*.

—— (2004c) 'Flag of Germany', *Encyclopædia Britannica*.

Sorek, T. (2004) 'The Orange and the "Cross in the Crescent": Imagining Palestine in 1929', *Nations and Nationalism*, vol. 10: 269–91.

Sørensen, Ø. (ed.) (1998) *Jakten på det norske: Perspektiver på utviklingen av en norsk nasjonal identitet på 1800-tallet*, Oslo: Ad Notam Gyldendal.

Southern Poverty Law Center (2006) 'Sons of Confederate Veterans Protest', *Intelligence Report* no. 8.

Stanton, M. (1998) *From Selma to Sorrow: The Life and Death of Viola Liuzzo*, Athens, GA: University of Georgia.

Sturken, M. (1998) 'The Wall, the Screen, and the Image: The Vietnam Veterans Memorial', in N. Mirzoeff (ed.) *The Visual Cultural Reader*, London: Routledge.

Swedish Institute (1997) *The National Emblems of Sweden*, Fact Sheets on Sweden, Stockholm: Swedish Institute.

Talocci, M. (1995) *Flaggor från hela världen* (translation of *Bandiere di tutto il mondo*), Stockholm: Natur och Kultur.

Taylor, C. (2004) *Modern Social Imaginaries*, Durham, NC: Duke University Press.

Tenora, J. (n.d.) 'Time to cut the umbilicus between heraldry and vexillology', in *The Flag Man*, Portsmouth: Bruce Nicholls.

Till, K. E. (2003) 'Places of Memory', in J. Agnew, K. Mitchell, and G. Toal (eds) *A Companion to Political Geography*, Oxford: Blackwell.

Turner, V. (1967) *The Forest of Symbols*, Ithaca, NY: Cornell University Press.

—— (1969) *The Ritual Process: Structure and Anti-Structure*, Ithaca, NY: Cornell University Press.

—— (1974) *The Ritual Process: Structure and Anti-Structure*, Harmondsworth: Pelican.

Understanding Global Issues (1994) *Flags of Europe: Their History and Symbolism*, Cheltenham: European Schoolbooks Publishing.

Varouxakis, G. (2001) 'Patriotism', in A. S. Leoussi (ed.) *Encyclopedia of Nationalism*, New Brunswick, NJ: Transaction.

Vermorel, F. and Vermorel, J. (1987) *Sex Pistols: The Inside Story*, London: Omnibus.

Walton, A. (1996) *Mississippi: An American Journey*, New York: Vintage Books.

Ware, V. and Back, L. (2001) *Out of Whiteness: Color, Politics, and Culture*, Chicago, IL: University of Chicago Press.

Warf, B. and Grimes, J. (1997) 'Counterhegemonic Discourses and the Internet', *Geographical Review*, vol. 87: 259–74.

Warner, L. (1962) *American Life: Dream and Reality*, Chicago, IL: University of Chicago Press.

Webster, G. R. (1997) 'Religion and Politics in the American South', *Pennsylvania Geographer*, vol. 35: 151–72.

—— (2004) 'If First You Don't Secede, Try, Try Again: Secession, Hate, and the League of the South', in C. Flint (ed.) *Spaces of Hate: Geographies of Discrimination and Intolerance in the U.S.A.*, New York: Routledge.

—— (2006) 'Sports, Community, Nationalism and the International State System', in L. DeChano and F. Shelley (eds) *The Geography-Sports Connection: Using Sports to Teach Geography*, Jacksonville: National Council for Geographic Education.

Webster, G. R. and Leib, J. I. (2001) 'Whose South is it Anyway? Race and the Confederate Battle Flag in South Carolina', *Political Geography*, vol. 20: 271–99.

—— (2002) 'Political Culture, Religion, and the Confederate Battle Flag Debate in Alabama', *Journal of Cultural Geography*, vol. 20: 1–26.

—— (2007) 'The Confederate Battle Flag and the Neo-Confederate Movement in the South,' in E. Hague, H. Beirich and E. Sebesta (eds) *The Neo-Confederate Movement in the United States*, Austin: University of Texas Press.

Webster, G. R. and Webster, R. H. (1994) 'The Power of an Icon', *Geographical Review*, vol. 84: 131–43.

Weight, R. (2002) *Patriots: National Identity in Britain, 1940–2000*, London: Macmillan.

Weitman, S. R (1973) 'National Flags: A Sociological Overview', *Semiotica*, vol. 8: 328–67.

Welch, M. (2000) *Flag Burning: Moral Panic and the Criminalization of Protest*, Somerset, NJ: Aldine Transaction.

Wellikoff, A. (1994) 'The Object at Hand,' *Smithsonian*, 25 April, 1994.

Wellman, D. T. (1977) *Portraits of White Racism*, Cambridge: Cambridge University Press.

Western, J. (1997) *Outcast Cape Town*, Berkeley, CA: University of California Press.

Wetzel, D. (2006) 'Red Flag', *Yahoo Sports*, October 9, 2006, http://sports.yahoo.com/nascar/news?slug=dw-confederateflag100906&prov=yhoo&type=lgns

Wilk, R. R. (1993) 'Beauty and the Feast: Official and Visceral Nationalism in Belize', *Ethnos*, vol. 58: 294–316.

Williams, R. (1965) *The Long Revolution*, Harmondsworth: Pelican.

Wilson, R. (2000) *Flagging Concern: The Controversy over Flags and Emblems*, Belfast: Democratic Dialogue, http://www.democraticdialogue.org/working/flags.htm

Wolstenholme, K. (1998) *They Think It's All Over . . .: Memories of the Greatest Day in English Football*, London: Robson.

Wood, M. (1999) *In Search of England: Journeys into the English Past*, Harmondsworth: Penguin.

Woodcock, T. and Robinson, J. (eds) (1990). *The Oxford Guide to Heraldry*, Oxford: Oxford University Press.

Wray, M. and Newitz, A. (1997) *White Trash: Race and Class in America*, New York: Routledge.

Young, I. M. (1990) *Justice and the Politics of Difference*, Princeton, NJ: Princeton University Press.

Yuval-Davis, N. (1997) *Gender and Nation*, London: Sage.

Zephaniah, B. (1996) *Propa Propaganda*, Newcastle upon Tyne: Bloodaxe.

Index

Some subjects are generic, occurring throughout this book, and have not been separately indexed, because to do so would be to index almost every page. These are: 'identity', 'flags', and 'nationalism'. For similar reasons, we have not indexed authors' citations of their own work.

Adams, Gerry 105, 106
Alabama (US state) 34, 35, 39, 41–2, 43, 45, 46, 49–50, 51
Andersen, Hans Christian 134
Anderson, Barbara Gallatin 134
antiquity, flags in 15–17
Arab development of flags 17–18
Austro-Hungarian flag 19–20
Ashe, Arthur 37
Augustine, Saint 18
Ayling, Bob 78

banal nationalism 7–8, 55, 115–16, 131–2, 137
Barcelona (Catalonia, Spain) 6
Barnes, Roy 36, 49
Belfast (Northern Ireland) 104, 106, 111, 113
Berger, Peter 127
Bessinger, Maurice 37
Billig, Michael 2, 3, 7, 8, 55, 115, 116, 131, 132–3, 137
Bjørnson, Bjørnstjerne 159
Bodnar, John 40, 54
Bomann-Larsen, Tor 12
Borneman, John 115
Borg, Björn 5
Bourdieu, Pierre 127
Bosnian flag 9, 25, 30n
Bowie, David 77
British flag (Union Flag, Union Jack) 6, 9, 10, 13, 13n, 29n, 68–87, 95, 102, 104, 105, 114, 126, 172
Brooke, Henry 80
Bryan, Dominic 5, 8, 10, 115, 174

Bryson, Lucy 115
Bulgarian flag 25
burning flags 12–13, 54, 55, 57, 60, 64–5, 91, 115, 138, 140

Caine, Michael 74
Carl Johan 147, 148
Carter, Angela 73
Catalonian flag 6, 11
Chamberlain, Neville 44
Charlemagne 18
Charles, Prince 80, 83
Chinese flags (ancient) 16–17, 18
Christianity 10, 17, 21–2, 29n, 121, 130, 147, 171
Christie, Julie 73
Christmas, use of flags at 3, 133–4n, 140, 156, 165, 166
civil society (see also: 'the state') 9–10, 119, 121, 122, 130, 139–40, 153, 157–70
'clash of civilisations' 1
Cohen, Anthony P. 53, 54, 58, 115, 116, 122
commercialisation of flags 9, 71–9, 84, 123–7, 131, 140–1
Confederate Flag (Southern Cross) 2, 5, 8, 11, 31–52, 143
conflict 10–12, 31–52, 88–101, 102–14, 115, 116–17, 118–19, 142–3, 146–56, 157–8
Connell, Richard 78
Constantine, Emperor 17, 22
consumerism 9, 71–9, 84, 123–7, 131, 140–1

Coward, Noël 69, 74
Croatian flag 25
'cross flags' in Europe 21–2, 147–8
Crusades 18, 19, 20, 29n
'culture wars' in US 40–1

Danish flag (Dannebrog) 4, 6, 9, 13,
    21–2, 27, 115–35, 146, 172
Deep South of the USA 8, 11, 31–52,
    115
Denmark 11, 115–35, 138, 142, 146,
    148
Derry (Londonderry, Northern Ireland)
    114
desecration of flags 12–13, 54, 55, 57,
    60, 64–5, 90, 91–4, 98, 115, 138,
    140
destruction of flags 91–4, 98
Diana, Princess of Wales 85
Drachmann, Holger 135
Du Bois, W. E. B. 66
Duara, Prasenjit 115
Durkheim, Emile 3
Dutch flag 22–3, 27

early modern Europe 19–21
Egypt, ancient 15
Elgenius, Gabriella 9, 118
Eliot, T. S. 68
Elizabeth II, Queen 69, 75, 80
emotion 31, 115–35
England 73, 74, 75, 82, 83
English (St George's) flag 2, 6, 10, 19,
    20, 21, 22, 27, 29n, 79, 82–3, 85,
    102
Eriksen, Anne 11, 172
Eriksen, Thomas Hylland 115, 132
ethnicity 53, 67n, 115
Europe, early modern 19–21; medieval
    17–19
European Union 6, 75, 123, 141, 144
European Union flag 6
Eusebius 17
everyday nationalism 7–8, 115

Farrow, Malcolm 87
Festival of Britain (1951) 69
Finnish flag 126, 147
Firth, Raymond 25
flag burning 12–13, 54, 55, 57, 58, 60,
    64–5, 91, 115, 138, 140
flag rules 85, 91–2, 109–13, 120, 130,
    132–3, 141, 165–6
Foucault, Michel 173

France 11, 24
France, Brian 48
Frederick II, Duke 20
Frederik VI, King 118, 119, 127
Friedman, Danny 76
French flag 21, 23, 24, 27, 172
French Revolution 14, 148

Gallagher, Noel 77
Garvey, Marcus 84
Geertz, Clifford 8
gender 157–70
Genghis Khan 18
George V, King 81
Georgia (US state) 34, 35–6, 39, 41, 43,
    44, 45, 46, 50, 51
German Democratic Republic
    (East Germany) 25
German flags 11, 24
Germany 73, 117, 130, 142, 163–4
Gilmour, John 68
Goldstein, Robert J. 54
'Good Friday Agreement' (Multi Party
    Agreement), Northern Ireland 106–8
Gottmann, Jean 39
Great Britain 68–87
Grimnes, Ole Kristian 5, 11, 157, 172
Groom, Nick 6, 9, 140
Grundtvig, N. F. S. 134
Gustav Vasa, King 22

Halliwell, Geri 77
Harrison County, Mississippi (USA)
    37
Henry II, King 19
Henry V, King 22
Henry VII, King 79
heraldry 18–19, 29n, 30n
'heritage' 41–3, 97–100
Hillary, Sir Edmund 70
historical origins of flags 14–30
Hitler, Adolf 44
Holmes, Alvin 49
Holy Roman Empire 19, 20, 22, 24
Home, Stewart 84
Hume, Mick 87
Hungarian flag 24
Huntington, Samuel 1

Iceland 10
Icelandic flag 147
iconography 39–41
Ignatieff, Michael 25
Ingle, David W. 54, 55, 115, 172

Irish (St Patrick's) flag 6, 79, 81, 85
Irish (tricolour) flag 10, 25, 85, 89, 91,
    93, 102, 104, 105, 108, 114
Islam 9, 13, 17–18, 29n
Israeli flag 6, 7, 82, 89
Italian flag 11, 25

James I, King 103
Japanese flag 13
Jarman, Derek 76
Jarman, Neil 5, 8, 10, 115
Jenkins, Richard 4, 6, 9, 11, 67,
    137
Jensen, Knud Møller 126
Johns, Jasper 72, 73
Johnson, Eric 43
'Jolly Roger' 173–4
Jørgensen, Kai 120

Kapferer, Bruce 8
Kennard, Peter 86
Kennedy, Robert F. 35
Khan, Shajaad 78
Khan, Amir 78
Knud, Duke 118
Kolstø, Pål 1, 7, 9, 11
Kristiansand (Norway) 160

Lake City, Florida (USA) 37
Larsson, Henrik (Henke) 89
Laurin, Carl G. 137
Law, Denis 74
Lee, Laurie 69
Lee, Robert E. 37
Leib, Jonathan 5, 8, 11, 115
Leopold V 19
Lévi-Strauss, Claude 3
Lisburn (Northern Ireland) 111–12
Liuzzo, Viola 37
Löfgren, Orvar 4, 11, 172
Low, David 86
Lowery, Joseph 50
Luckmann, Thomas 127

McCartney, Clem 115
McCartney, Paul 75
McConnell, Glenn 44
McGuinness, Martin 105
McKinney, Billy 44
McLaren, Malcolm 75–6
Madriaga, Manuel 10, 11
Malta 171
Mandelson, Peter 77
Manis, Andrew 40

Marchbank, Pearce 71, 73
Marvin, Carolyn 12, 54, 55, 115, 138,
    172
Maryville, Tennessee (USA) 37
Mauritian flag 12
Mauritius 8, 10, 12
Mauss, Marcel 3
Maxentius 17, 22
medieval Europe 17–19
Melly, George 72
Mercury, Freddie 77
Mexican flag 1, 63–4
Miller, Zell 35–36
Mississippi (US state) 34, 36, 45, 46,
    51
Mitchell, Don 40
'Mohammed cartoons' controversy 13,
    132–3
Mohammed, Prophet 17, 18
Mongol Empire 18
Moon, Keith 72
Morrison, Van 123
Morrissey 77
Moseley-Braun, Carol 38, 49
Mosley, Oswald 82
multi-national organisations, flags of
    173
Murphy, Conor 109
Murphy-Roud, Kenny 84

Nansen, Fridtjof 155
nation, concept of the 14–15, 25–6,
    27–8, 31–2, 115–16, 130–1,
    171–2
Nepali flag 173
Neumann, Iver B. 5
Newtownabbey (Northern Ireland)
    102, 111, 114
Nietzsche, Friedrich 173
non-governmental organisations
    (NGOs), flags of 173
Northern Ireland 6–7, 8, 10–11,
    88–101, 102–14, 115
Northern Irish flag 105, 111
Norway 6, 7, 11–12, 117, 142–3,
    146–56, 157–70
Norwegian flag 4, 5–6, 13, 25, 126,
    146–56, 157–70, 172
Nuttall, Jeff 71

O'Dell, Tom 140
O'Leary, Cecilia E. 55, 65
Ortner, Sherry 5
Oscar I, King 158

Oslo (Christiania or Kristiania, Norway) 153, 158, 159, 160, 161, 164

Paisley, Rev. Ian 104, 109
Palestinian flag 6–7, 11, 82, 89
Patten, Chris 113
Pamphilon, Denis 81
Philip, Count 19
Philip Augustus, King 19
Pierce, C. S. 171
Polish flag 30n
Pop Art 71–3
popular culture 41–3, 70–9, 122–3, 143–4
public memory 39–41
punk 75–6

Quisling, Vidkun 12

'race' 31–52, 53–67, 83–4, 136
racism 43–6, 77, 136, 137, 141
Rauschenberg, Robert 73
Red Brigades flag 174
Reid, Jamie 75, 76
Richmond, Virginia (USA) 37
right-wing political groups 4, 34, 37–8, 42, 75, 77, 82–3, 88–101, 102–14, 137, 138, 141
Roman flags 17
Roman military symbols 15, 16, 29n
Romanian flag 24, 25
royalty 69–70, 119, 130
Russian flag 1, 9, 23, 27

sacred character of flags (see also: 'desecration of flags') 12–13, 54, 57, 61, 65, 132–3, 138
Sami (minority population in Norway) 4
Sarajevo (Bosnia) 1
Saudi Arabian flag 1, 171
Scanian flag (Swedish region) 142–3
Scotland 74, 75
Scottish (St Andrew's) flag 6, 79, 81, 89
Scouting movement 119, 120, 163
Skive (Denmark) 116–35
Slovak flag 25
South Carolina (US state) 34, 35, 39, 41, 44, 45–6, 51
southern states of the USA 8, 11, 31–52, 115
Spanish flag 6

sport 3, 5, 7, 46, 47–8, 60, 73–4, 75, 117, 174
'Stars and Stripes' 2, 7, 10, 11, 23–4, 37, 53–67, 91–2, 126, 137
state, the (see also: 'civil society') 9–10, 121, 122, 130
Stenmark, Ingmar 5
Stewart, Rod 75
Sweden 5, 8, 11, 117, 136–45, 146, 157, 161
Swedish flag 4, 22, 136–45, 146–53, 172
Swiss flag 22
Switzerland 117
symbolism 3–7, 10, 14–30, 31–2, 39–41, 54–5, 58–9, 65, 93–4, 116, 143–4, 151–6, 159, 171–4

Talocci, Mauro 23
tartans, in Scotland 3, 75
Tenzing, Sherpa 70
totemism 3, 16, 28n
Townshend, Pete 73
transnational corporation flags 173
tricolour flags in Europe 22–3
Tromsø (Norway) 160
Trondheim (Norway) 158
Turkish flag 1, 138
Turner, Victor 3, 10, 67

Ukrainian flag 26, 174
Ulster flags 81–2, 88–101, 102–14
'Union Jack' (the Union Flag) 6, 9, 10, 13, 13n, 29n, 68–87, 95, 102, 104, 105, 114, 126, 172
United States of America 1, 8, 11, 31–52, 53–67, 117, 137; southern states 8, 11, 31–52, 115
United States flag 2, 7, 10, 11, 23–4, 37, 53–67, 91–2, 126, 137
unwaved and waved flags 3, 7–9, 137

Valdemar II, King 21, 117
veterans, military 56–7
vexillodule 12
vexilloids 15–16
vexillophobe 12
vexillology 15, 28n
Vidal, T. E. 79

Wallace, George 35, 42, 43
warfare, flags in 15, 16, 18, 19, 20, 27, 32–3, 53–67, 70, 79, 85, 138, 146

Watson, Tom 87
waved and unwaved flags 3, 7–9, 137
Webster, Ben 5, 8, 11
Weight, Richard 86
Welsh flag 79–81, 89
Western, John 31
Westwood, Vivienne 84
'whiteness' 44–5, 53n, 53–67
Wilk, Richard 115
William, Prince 78

William I, King ('the Conqueror') 18
William III, King ('of Orange') 23, 98, 103
Williams, Hank Jr. 47
Williams, Raymond 132
Wilson, Harold 85

Young, Andrew 50

Zephaniah, Benjamin 87